Revelation, History, and the Dialogue of Religions

FAITH MEETS FAITH

An Orbis Series in Interreligious Dialogue

Paul F. Knitter, General Editor

In the contemporary world, the many religions and spiritualities stand in need of greater communication and cooperation. More than ever before, they must speak to, learn from, and work with each other in order both to maintain their vital identities and to contribute to fashioning a better world.

FAITH MEETS FAITH seeks to promote interreligious dialogue by providing an open forum for exchanges among followers of different religious paths. While the series wants to encourage creative and bold responses to questions arising from contemporary appreciations of religious plurality, it also recognizes the multiplicity of basic perspectives concerning the methods and content of interreligious dialogue.

Although rooted in a Christian and Maryknoll theological perspective, the series does not endorse any single school of thought or approach. By making available to both the scholarly community and the general public works that represent a variety of religious and methodological viewpoints, FAITH MEETS FAITH seeks to foster an encounter among followers of the religions of the world on matters of common concern.

FAITH MEETS FAITH SERIES

Revelation, History, and the Dialogue of Religions

A Study of Bhartṛhari and Bonaventure

David Carpenter

ORBIS BOOKS
Maryknoll, New York 10545

The Catholic Foreign Mission Society of America (Maryknoll) recruits and trains people for overseas missionary service. Through Orbis Books, Maryknoll aims to foster the international dialogue that is essential to mission. The books published, however, reflect the opinions of their authors and are not meant to represent the official position of the society.

Published in the United States by Orbis Books, Maryknoll, New York, U.S.A.

Manufactured in the United States of America

Library of Congress Cataloging-in-Publication Data

Carpenter, David, 1949-
Revelation, history, and the dialogue of religions : a study of Bhartṛhari and Bonaventure / David Carpenter.
p. cm.
Includes bibliographical references and index.
ISBN 1-57075-039-4 (alk. paper)
1. Revelation (Hinduism) 2. Revelation—Comparative studies.
3. Bhartṛhari. 4. Bonaventure, Saint, Cardinal, ca. 1217-1274.
I. Title. II. Series: Faith meets faith.
BL1215.R4C37 1995
291.2'11–dc20 95-21567
CIP

To my mother, Vera,
and to the memory of my father,
Jess L. Carpenter

To light a candle is to cast a shadow.

— URSULA K. LE GUIN, *A Wizard of Earthsea*

Therefore concord alone is commendable,
for through concord men may learn and respect
the conception of Dharma accepted by others.

— AŚOKA ROCK EDICT XII

Contents

Acknowledgments **xi**

Introduction **1**

Revelation as a Historical Problem: Beyond the Experience of the Sacred 5

Revelation as a Theological Problem: Beyond the Theology of Religions 9

The Study Ahead 14

I

BHARTṚHARI

1. Bhartṛhari on Vedic Revelation: Introduction **21**

Bhartṛhari's Historical Context 22

Bhartṛhari's Intellectual Context 24

Bhartṛhari the Grammarian 28

2. Bhartṛhari's Doctrine of Revelation **35**

The Metaphysical Foundation: The True Word 35

Bhartṛhari and the Tradition: The Mediation of Revelation 49

3. The Reception of the Language of Revelation: From Words to the Word **58**

The Nature of Language 59

The Experience of Language: Pratibhā 64

The Dialectic of Language and Vision 67

Conclusion 75

II
BONAVENTURE

4. Bonaventure on Christian Revelation: Introduction **81**
Bonaventure's Historical Context 81
Bonaventure's Intellectual Context 84
Bonaventure the Franciscan 89

5. The Metaphysics of Revelation **92**
Prologue in Heaven: Bonaventure's Theology of the Trinity 92
The Doctrine of the Threefold Word 97
The *Verbum Increatum:* The Word as Exemplar 98
The *Verbum Incarnatum:* The Word as Redeemer 102
The *Verbum Inspiratum:* The Word as Revealer 105

6. The History of Revelation **115**
Revelatio 115
Prophetia 119
Christus Magister 126

7. The Reception of the Language of Revelation **131**
Scripture 132
Preaching 139
Prophecy 144
Conclusion 152

III
COMPARING BHARTṚHARI AND BONAVENTURE

8. Bhartṛhari and Bonaventure in Comparison **157**
Theory 158
Reception 163

9. Interpreting the Comparison **176**
Difference: A Question of History 176
Similarity: The Question of Truth 192
Similarity in Difference: From Revelation to Dialogue 200

Index **203**

Acknowledgments

It is a pleasant task to acknowledge those who have contributed in various ways to the following study. This book began as a dissertation at the University of Chicago, and there are many people at that institution who deserve my thanks. I am deeply indebted to Bernard McGinn and to Edwin Gerow (now at Reed College) for agreeing to oversee the project as co-advisors and to Wendy Doniger and David Tracy for agreeing to read the results. Bernard McGinn's own high standards as a scholar, his openness to new ideas, and his personal kindness were and remain an inspiration. I have James Fitzgerald to thank for my introduction as a graduate student into the enchanted forest that is the Sanskrit language, and for continued encouragement and stimulating conversation since. I am also indebted to Frank Reynolds and Ronald Inden for their many lessons and for the generosity and enthusiasm that they show to their students. The American Institute of Indian Studies made possible a year of study in Pune, India, and I am particularly grateful to G. B. Palsule, then of the Center for the Advanced Study of Sanskrit at the University of Poona, who read Bhartṛhari's difficult text with me during that year.

Parts of chapters 8 and 9 appeared in "Revelation in Comparative Perspective: Lessons for Interreligious Dialogue," *Journal of Ecumenical Studies* 29 (1992): 175–88.

I have learned much over the years from ongoing conversations with a number of colleagues, including Gregory Alles, Frank Clooney, Stephen Lestition, Michael Sells, and Brian K. Smith. Michael Sells in particular read the final manuscript and made many valuable comments. I am indebted to William Burrows and Paul Knitter, editor of Orbis's Faith Meets Faith series, for their encouragement and assistance in seeing the manuscript through to publication. Finally, I owe a great debt to my mother, Vera, and to my wife, Eileen, for their unfailing support and encouragement.

Introduction

Religious diversity is a fact, one might almost say a primordial fact. When one considers the history of religions in its full historical sweep, diversity appears to be the norm. The earliest forms of religious belief of which we have any evidence were inseparable from the tribal groups that transmitted them orally to their own descendants from generation to generation. There were as many "religious worlds" as there were distinct tribes and languages. How many is now impossible to tell, but a contemporary inventory of distinct world cultures — most of them tribal — puts their number today at well over a thousand.[1] Throughout most of human history the myriad totalizing forms of religious life have existed in relative isolation from one another. Diversity has been a fact, but not a problem. In fact, given what ecologists today tell us about the importance of biological diversity it seems to make more sense to view such human and religious diversity as originally an asset.

To a degree religious diversity begins to become a problem when tribal units begin to be consolidated into kingdoms and especially into empires. Unified rule requires a unified ideology for its legitimation, and just as the king or emperor must subordinate his rivals in a hierarchically arranged power structure, so too the plethora of pre-conquest deities must be ordered into a new divine hierarchy that gives pride of place to the heavenly patron of the earthly "king of kings." Similarly, pre-conquest tribal cosmologies must give way to the more encompassing cosmology of the victors. Religious diversity, then, first becomes a problem, in a political sense, as a potential obstacle to hegemony, and the rationalized theologies of the great national religions served to overcome this obstacle. One cannot, for instance, read the *Enuma Elish* without realizing that it is as much about the legitimacy of Babylonian and, later, Assyrian rulers and

1. According to George Peter Murdock's *Atlas of World Cultures* (Pittsburgh: University of Pittsburgh Press, 1981), there were in 1971 at least 1,264 distinct cultures on the planet, and since the majority of these cultures are tribal with distinct forms of religious beliefs and practices, it is safe to say that at least a thousand different religions have survived into the twentieth century. How many more have perished without a trace is impossible to determine, but the number is probably quite large.

their empires as it is about the creation of the world and the supremacy of Marduk among the gods.

In such a context, where religion is pressed into service on behalf of imperialism, a troublesome diversity of religious traditions has a straightforward solution, namely, the imposition through force, if not of uniformity then of a hierarchical subordination (political exclusivism or inclusivism, one might say). But there is another important dimension to the "problem" of religious diversity, and this is the appearance of the so-called "axial age" or "world religions."[2] Often in direct opposition to the earlier nationalist (as well as tribal) religious ideologies, these new religions are armed with a vision that is presented as universal in scope, as transcending political boundaries, and intended to serve as a blueprint for a new way of life for all who respond to the call. To be sure these new religions are deeply rooted in the local conditions that witness their birth and soon enough accommodate themselves to the ways of this world, taking their turn at the legitimation of the political status quo. But it is their claims to possess a universally valid truth, expressed through a universally valid way of life, that bring the problem of religious diversity to a head. It is one thing to have a plurality of tribal traditions, each content to go its own way, or a plurality of nationalist ideologies, limited in its scope by the practical limitations of conquest and rule. It is quite another thing to encounter a preacher during one's travels along the Silk Road or while crossing the Aegean or the Arabian Sea who proclaims a universal truth that is said to transcend all ethnic and political boundaries and that seemingly obliges one to choose between truth and error. This is especially the case when these universal messages come to be involved, as they eventually do, with the legitimation of an imperial rule that sees itself as possessed of an equally universal mandate.

Christianity is one such religion, and among Christian theologians the fact of religious diversity has typically been viewed as a theological problem. Christians have traditionally celebrated the revelation of Jesus of Nazareth as a universal or "final" revelation of the divinely willed destiny of creation. Not only has Jesus of Nazareth been believed to be the Christ, the Messiah, but he has also been celebrated as "Christ the King," the imperial Christ whose rule is universal and upon the grace of whom the salvation of all humanity depends. And yet what the followers of Jesus Christ have claimed for him in theory they have been

2. The term "axial age" originates with Karl Jaspers. For more recent explorations on this theme, see S. N. Eisenstadt, *The Origins and Diversity of Axial Age Civilizations* (Albany: State University of New York Press, 1986).

unable to gain for him in practice. In our contemporary fragmented post-colonial, post-Christian world, with its global forms of communication and cultural and religious interaction, the rule of this Universal Lord is increasingly contested, sometimes by Christians themselves. Nor have any of the other great "world religions" won universal acceptance for their universal messages. In our contemporary situation, as the inheritors of these great religions and inhabitants of the one world that they in some ways helped to create, religious diversity has become an important religious problem. For those attempting to preserve a coherent religious identity within the radically plural conditions of the present it is perhaps not too much to say that religious diversity, especially in its increasingly strident manifestation as religious communalism, has become *the* theological problem of our day.

I have tried to sketch the broadest historical context of this problem in order to make a point, namely, that the problem is rarely dealt with from a historical perspective. Rather, the theologians or "representative intellectuals" (to borrow Paul Griffiths's phrase[3]) of the traditions concerned generally presuppose the universal validity of the essential doctrines and practices of their respective traditions, since such claims are typically supported by the further claim that they are grounded in some form of disclosure of the ultimate nature of things, a disclosure that lies at the origin of the tradition concerned and thus provides its sure, typically scriptural, foundation. Furthermore, the acceptance of the "revealed," canonical, or otherwise authoritative status of the tradition's scriptures is part and parcel of the identity of a thinker as a theologian or "representative intellectual" of that tradition. The task for such a thinker then is not to question the authoritative status of the tradition's revealed truths but to apply them to the evaluation of the status, and perhaps also the specific claims, of the religious other. Since the pursuit of such a task presupposes the prior acceptance of the truths of the tradition as authoritatively given, the question of their historical foundations is often of little interest.

For the historian of religions, however, viewing this situation against the backdrop of the global history of religions, such an appeal to an authoritative foundation in revelation is itself an interesting phenomenon, since the claim to possess a revealed truth is not unique to a single religion, or even to the so-called "axial age" religions. Such claims are in fact only one aspect of the rich phenomenon of revelation itself, considered precisely as a historical *phenomenon.* The goal of the following study is in

3. See his *An Apology for Apologetics* (Maryknoll, N.Y.: Orbis Books, 1991), pp. 3–9.

a sense to "go behind" the authoritative claims that are typically founded upon some form of revelation and to examine revelation itself as a concrete historical phenomenon. Since the actual disclosive event or events that are said to lie at the origin of revelation in a particular religious tradition (e.g., the seer's visions, the prophet's call and commission, etc.) are not immediately available to us, we will have to rest content with a comparative study of how these events are represented by the members of the tradition, i.e., the forms in which revelation is theorized, and a comparison of the practical forms of its mediation and reception.

When one looks at revelation carefully as a religious phenomenon and begins to unpack it, one finds that in each of its instances it is rich and complex. It includes the processes through which disclosive experiences are given an authoritative interpretation by a community and expressed in canonical form for transmission to later generations. It also includes the later reception of these transmitted forms and their impact upon the recipient. Central to all of this is language, or what I will call the "language of revelation," and the practices through which it is received, preserved, and transmitted. Rather than an unquestioned, unmoving point of departure, then, a firm foundation upon which later theological elaboration is to proceed, revelation from a historical and comparative perspective may be viewed as a dynamic, linguistically mediated process, which needs to be located within the historical horizons of the religious traditions in which it is found. Rather than begin with revelation as a presupposition of theological discourse, then, the study that follows will begin with revelation as a historical phenomenon, a phenomenon that is to be found in many religious traditions and that is therefore open to comparative historical investigation. Consequently this study is not conceived primarily as an exercise in the theology of religions, or even in "comparative theology,"[4] but primarily as an exercise in the history of religions, and secondarily as an exercise of religious reflection in a pluralistic context. The attempt will be made to shed some light on the matter of religious diversity by examining what I take to be one of its most important aspects, namely,

4. The term "comparative theology" has been used most prominently of late by Francis Clooney, S.J., in particular in his outstanding study of Vedanta, *Theology after Vedanta: An Experiment in Comparative Theology* (Albany: State University of New York Press, 1993). Clooney's work represents an important move toward a careful and sophisticated comparison of specific texts from Christian and non-Christian traditions, and hence a move away from the theology of religions that historically has taken little interest in the details of the religious traditions whose truth and value it presumes to evaluate. His point of departure, however, is overtly theological and focuses upon the integral "Texts" of the two traditions, for which matters of historical context are of little importance.

the diversity of disclosive or revelatory phenomena and the forms of their mediation.

To a degree the perspective adopted here differs from the perspective that historians of religions often bring to the comparative study of religion. As is obvious, it also differs in some important ways from the more typical theological perspective from which revelation and doctrine are usually viewed, as well as from the approaches to interreligious dialogue that presuppose such a theological perspective. These differences in perspective require some explanation.

REVELATION AS A HISTORICAL PROBLEM: BEYOND THE EXPERIENCE OF THE SACRED

To one familiar with the landscape of the modern study of religion, it might seem odd to view revelation as a historical problem. One might assume — not without reason — that revelation, as a "normative" category, should be left within the citadel of theology, content to provide that fortress with its firm foundation. From its battlements theologians might look out over the less secure terrain below, where historians of religions are encamped, stalking their more exotic game: hierophanies, kratophanies, even theophanies: all interesting game worthy of pursuit, no doubt, but also wild and unruly. Occasionally an inquisitive theologian might lower the bridge and sally forth into the wilds or invite a passing historian in to dine and share tales of the hunt, but by and large the two groups should be content to remain within their respective worlds. And in fact, the problem of revelation has indeed remained predominantly the concern of those who would affirm the authority of revealed truth amid the unstable and unpredictable experiences of the *homo religiosus*. What then does the problem of revelation have to do with *history*, with the history of religions?

Everything. We have only to step back briefly from this conventional understanding of the concept of revelation to see that revelation is in fact a complex historical phenomenon with many different aspects and as such is a most promising subject for comparative study. Far from standing outside time, as a kind of *norma normans non normata* brought to bear on the vicissitudes of human experience, the phenomenon of revelation involves human experience in some of its most intense forms: the ecstatic experiences of shamans, the visions of seers, the inspired speech of poets and prophets, the pronouncements of sages, diviners, and incarnate gods.[5] On the other hand, the phenomenon of revelation cannot be reduced to such experiences. Far from being merely a subjective experience of a few gifted *religiosi,* revelation in its concrete historical form involves the objective mediations of language, itself a deeply social and even political reality. Disclosive experiences such as those just referred to occur amid and are in part constituted by specific social and historical conditions, often occurring within established religious communities or as sectarian reaction to such communities. These communities and sects in turn rely upon a whole host of institutions for the preservation and transmission of the primary linguistic expressions of such disclosive experiences. These expressions, as forms of language, are thus inseparable, both in their origin and in their transmission, from social, linguistic, and political structures: not only songs, chants, oracles and myths, but also the forms of their mediation through the institution of ritual; not just scriptures, but also the associated practices of study, preaching, and exegesis and their institutionalization; not just a body of authoritative knowledge, but a whole range of religious specialists entrusted with its authoritative transmission. Revelation, viewed as a phenomenon within history, is thus quite complex, involving a rich and multifaceted array of religious phenomena, which are themselves rooted in the historical, social, political, and economic realities of the worlds in which they are found. Given this level of historical complexity we shall find it most appropriate to think of revelation not as an experience, nor as an objective form of knowledge or social institution, but as first and foremost a historical process that involves each of these but is reducible to none of them.

•

The phenomenon of revelation has not remained totally foreign to historians of religions. The more immediate and experiential aspects of the

5. Understood in this way, there arguably already exists an enormous literature on "revelation" in the history of religions, although it exists in the form of a number of disparate works that have not been thematized as such. One thinks, for instance, of Mircea Eliade's masterful study of shamanism, Gilbert Rouget's suggestive work on music and trance, the literature on Native American vision quests, etc. One can get a sense of the possibilities by consulting the heading "Revelation and Divination" (787) in the *Outline of Cultural Materials* compiled by George P. Murdock et al. (New Haven: Human Relations Area Files, 1982), where these terms are understood to refer to "practices reflecting anxiety about the future and often also a sense of inspiration; quest for visions and guardian spirits; hallucinatory revelations; communication with spirits (e.g., through spirit possession, through inspired oracles, through mediums); prophesy; clairvoyance; acquiring mystic insight through concentration and contemplation; interpretation of dreams; omens and their interpretation; divinatory practices and techniques (e.g., geomancy, haruspicy, heptoscopy, necromancy, scapulimancy, scrying, sortilege, astrology); etc." And as if this were not enough, the "see also" refers the reader to related entries on the cult of the dead, on diviners, seers, and messiahs, on guardian spirits, and more.

phenomenon have been incorporated to an extent into their conceptuality under the rubric of "hierophany," or the manifestation of the sacred.[6] But while it would be hard to deny the utility of the vague but ubiquitous notion of the sacred for creating a distinctive space for the discourse of historians of religions,[7] its use is nevertheless not without its drawbacks, not the least of which is its tendency to obscure the distinctive linguistic, social, and political structures associated with a phenomenon such as revelation. For to the extent that revelation is understood solely as a manifestation of the sacred its distinctive character is lost. One sometimes feels that in the discourse of historians of religions, the category of the sacred in fact functions as a place-holder that defines a theoretical space left empty of any more determinate historical phenomenon.

The problem becomes particularly acute when one considers the relationship between the phenomenon of revelation and religious authority. Revelation after all is not just another passing religious experience of *homo religiosus,* however profound. As theologians know quite well, revelation *matters* not only because it provides a primordial orientation in sacred time and space (when in fact it does), but also because it in some way provides a foundation for a religious tradition. To say that something is "revealed" is to say in the same breath that it has authority, that it provides norms for a community of believers, that it is *true.* It is precisely for this reason that revelation has generally been viewed as a properly theological category falling outside the range of a historian's legitimate interests. In this connection it is important to remember that the history of religions discipline, as a "child of the Enlightenment" growing up amid the larger religious, cultural, and intellectual currents of eighteenth- and

---

6. It is instructive in this regard to reread the opening paragraphs of Mircea Eliade's *The Sacred and the Profane,* where the concept of hierophany is explained in terms of religious experience and revelation: "It must be said at once that the religious experience of the nonhomogeneity of space is... not a matter of theoretical speculation, but of a primary religious experience that precedes all reflection on the world. For it is the break effected in space that allows the world to be constituted, because it *reveals* the fixed point, the central axis for all future orientation. When the sacred manifests itself in any *hierophany,* there is not only a break in the homogeneity of space; there is also *revelation* of an absolute reality" (emphasis added). Eliade goes on to say that the hierophany *"reveals"* a center, and refers repeatedly to the *"revelation* of a sacred space." See *The Sacred and the Profane* (New York: Harcourt, Brace & World, 1959), pp. 20–23 and *passim.* The term "revelation" appears frequently in this work as a synonym of hierophany.

7. It is precisely the vagueness of the term that makes it so useful. See, for instance, the remarks of Mircea Eliade, who coined the term, and Lawrence Sullivan, in their joint article, "Hierophany," in *The Encyclopedia of Religion,* ed. Mircea Eliade, 16 vols. (New York: Macmillan, 1987), 6:313: "Hierophany... is a term designating the manifestation of the sacred. The term involves no further specification. Herein lies its advantage: it refers to any manifestation of the sacred in whatever object, throughout history."

nineteenth-century Europe, was also a child of the Enlightenment critique of religious authority, and in particular of authoritative revelation. The ticket of entry to the "serious" study of religion was the abandonment of the traditional account of its origin in a divine revelation — whether the "primordial revelation" made to Adam and his descendants or the "historical revelation" made to later Jews and Christians. The quest for origins that typified the early historical-critical study of religion precluded any serious interest in a phenomenon that was still viewed as inseparable from uncritical, ahistorical claims of authority. Those charged with the emancipation of the new discipline from the intellectual hegemony of normative Christianity could hardly be expected to give much attention to what was for them an exclusively normative and Christian concept. It is not surprising, then, that it is precisely this normative aspect of revelation that escapes the conceptuality of the sacred, of hierophany, and of the immediacy of religious experience, elements that have played such a prominent role in the history of religions discipline. Nor should it be surprising that in those cases where the concept of revelation *has* been used, it has often been by those close to the Christian theological tradition.[8] Nevertheless

8. This has not always encouraged objectivity. Thus Nathan Söderblom, who is often claimed as a historian of religions, was interested in the category of revelation in the history of religions primarily for Christian apologetic reasons. This becomes obvious in the first chapter of Söderblom's monograph *The Nature of Revelation* (New York: Oxford University Press, 1933). While the archbishop can affirm that "a revelation of God is present wherever a real religion is found" (p. 6), nevertheless for him the "clear story of the history of religion" teaches that "no nature-god or culture-god has ever been able to achieve a real monotheism of universal or spiritual nature. For this achievement there was demanded the revelation of the prophets" (p. 19). The connection with Christian theology has not always been so direct, however. In a critical discussion of Max Scheler's proposal for an "essential phenomenology of religion" that would include a study of the forms of revelation, Joachim Wach expressed his support for a strictly historical study of the types of revelation and distinguished it from Scheler's more philosophical project: "In my view, a theory of the types of revelation is a task for the history of religions, a task that must be undertaken independently from the philosophical question about the essential nature of revelation" (*Religionswissenschaft: Prolegomena zu ihrer wissenschaftstheoretischen Grundlegung,* originally published in 1924, trans. Gregory D. Alles, *Introduction to the History of Religions* [New York: Macmillan, 1988], p. 93). While Scheler's original proposal clearly presupposed a Christian apologetic view of revelation, Wach seemed to be interested in a study of the forms of revelation that would be independent not only of Christian theology, but of philosophy as well. In Wach's case, however, such a projected study remained unrealized. Instead, toward the end of his life, he seemed to view the matter from a fairly traditional apologetic perspective. In his 1953 lecture to the National Association of Biblical Instructors, for instance, he appealed to the theological concept of general revelation in order to explain the work of historians of religions, referring in particular to Söderblom, Otto, and van der Leeuw. See Joachim Wach, "General Revelation and the Religions of the World," first published in the *Journal of Bible and Religion* 22 (1954), and reprinted in *Understanding and Believing,* ed. Joseph M. Kitagawa (Westport, Conn.: Greenwood Press, 1975), pp. 69–86. Wach called particular attention to the achievement of Rudolf Otto: "Rudolf Otto... has, as the first among modern historians of religions, given real content to the notion of general revelation by his analysis of religious experience

it is the authoritative character of revelation that raises questions about the mediating structures of language and community, questions about legitimacy and power — questions concerning the ideological dimension of revelation — that have figured much less prominently in the discipline. My own view is that the authoritative status of revelation, far from making it the exclusive preserve of confessional theology, is itself an important part of the phenomenon as a whole and adds to its interest and significance as a subject of comparative historical inquiry.

REVELATION AS A THEOLOGICAL PROBLEM: BEYOND THE THEOLOGY OF RELIGIONS

While revelation may thus be a legitimate subject of comparative historical study, it remains true that in the Christian tradition it has been understood primarily not as a subject of historical interest but as the authoritative foundation of the tradition and its theological reflection. This is not to say that its position has gone unquestioned. Especially since the eighteenth century, revelation has been the subject of a great deal of scrutiny, both by critics of the Christian tradition and increasingly by its defenders. Under the influence of Karl Barth, revelation became such a prominent topic for theological debate that as early as 1941 Paul Althaus could speak of the "inflation" of the concept of revelation,[9] and more recently Ronald Thiemann has written of the "revelation-weariness" of the theological community since the 1960s, even though he himself defends the category as crucial to the theological enterprise.[10] Yet whether revelation is thematized as a central concern of theology or not, as the presupposition underlying the authority of scripture and doctrine, it continues

---

as a communion with the holy, and his demonstration of the ubiquity of the *sensus numinis*" (ibid., p. 71). He offers a very similar assessment of the significance of his own analysis of "universals in religion" in his *Types of Religious Experience* (Chicago: University of Chicago Press, 1951), p. 47. Here Wach's earlier interest in revelation as a historical category, along with its projected typology, seems to be replaced by an interest in the theological category of general revelation. Furthermore, the category of general revelation is correlated with the notions of the Holy and the numinous, whence our present-day category of the sacred. In the process, the question of a distinct category of revelation appropriate for the history of religions discipline seems to have been dropped.

9. See his article, "Die Inflation des Begriffs Offenbarung in der gegenwärtigen Theologie," *Zeitschrift für Systematische Theologie* 18 (1941): 134–49.

10. See his *Revelation and Theology: The Gospel as Narrated Promise* (Notre Dame: University of Notre Dame Press, 1985), p. 1. For overviews of the debate on this matter see John Baillie, *The Idea of Revelation in Recent Thought* (New York: Columbia University Press, 1956), and Avery Dulles, *Models of Revelation* (Garden City, N.Y.: Doubleday, 1983).

to play an important role in theological discourse. Indeed, it is the prior acceptance of a revelation as normative that has traditionally constituted theological discourse as theological.

As noted above, this is in itself, for the historian of religions, an interesting phenomenon, for there are in fact many "normative" revelations and many theological traditions that stem from them. From the historian's point of view, it is difficult to see why one should view the Christian claim to possess "the" normative revelation any differently than one would view the analogous claims made by Muslims in regard to the Qur'an and the role of Muhammad as the "seal of the prophets," the claims of the Gelukpa Tibetan Buddhist about the superiority of the Prasaṅgika School of Mādhyamika Buddhist thought, the Mīmāṃsaka's claims for the eternality and trans-human status of the Veda, or other similar claims for the superior or final status of a particular religion's positions.

Nevertheless, as a branch of theology the theology of religions accepts a specific revelation as regulative for its own reflection, and it is this fact that makes it difficult to pursue the issue of revelation in a critical and comparative manner within the confines of a theology of religions. Revelation, or more accurately, Jesus Christ as the definitive self-revelation of God, as witnessed to in Christian scripture, is the presupposition that makes the entire endeavor both possible and meaningful. Thus in most of the work produced within this field, revelation, and the scriptures and doctrines that mediate it, are simply taken as secure points of departure. This is especially true of a mainstream "inclusivist" theologian like Karl Rahner. While Rahner developed a sophisticated and nuanced theology of revelation, which played an important role in his attempt to sketch out a theology of religions, the final criterion for judgment is the normative revelation in Christ as mediated through scripture and doctrine.

It is one of the distinctive features of so-called "pluralist" theologians to have broken with this basic presupposition, in that the finality and normativity of the revelation in Jesus Christ is explicitly denied, at least as a presupposition for engagement in religious reflection and interreligious dialogue. To this extent it may be misleading to view these thinkers as engaged in the same enterprise as are the inclusivist theologians of religions. John Hick, perhaps the most influential "pluralist," is probably best classified as a philosopher of religion rather than as a theologian engaging in the subdiscipline of theology of religions. And Wilfred Cantwell Smith, another thinker commonly classified as a pluralist, has explicitly called a Christian theology of religions "an inherently inadequate concept."[11] Nevertheless, this rejection of the normativity of Christian revelation as a working hypothesis has given these thinkers a greater degree of freedom in approaching the problem of religious diversity. They have, for instance, on occasion turned a critical eye toward the foundations of their own tradition in order to find grounds for a more radical openness to the claims of other religions.[12] One of the charges made against such pluralists, however, is that they sometimes bypass the "positivities" of scripture and doctrine in order to appeal either to religious experience as a kind of human universal[13] or to a single religious "object" (e.g., God, the Real) that would underlie a diversity of religious expressions, in either case downplaying the differences that distinguish the different religious traditions.[14] This is the message of some of the most recent, and in some ways most impressive, of the theological work being done in this area. Thus of late Paul Griffiths, J. A. DiNoia, and Francis Clooney have each in his own way called into question the presumption of a "common essence" underlying the different religions and the privileging of sameness over difference. Each has made a plea for greater attention to the differences that distinguish the religions, as these are to be discerned through the careful, comparative study of specific texts and doctrines.[15] Such criticisms of the pluralist approach are to be taken seriously. To the extent that similarity is privileged over difference, generalizations are substituted for specifics, and abstract, *a priori* judgments about the nature of religion take the place of careful historical-critical analysis of the religions in all their diversity and concreteness, the pluralist approach runs the risk of

---

11. Wilfred Cantwell Smith, *Towards a World Theology: Faith and the Comparative History of Religions* (Maryknoll, N.Y.: Orbis Books, 1989), p. 110. See also, ibid., p. 103: "A Christian theology of comparative religion is, therefore, not a view from within one tradition or community out upon the others. To conceive it so has been the chief error until now.... Rather, that theology, if it is to be true, becomes a Christian view (and I stress the adjective) from within all. It postulates that we see ourselves as participants in one community, the human: that the Christians see the Christian group and other groups as fellow participants in that one community."

12. I have in mind here the critical examination of the scriptural status of Jesus as the Christ by both John Hick and Paul Knitter.

13. One thinks here of Wilfred Cantwell Smith's understanding of a single "faith," which he contrasts with the diversity of "cumulative traditions."

14. Here one thinks of John Hick and his distinction between the noumenal object of religion and the many phenomenal expressions of the experience of this object.

15. See Paul J. Griffiths, *An Apology for Apologetics: A Study in the Logic of Interreligious Dialogue* (Maryknoll, N.Y.: Orbis Books, 1991), J. A. DiNoia, *The Diversity of Religions: A Christian Perspective* (Washington, D.C.: Catholic University of America Press, 1993), and Francis X. Clooney, S.J., *Theology after Vedanta: An Experiment in Comparative Theology* (Albany: State University of New York Press, 1993).

subsuming the religious other into the abstract sameness of religion "in general." Clearly in an approach that succumbed to these dangers, revelation as a concrete historical phenomenon in the sense given it above, along with its objective mediations through scripture and doctrine, would be lost from view. This does not mean, however, that the only position that "takes differences seriously" is the inclusivist one. Far from it. On the contrary, it could be argued that the inclusivist position fails to do precisely this, in failing to invest the religious other with sufficient authority as to necessitate a fundamental rethinking of the *foundations* (as distinct from the particulars) of one's own theological tradition, i.e., in the present case, to necessitate a critical examination of the category of revelation and the concept of authority that is connected with it. Thus none of the aforementioned thinkers interrogate the basis and claim to authority of the fully developed doctrinal and theological traditions that they take as their points of departure.

It seems to me that neither presupposing revelation as an objective datum, as a secure foundation upon which dialogue with the "other" is to proceed, a *norma normans non normata* that establishes the parameters and guidelines for dialogue (which seems to be required of the inclusivist approach), nor implicitly identifying it with a supposedly universal feature of human experience (which is the mistake of at least a certain type of pluralist approach) leaves much room for an appreciation of the complex and dialectical character of revelation as it actually appears in history, or its implications for the issue of religious diversity. It is perhaps not altogether untrue to say that in the case of both inclusivists and pluralists, whether their approach is made through doctrine (an approach favored by the inclusivists) or through religious experience (an approach more often found among the pluralists), appeal is made to fundamental criteria that resist being drawn into the ambiguities and particularities of concrete historical, social, and political existence. Whether the foundation is identified in mystical experience, Holy Writ, or conciliar decree, the net result seems to me to be the same: there are certain presuppositions that are brought to the dialogue table that are themselves not open to question, partly because both parties to the dialogue are very likely to share similar presuppositions concerning the foundational and non-negotiable character of the basic premises of their respective traditions. Accepting such things is assumed to be part of what it means to be religious, to be a person of faith with a well-formed religious identity. It is precisely here that one reaches an impasse. *De revelationibus non disputandum!*

Revelation and its authority are thus normally taken as givens, as conditions for the possibility of serious interreligious dialogue, whether this revelation comes from the Word on high or from the Word within. Because those involved in interreligious dialogue tend to assume that they have a secure basis for dialogue in the foundational truths of their own tradition or their own experience, the most radical presuppositions of their traditions or their experience often remain unconscious and unquestioned. But what if revelation ceases to function theologically as a presupposition and rather is thematized as an object of historical-critical scrutiny? In particular, what would a comparative historical examination of revelation in two quite different traditions reveal, and what impact would such a study have on the practice of interreligious dialogue? A serious grappling with the problem presented by the very plurality of claims of revelatory foundations might serve to de-familiarize the concept of revelation itself, in its unquestioned immediacy, and contribute to the attitude of radical openness and questioning that I believe is called for by the present situation. One might then expect, as a result, a de-centering of the religious traditions themselves, and consequently of the individual historical subjects who are to an extent constituted by these traditions. We must ask then whether any given tradition's "revelation," taken as an unanalyzed *datum,* can be taken as the secure point of departure for dialogue with the other traditions, or whether this is starting too late, i.e., leaving unexamined the thing that should be the very focus of examination, the nature of revelation itself and of the claims based upon it.

In the study that follows I will attempt to show that such an examination makes necessary a revision of conventional theological views of revelation, whether in the Hindu or Christian camp, and that this in turn fundamentally alters the subject matter of interreligious dialogue, shifting it away from the established doctrines or representations of the respective traditions and toward both the experiential resources of these traditions and the historical, social, and economic underpinnings of their traditional representations. At the same time, this kind of historical-critical study of revelation blurs the boundaries between the "neutral" approach of the historian of religions and the confessional approach of the traditional theologian and makes clear the need for a continued rethinking of the nature of religious truth, which for some at least, come of age under the radically plural conditions of the global village, can be adequately expressed neither by a particular set of propositions or "rules" of doctrine, Christian or otherwise, nor presumed to be available to a "view from nowhere," namely, to the "objective" and value-free perspective of a science of religion.

THE STUDY AHEAD

In spite of the increasing volume of literature being produced by theologians on the topic of interreligious dialogue and the theology of religions, and in spite of the large number of monographs produced yearly on particular aspects of individual religious traditions on the part of historians of religions, detailed comparative studies are still relatively few. This may in part be explained by the fact that some of the earliest attempts at comparison suffered from rather obvious apologetic motivations (whether religious or rationalist) that led to distortions of the traditions under study. Whether the outcome of such studies was a self-serving "demonstration" of the uniqueness and superiority of Christianity or a facile affirmation of the essential unity of all religions, the net result was to discredit attempts at comparison in the eyes of many, especially those who were becoming increasingly specialized in the study of the specific non-European traditions that were serving as grist for the apologetic mill. As a reaction against such tendencies within the field that came to be known as "comparative religion" or "history of religions," many scholars turned to detailed analyses of specific aspects of individual religious traditions, under the assumption that to compare different traditions entailed the unwarranted assumption of an underlying commonality that was purely speculative. More recently, however, and in part thanks to our improved knowledge of a large number of non-European religious traditions that have been the subjects of in-depth historical studies, there has been a growing recognition that comparison carried out in the light of this improved knowledge need not necessarily privilege sameness over difference, but on the contrary may just as readily serve to highlight the important ways in which traditions differ from one another. When attention to similarity and difference are kept in balance and one allows oneself, to some degree at least, to be taken over by the dialectic of the comparative process itself, comparative studies are capable of yielding insights into the traditions compared that are unavailable in any other way. The study that follows represents an attempt to do comparison in a way that attends to the specific details of the figures compared and thus "takes differences seriously," but at the same time remains open to the discovery of genuine similarity.

Granted the need to keep both similarity and difference fully in play, how one best goes about such comparison remains very much an open question. It would be a mistake to assume that, within the notoriously eclectic discipline of the history of religions, there was one "right" way that alone would guarantee fruitful results. In the specific instance of the comparative study of revelation, however, there has been one approach, now somewhat dated, that has been tried and, in my opinion, found wanting. I have in mind a phenomenological approach that surveys a large number of traditions in order to derive a typology of forms. This is the approach adopted by Gustav Mensching in his essay entitled "Typology of Revelation in the History of Religions"[16] and continued by Theodorus Petrus van Baaren in his Utrecht dissertation, described as a phenomenological study of the representations of revelation.[17] Van Baaren built on Mensching's work to develop a typology of thirteen distinct types of revelation, subdivided into three groups: dynamistic, polytheistic, and monotheistic. These types are derived through an analysis in terms of the author, instrument, content, and recipient of revelation, as well as the response of the recipient of revelation.

If space permitted, van Baaren's contribution would warrant a more detailed discussion. His analysis of the representations of revelation in terms of author, instrument, etc. represents, to the best of my knowledge, the most extensive study of revelation that has thus far been undertaken by a historian of religions. It suffers the weakness, however, of being ahistorical, remaining on the level of a phenomenological description of traditional representations of revelation.

While in no way denying the importance of van Baaren's analysis on its own level, I would argue that the study of the representations of revelation must be rooted in a more fundamental historical analysis if it is to be productive of a deeper understanding of the phenomenon of revelation itself. This would seem to be impossible as long as one aspires to the kind of encyclopedic scope that is typical of the phenomenological approach adopted by van Baaren. Such an approach shares much in common with the theological approach that I have criticized above. Whereas the theologian traditionally presupposes the validity of his or her tradition's representation of revelation, in scripture and doctrine, van Baaren similarly takes at face value a large number of such representations (though in his case mythological rather than doctrinal) and juxtaposes them in an attempt to derive a typology. In neither case is the historical context of the

16. Originally published in Gustav Mensching, *Gott und Mensch: Vorträge und Aufsätze zur vergleichenden Religionswissenschaft* (Vieweg Verlag, 1948), pp. 11–36, and reprinted in his *Topos und Typos: Motiv und Strukturen religiösen Lebens* (Bonn: Ludwig Röhrscheid Verlag, 1971), pp. 178–96.

17. Theodorus Petrus van Baaren, *Voorstellingen van Openbaring Phaenomenologisch Beschouwd* (Representations of Revelation Phenomenologically Considered) (Utrecht: Drukkerij Fa. Schotanus & Jens, 1951).

representations taken into account. By contrast, one way of characterizing the approach taken here is that it attributes a great deal of importance to the historical context of the representations compared and to the *uses* to which these representations are put by the traditions involved.

Consequently what follows is not an encyclopedic survey of the place of revelation within the different religions but rather an in-depth study of the theories and practices related to revelation in two specific individuals, each an important representative of a major religious tradition. Each figure is studied independently and in-depth prior to the attempt to engage in explicit comparisons. Such an approach obviously precludes any pretense to comprehensiveness. Nevertheless, it is hoped that by selecting two outstanding thinkers, each centrally located within a major religious tradition, it will be possible to arrive at some conclusions that, while in no way universal in significance, will nevertheless be enlightening and suggestive. As noted above, the representations of revelation, whether mythical or theoretical, are only a part of revelation considered as a complex historical phenomenon. Nevertheless the following study devotes a good deal of attention (perhaps more than some would wish) to the theories of the two thinkers compared, the medieval Christian theologian Bonaventure and the classical Indian grammarian and philosopher of language Bhartṛhari. Indeed, it is my hope that the two studies of Bhartṛhari's and Bonaventure's ideas, which are more or less independent of one another, will each make a useful contribution, in their own right, to the history of the religious thought of their respective traditions, whatever one might make of the larger comparative project of which they are a part. In this attempt to treat the ideas of each thinker fully in their respective intellectual context, I hope to make it clear that I am in full agreement with those who insist that the specific theoretical positions of the different religions must be taken seriously in their own right.[18] But to stop here, to rest content with the comparison of fully formed representations of revelation, without asking for their "birth certificates" (to borrow a phrase from Heidegger[19]), is to accept an ahistorical approach to what is, as I have suggested, a deeply historical phenomenon. Accordingly, a good deal of attention is also given to the historical context of each thinker and to the role that the representations of revelation play in the life of their respective traditions.

Particularly important, I believe, is the attention given to what I will be referring to as the "language of revelation." As noted above, by this I

18. Here I have in mind in particular Paul Griffiths and J. A. DiNoia.

19. See Martin Heidegger, *The Basic Problems of Phenomenology* (Bloomington: Indiana University Press, 1982), p. 100.

do not mean primarily the "sacred scriptures" of the respective traditions, though especially in the case of Bonaventure the notion of scripture will be quite important. What I intend by this phrase is the linguistic mediation of revelation as a process. The language of revelation is thus understood to include speech as much as text and to be as much an *activity* as an artifact. The *practices* connected with the language of revelation will thus also be of central importance.

The study itself is divided into three parts: two parts devoted to in-depth studies of our two thinkers and a third part devoted to their comparison. The individual studies of Bonaventure and Bhartṛhari are organized similarly. Each begins with an attempt to place the thinker into his individual historical and intellectual context and then goes on to investigate first his theory of revelation and then his reception of the language of revelation in his own historical context. Thus each of the independent studies examines *both* theory *and* practice, and this double focus will prove important in the comparison that follows.

Finally, perhaps something needs to be said about the choice of these two specific figures and these two specific religious traditions and about the motivation behind the study. That one of the figures is Christian is related not only to the fact that my own personal religious roots are in the Christian traditions (both Methodist and Catholic), but also to the fact that when this study was first conceived it was conceived as what one might call a historical version of a theology of religions. Namely, it was my initial intent to engage in a retrieval of the Logos theology of Bonaventure so as to use a Bonaventure-inspired theological perspective normatively to evaluate a non-Christian theology of revelation. My expectation was that I would be able to provide a positive evaluation of non-Christian claims to revelation within the framework of such a Christian theology, with an outcome that would be "inclusivist" though not "pluralist" (to use these terms once again). The initial study, however, convinced me of the futility of such an approach and pushed me in the direction of the more "non-theological" approach that I have outlined above. I would repeat that this was in no way seen as an abdication of questions of truth in the interest of "objective" description. Rather it represents my own conviction, arrived at in the course of this study, that the question of truth cannot be adequately addressed from within the confines of a theology of religions as it has traditionally been conceived, i.e., from a perspective that *begins* with the assumption that the "full" truth is already known in some final, authoritative (even if necessarily imperfect) form and can be used to evaluate other truth claims that are more or less imperfect or incomplete. As the following study will argue, Christian revelation, like other forms of revelation, should be understood as a dynamic historical process subject to ideological distortions and in continuous need of critique. If this is indeed the case, then it undoubtedly serves as a potential *witness* to truth, but it is unclear to me just how it can anymore serve as an *authoritative foundation* for truth.

The choice of the Hindu (or more accurately, the Brahmanical) tradition of India was motivated by the desire to find a sophisticated tradition that had not been significantly influenced by the religious traditions of the West and that nevertheless made quite explicit claims to be grounded in revelation (in this case the Veda or *śruti*). Bhartṛhari seems a good counterpart to Bonaventure in that, like the latter, he lived at a time of great intellectual effervescence and developed his positions in dialogue with many of the most distinctive voices of his tradition. Originally I was also attracted to Bhartṛhari because he seemed to represent a sort of Indian counterpart to the Christian tradition of Logos theology, of which Bonaventure is a prime exemplar. As it turned out, however, and as will be seen below, it was the differences that divided these two thinkers that proved most intriguing. It was the need to account for these differences that led beyond their explicit theories and into a deeper consideration of their historical contexts. Their differences thus proved quite productive for the project as a whole. It might be expected that a comparative study of revelation would begin with the earliest sources available, namely, the canonical scriptures of the respective traditions. There would indeed be much merit in a comparative study of the canonical processes that led to the authoritative forms of the Veda and the Christian scriptures known respectively to Bhartṛhari and Bonaventure, and to us today. In fact, the present study points up the need for such a further study, but it is not something that could be made to fit within the confines of the present work. There will be occasion to refer to these processes in passing, as providing important background for an understanding of our main figures. But a full comparative study of them in their respective historical contexts remains a *desideratum*. On the other hand, the choice of Bonaventure and Bhartṛhari provides the opportunity to compare two complete and very sophisticated systems of thought that presuppose centuries of elaboration within their respective traditions. In the mature thought of these two men we find the underlying assumptions of each tradition developed in full.

PART I

Bhartṛhari

1

Bhartṛhari on Vedic Revelation: Introduction

To speak of revelation in India is to speak of the Veda. The term *veda,* which literally means "knowledge," is applied to a collection of compositions that were composed over a period of many centuries, but that all have in common, in the eyes of the later tradition, the quality of being equally *śruti,* a word that literally means "hearing" but, as we shall see, refers to their status as inspired compositions passed down orally and thus "heard" by each succeeding generation. The Vedic corpus as a whole consists of four major sections, each section in turn being comprised of a number of distinct texts. The earliest compositions of the Veda, the hymns now contained in the Ṛg Veda and composed by inspired seers, or *ṛṣi*-s, date from the late second millennium B.C.E. and together comprise the first major section of the Vedic corpus per se, the *Saṃhitā*-s, or "Collections." Of somewhat later origin are three other such collections, the Yajur Veda, the Sāma Veda, and the Atharva Veda. In addition to these four distinct "Vedas," or "Collections," the corpus of the Veda also includes a large number of ritual texts known collectively as the Brāhmaṇa-s. These texts, dating from the early centuries of the first millennium B.C.E., composed and transmitted exclusively by Brahmin priests, provide interpretations of the significance of the Vedic sacrificial cult over which the Brahmins presided and which was at the heart of the "Brahmanical" socio-religious order. The speculations begun in them are continued in the third major section of the Vedic corpus, comprised of the Āraṇyaka-s, or "Forest Texts." Finally come the more familiar Upanishads, which make up the final section and which contain increasingly self-critical reflections on the significance of the Brahmanical world order and the place of the individual within it. Passed down together orally for centuries and thus varying widely in content and style, these Vedic texts have been viewed as an authoritative source of revealed knowledge by the majority of the inhabitants of the Indian subcontinent for more than three thousand years.

Though far distant from the age that saw the actual composition of the Vedic texts, the period of the Gupta Empire (fourth and fifth centuries C.E.), sometimes referred to as India's "Golden Age," was an age in which the nature of Vedic revelation had become a matter of lively debate. The grammarian and philosopher of language Bhartṛhari (fl. c. 450–500 C.E.) was a major participant in that debate. As Madeleine Biardeau has noted, in the fifth century Bhartṛhari's work was "like a crucible where notions and theories from all points of the horizon come to be melted down."[1] A careful study of Bhartṛhari's doctrine of Vedic revelation and of his view on the reception of Vedic revelation in his own period will, when supplemented with a parallel study of the doctrine and practice of the medieval scholastic St. Bonaventure (1221–74), allow us to compare the two thinkers in some detail and to raise some important questions about the nature and function of revelation as we find it in these two traditions. We begin with Bhartṛhari and a brief survey of his own historical and intellectual context.

BHARTṚHARI'S HISTORICAL CONTEXT

Bhartṛhari can be dated with reasonable certainty to the fifth century C.E.[2] He lived in a sophisticated, pluralistic society which had for some time been experiencing relative peace and prosperity and in which the Vedic traditions that Bhartṛhari represented were undergoing something of a revival after a period of relative decline. The Gupta dynasty under which Bhartṛhari lived arose from a small principality in the region of Magadha in northeastern India to become an empire second in size and power only to the earlier Mauryan Empire, which had reached its apogee under Aśoka (268–230 B.C.E.). There was a crucial difference between the Gupta Empire and its predecessor, however. The political unification under Aśoka had brought the demise of the earlier Brahmanical tribal

1. In her outstanding study *Théorie de la connaissance et philosophie de la parole dans le brahmanisme classique* (Paris: Mouton & Co., 1964), p. 400.

2. Bhartṛhari's date has in the past been the subject of considerable discussion. While today he is assigned to the fifth century, he was for some time believed to have lived considerably later, in the seventh century. This mistaken view was based upon the report of the Chinese pilgrim I-Tsing, a report that is now viewed as erroneous. For a full discussion of the relevant evidence, see Carpenter, "The Light of the Word: A Comparative Study of the Phenomenon of Revelation," Ph.D. dissertation, University of Chicago, 1987, 1:94–98.

order that had provided the social and political context for the expansion of the Vedic religion and the gradual codification of the Vedic "canon."[3] In addition, it had encouraged the growth of the new religion of Buddhism, which had arisen in part as a reaction against the old Brahmanical order. The rise of the Guptas, by contrast, coincided with what has been called a "Hindu Renaissance." Whereas Aśoka had converted to Buddhism, as had many of his foreign successors, the Guptas were Hindu, sponsors of new theistic beliefs focused primarily on the Hindu gods Viṣṇu and Śiva. They were furthermore revivers of the Vedic past.[4] Through their patronage the Guptas encouraged a revival of past values and institutions that, in the new pluralistic yet peaceful environment of empire, gave rise to many of classical India's truly original cultural and religious creations. It was a sophisticated age and also a remarkably tolerant one. It was a time when Vaiṣṇava kings supported Śaiva poets and patronized both Buddhist and Jain scholars, and when the learned of all these traditions could participate freely in an increasingly common discourse through the *lingua franca* of classical Sanskrit.[5]

How did Bhartṛhari fit into this world? First of all he was most probably a Brahmin, a fact that speaks volumes to anyone familiar with Indian sociology. Bhartṛhari was a member of an educated elite. He was a scholar highly trained in the very exacting discipline of *vyākaraṇa,* or grammar. Such training required long years of careful study. Bhartṛhari's teacher, Vasurāta, is portrayed by the Buddhist biographer Paramārtha (499–569 C.E.) as a defender of correct Sanskrit and was undoubtedly a defender of the traditional form of Brahmanical education.[6] Vasurāta and his young pupil would most likely have been encouraged to preserve the

---

3. The term "canon" can be applied to the corpus of the Veda only with important qualifications. See David Carpenter, "The Mastery of Speech: Canonicity and Control in the Veda," in Laurie L. Patton, ed., *Authority, Anxiety, and Canon: Essays in Vedic Interpretation* (Albany: State University of New York Press, 1994), pp. 19–34.

4. Thus Louis Renou notes that "with the advent of the Guptas there is produced a sort of partial re-Vedisation of Hinduism.... The initiative for this goes back, perhaps in part, to the Smarta circles which were formed within the sects." See his *Études védiques et pāṇinéennes,* vol. 6: *Le destin du Véda dans L'Inde* (Paris: Éditions E. de Boccard, 1960), p. 5, and note 4. Both Samudra Gupta and the later Kumāra Gupta (415–50) are known from inscriptions to have performed the *aśvamedha,* or old Vedic horse sacrifice, which ritually established the newly won dominion of a king and was thus an important symbol of the old Vedic political order. Samudra Gupta was described as the performer of the *aśvamedha* "that had long been in abeyance." See J. F. Fleet, *Inscriptions of the Early Gupta Kings and their Successors* (Calcutta, 1888; reprint ed., Benares: Indological Book House, 1963), inscription no. 13.

5. On this theme, see Jean Filliozat, "Sanskrit as Link Language," *Cultural Forum* 15 (1972): 10–18.

6. See Paramārtha, "The Life of Vasubandhu," trans. J. Takakusu, *T'oung Pao* (1909), pp. 288–89.

ancient knowledge of the Vedas and the traditional methods of education through a program of royal land-grants offered by the Gupta kings. At the same time Bhartṛhari was clearly a man of his time, and a master of the forms of discourse common to the Gupta age. Even the most traditional of Brahmins could not help — if endowed with an intellect of the caliber of Bhartṛhari's — being affected by the new intellectual environment made possible by the Guptas. Furthermore, the prestige of the Sanskrit language and the virtually universal acceptance of Pāṇinian grammatical norms during the fifth century provided an exceptional opportunity for an original grammarian-cum-metaphysician like Bhartṛhari. In a context of open debate over diverse and often conflicting claims concerning the nature of revelation generally (e.g., Hindu vs. Buddhist), and the proper reception of Vedic revelation in particular, Bhartṛhari the grammarian was to re-examine his tradition and seek an answer at a deeper level, beyond the conflicting claims of the different *pravāda*-s, or schools of thought. Bhartṛhari was to examine the problem of revelation from the point of view of the language of revelation *as language,* which was for him both a form of *dharma,* the socio-cosmic order of the Brahmanical universe, and a self-manifestation of ultimate Reality that underlay that universe, Brahman.

BHARTṚHARI'S INTELLECTUAL CONTEXT

The intellectual context in which Bhartṛhari was to address the question of Vedic revelation was to a large extent determined by the Buddhist challenge to the traditional authority of the Veda. Two important aspects of this challenge were the Buddha's claim to direct religious experience, his direct insight into the nature of things, which the Buddhists, like their Vedic predecessors, referred to as the *dharma,* and his critique of the Vedic tradition precisely as *mere* tradition, having no basis in direct experience. Evidence for the truth of the first claim seemed to be found in the historical success of Buddhism itself. The "Buddhist experience" was received by so many, and with such enthusiasm, that it could not be ignored. Its influence reached down through the centuries, significantly determining the development of Hinduism and remaining a vital element in the religious universe of Bhartṛhari's fifth century. The second claim, although hardly an unbiased historical assessment, did in fact contain an element of truth. The Vedic tradition was in fact based to an extent upon direct experience, the Vedic seers' experiences of the gods and the cosmos, which were expressed and elaborated in the early Vedic hymns. Yet it is also true that the growing importance of the authoritative transmission of the sacred mantras taken from these hymns, as fixed *tradita,* endowed with an unquestioned authority and power, had tended to overshadow the visionary origins of the hymns themselves. As the Vedic tradition developed there was a tendency to relegate the seers and their visionary experiences more and more to a mythical past. The theistic accounts of the origin of the Vedas, which had developed by Bhartṛhari's day, gave expression to their transcendental authority but also placed the immediacy of the original experiences of the seers beyond the limits of possible human experience. In the later tradition, as John E. Mitchiner has shown,[7] the seers become quasi-divine beings who are actually the manifestations of the supreme Deity, no longer recognizable as normal human beings.

Side by side with the developing forms of Hindu theism, however, and preceding them, was the tradition that we may call "main-line" Brahmanism, the tradition elaborated in the Brāhmaṇa-s, texts, which, as noted above, belong to the corpus of the Veda and which provide interpretations of the Vedic sacrifice, the cultic center of the Vedic religious tradition. This tradition of Brahmanism, of which Bhartṛhari was a part, had its own development, as it moved into the post-Buddhist age of Hinduism. In its most authoritative form, as represented by the developing school of Mīmāṃsā, the school concerned with the exegesis of the Vedic ritual texts, it brought the aforementioned emphasis on the external verbal tradition to its most uncompromising formulation, explicitly rejecting the very possibility of an immediate, visionary experience of *dharma* (such as was claimed by the Buddha), and thereby not only implicitly accepting the Buddhist charge, but indeed elevating it into a virtue.

The Mīmāṃsā school of Vedic ritual exegesis limited itself to reflection on the ritual injunctions found in the Vedic texts. The focus was not on the innovative potential of the tradition, but on the conservation of the tradition, understood as a received "text" (although still orally transmitted) and a fixed form of ritual performance.

The earliest text of this school, the *Mīmāṃsāsūtra*-s of Jaimini, already presents us with a terse but self-conscious defense of Vedic revelation. For a detailed defense of the tradition from the Mīmāṃsaka viewpoint, however, we must wait for Śabara (c. fifth century C.E.), roughly contemporary with Bhartṛhari. In his commentary on Jaimini's *sūtra*-s, Śabara devel-

7. John E. Mitchiner, *Traditions of the Seven Ṛṣis* (Delhi: Motilal Banarsidass, 1982), pp. 296–311.

oped a defense of Vedic authority based on the Veda's eternity (*nityatva*) and its non-human origin (*apauruṣeyatva*). The Veda, understood as the discrete collection of mantras, injunctions (*vidhi*-s) and commendatory statements (*arthavāda*-s), actually handed down orally by the tradition, is quite literally eternal, having had neither beginning nor author. As for the tradition (*smṛti,* literally "memory") it names not so much a process of transmitting and applying the Veda to changing circumstances as the literal memory of the Vedic texts that have now been lost. The "lost" texts are postulated as the source of those current practices that are not mentioned in the Vedic collections now extant. Revelation is now taken to be a wholly extrinsic authority, under the control of the Brahmin priests. *Dharma* is defined as that which is enjoined by the Vedic injunctions. The possibility of any direct experience of it is explicitly denied.

It is impossible to know just how influential this quite conservative position was. It is possible, and indeed probable, that it had a rather limited appeal. This appears likely in light of the fact that a quite different position — equally "orthodox," inasmuch as it accepted Vedic authority — was developing at the same time. This was the position developed in the Nyāya, or school of logic, which found its first major expression in the commentary on the Nyāya Sūtras of Gautama, written by Vātsyāyana (c. fifth century C.E.), again, roughly contemporary with Bhartṛhari. The very different approach taken by Vātsyāyana is undoubtedly linked to the origin of the Nyāya school. Unlike the Mīmāṃsā, Brahmanical to the core, Nyāya arose in a more "secular" context, with looser ties to the Brahmanical tradition. It originated in the study of the rules governing debate, rules that knew no party but were applied equally to all, be they Brahmin or Buddhist. Nyāya therefore developed in relative independence of strictly Vedic concerns, and this is reflected in its theory of Vedic revelation. For the Nyāya, it is not the Veda as a concrete tradition that is authoritative as such. The Veda is not self-validating, as the Mīmāṃsaka would have it. It is rather the *experience* of a trustworthy witness that grounds the Veda's authority, as well as the authority of the various *smṛti*-s, or traditions. Whereas Mīmāṃsā had created an absolutism of the spoken word, i.e., of the concrete audible words of the Veda as self-authenticating, by virtue of the knowledge that they cause to arise in the listener, the Nyāya took this confidence in the language of tradition to be misplaced (as had, interestingly enough, the Buddha). Language, even the "sacred" language of the Veda, conveys knowledge only on the basis of convention, and it is the experience of the one who uses language that is crucial, whether this be an *ṛṣi,* or Vedic "seer," or, at a later period, God, who is responsible for establishing the conventions in the first place. In its emphasis on direct experience, Nyāya shows the influence upon it of the various traditions of renunciation, such as Buddhism, not to mention the apophatic traditions found in the Upaniṣads. It is significant that the Nyāya, like its sister discipline the Vaiśeṣika, did not claim to arise out of reflection on revelation, as did the Mīmāṃsā. Since its origin was in the examination of argument, a wholly human activity, its perspective was that of the individual investigator, and its theory of the Veda was a secondary application to Vedic tradition of ideas developed elsewhere.

The divergence of the Mīmāṃsā and Nyāya schools over the nature of Vedic revelation illustrates the growing complexity of the post-Vedic world, even among the "orthodox." Their views represent the further elaboration of tendencies in the late Vedic period, namely, the tendency to interpret revelation exclusively as either individual experience or social institution. The Mīmāṃsā eternalizes the very words of the Veda and rejects any claim to an "experience" of *dharma* beyond what is mediated externally through the Vedic institutions of speech and action. Nyāya accepts the authority of this external tradition, but only to the extent that it can be traced to the immediate experience of an *āpta,* or trustworthy witness, be this a seer or a god. The influence of yoga is evident here, probably mediated to Nyāya by way of the Vaiśeṣika system. A Buddhist influence is also discernible. The emphasis is on individual experience, whereas the emphasis in Mīmāṃsā is on the collective tradition.

What unified the diverse Brahmanical responses to the Buddhist challenge, however, was a common allegiance to the Veda and, especially in the case of the Mīmāṃsakas, an allegiance to the social order derived from it. This allegiance entailed, obviously but also quite importantly, an allegiance to Sanskrit, the "Divine Speech" of the Veda and the privileged medium of Vedic culture. This unifying aspect of Vedism came to be expressed in the syllable *Oṃ,* as a sort of symbol of Vedic (and thus Sanskritic) revelation. Thus while the Buddhist success, particularly its rising popularity among the growing urban population and among the rulers of the Mauryan Empire, had brought an end to the strictly Vedic culture of the past, the revivalistic and self-assertive Brahmanism that Bhartṛhari inherited in the fifth century shared a common allegiance to the Vedic tradition and a common concern to clarify the exact nature of its authority. As a grammarian, Bhartṛhari's own approach to this problem was through the medium that tied the Brahmanical tradition together: language.

BHARTṚHARI THE GRAMMARIAN

In the Brahmanical tradition to which Bhartṛhari belonged, the language of the Veda was understood primarily as ritually powerful speech. The Vedic texts themselves often personified language as a goddess. Whether the early Indians considered language in its divine or human aspect, however, they understood it primarily as *sound,* and only secondarily as a system of signs. True speech conveyed meaning by embodying vision and enjoining action. The inspired speech of the seer, also known as a *vipra,* literally one who "quakes," arose out of a powerful experience rather than out of a purely mental act of conceptualization. An original unity of vision and language endowed spoken language with an ontological importance that is perhaps better captured by speaking of "speech-acts"[8] rather than of "language" with its mentalistic connotations. Language in India has traditionally been viewed as more a form of *activity* than as an instrument of thought or representation. This different experience of language accounts for the fact that the earliest linguistic science to develop in India was phonetics (*śikṣā*), which as a science is virtually unknown to Western antiquity and appeared clearly in Europe only in the nineteenth century.[9]

It is important to keep these facts in mind as we locate Bhartṛhari in the grammatical tradition to which he belonged. Grammar (*vyākaraṇa*), like the science of ritual order (*kalpa*) and the science of phonetics, was one of the six *vedāṅga*-s, or auxiliary sciences, of the Veda. Like the other *vedāṅga*-s it originally had the practical concern of preserving "correct" usage in the context of the sacrifice. In the case of *vyākaraṇa* this idea of "correctness" derived originally from the idea of ritually potent speech. Correct speech was inseparable from the correct mode of being, constituted by correct action. The discipline of grammar thus had its roots in the ritual world of the Vedic sacrifice. Both the science of ritual and the science of grammar consisted of a system of interlocking, hierarchically ordered rules that allowed for the marshaling of a diverse set of basic elements to the achievement of a single end. In the science of ritual, this end was a successfully accomplished sacrifice having a single result or "fruit" (*phala*). In the case of grammar, the desired end

---

8. For a discussion of the theory of speech acts as applied to the language of Vedic ritual, see Wade Wheelock, "The Problem of Ritual Language: From Information to Situation," *Journal of the American Academy of Religion* 50 (1982): 49–71.

9. On phonetics in early India, see Jan Gonda, gen. ed., *History of Indian Literature,* vol. 5, fasc. 2: *Grammatical Literature,* by Hartmut Scharfe (Wiesbaden: Otto Harrassowitz, 1977), p. 78.

was a fully and correctly derived utterance, expressing a single action. Both were centrally concerned with action, each having a discrete act — whether the sacrificial act or the "speech-act" — as its *telos.* As intellectual disciplines, both were essentially rule-governed and injunctive in character, and the ideal seems to have been the attainment of a virtually self-governing system that placed great value on the order intrinsic to the subject matter — be it the sacrifice or the Sanskrit language — and de-emphasized the subjectivity of the investigators. This is made clear in part by the fact that the *Aṣṭādhyāyī,* the early authoritative work of the grammarian Pāṇini (c. fifth century B.C.E.), which stands at the head of the Pāṇinian grammatical tradition to which Bhartṛhari belonged, does not recognize a grammatical subject, the key category being rather the *agent,* which need not be personal and may indeed, in certain cases, be identified with the action itself. Just as in the science of the sacrifice, it is the intrinsic order of the sacrifice itself, its *dharma,* that is most important and not the subjective motivations of the individual priests and sacrificers, so too in the grammar, the speaker's subjective intention serves only to set the rules in motion. Once initiated, the process of derivation is virtually automatic. Pāṇini brings the quest for system to its highest development — a fact that has made him particularly popular with structural linguists in the West. His rules are intended to be present as a whole, as a system, at all times, at every step of the derivational process. This presupposes that the entire system of approximately four thousand *sūtra*-s be memorized prior to its actual employment. The *whole* necessarily precedes the *part,* and each part, each *sūtra,* and each derivational operation presupposes the whole and is indeed unintelligible if taken in isolation.

The Vedic notions of ritually potent speech and of the systematic order of the sacrifice are thus reflected in the structure and method of the science of grammar, as well as in other early Vedic auxiliary sciences, or *vedāṅga*-s. But already by Pāṇini's time the subject matter of grammatical science went beyond the strictly ritual use of language. Pāṇini's *Aṣṭādhyāyī* in fact describes the language actually spoken in his day, and only a small proportion of its rules applies specifically to the by then archaic language of the Vedic mantras. Whereas the sciences of phonetics and ritual were in Pāṇini's day restricted to specific Vedic schools, or *śākhā*-s, Pāṇini's grammar was intended to serve *all* schools, indeed, all speakers within the Sanskrit language community, and not merely particular ritual traditions within it. Pāṇini's commentator Patañjali (c. 150 B.C.E.) makes this point clear: "the grammatical science belongs to all the Vedic schools; it is not possible to resort to one single way."[10]

Thus Pāṇini's grammar not only reflected the deepest structures of the Vedic ritual world and its experience of language as powerful speech, but it also projected these structures beyond the strictly ritual world into the larger language community. We shall see that this potential of grammar to mediate Vedic structures to a broader community provided Bhartṛhari with a powerful apologetic tool when he came to develop his theory of Vedic revelation.

Pāṇini's great commentator Patañjali composed his *Mahābhāṣya,* or "Great Commentary," on Pāṇini's *Aṣṭādhyāyī* sometime in the second century B.C.E., as a response to criticisms of the latter work made by the intervening grammarian Kātyāyana. Kātyāyana is known to us only through Patañjali's work. He is of interest primarily because of the discursive style that he introduces into grammatical discourse. From his time on, Pāṇini's *sūtra*-s become the subject of commentaries employing a dialectical style of question and answer, remarkably similar to the Western scholastic style of the *quaestio.*

Patañjali himself is important to us not only because his *Mahābhāṣya* is the last great work in the Pāṇinian tradition prior to Bhartṛhari's *Vākyapadīya,* but also because his work provides us with evidence of a transformation in the understanding of the language of Vedic revelation in which form almost completely overshadows content, a transformation that Bhartṛhari will take for granted. It seems clear that Patañjali saw himself as part of a movement to reassert the norms of correct Sanskrit, as codified by his mentor Pāṇini, as an essential feature of the new social and religious order that had to be forged after the onslaught of Buddhism and the loss of political control marked by the rise of the Mauryan rulers and their foreign successors. The use of correct Pāṇinian Sanskrit, regardless of its material content (Vedic or otherwise), becomes for him a principal form of the performance of *dharma.* Thus the linguistic practice of the individual Brahmanical scholar, or *śiṣṭa*, through study and teaching, becomes a principal form of *religious* practice, precisely when earlier forms of religious practice, e.g., the elaborate sacrificial rituals prescribed in the Vedas, are becoming increasingly uncommon. In the process the authority of the Veda, as a discrete corpus of texts, is conferred upon the Sanskrit *language* of the Veda as such, as codified by Pāṇini and em-

10. The *Vyākarana-Mahābhāṣya* of Patañjali (hereafter MBh), ed. F. Kielhorn, 3 vols. (Bombay: Government Central Press, 1880–85; reprint ed., Poona: Bhandarkar Oriental Research Institute, 1962–72), 1:400, 10–11. See also MBh 3:146.

ployed by the *śiṣṭa.* Pāṇini himself comes to be seen as an inspired seer in his own right.[11] This reassertion of Brahmanical linguistic (as well as, unavoidably, social) norms will provide a necessary foundation for the later "Hindu renaissance" under the Guptas of which Bhartṛhari was a part, a renaissance that can thus equally be viewed as a "Sanskrit renaissance."[12]

Bhartṛhari wrote a commentary on Patañjali's work and clearly recognized him as an authority. Many passages of the *Vākyapadīya* itself must be read as direct commentaries on the *Mahābhāṣya.* Bhartṛhari's work, in fact, follows close upon a major revival in the study of Patañjali's commentary. In order to better understand Bhartṛhari's own position in the Pāṇinian grammatical tradition, however, we must turn to the description of the fate of that tradition, its decline and subsequent revival, presented toward the end of the second book of his major work, the *Vākyapadīya.*[13] I will first offer a translation of the relevant verses and then discuss their significance in the light of what we know about their historical context. We will then be in a position to understand how Bhartṛhari's place within the Pāṇinian tradition connects with his general historical setting in the last half of the fifth century.

At *Vākyapadīya* 2.481–87, we find the following description of the history of the grammatical tradition prior to Bhartṛhari:

> After the *Saṃgraha* [of Vyāḍi, a lost compendium of grammar] had come into the hands of grammarians mostly interested in making abridgments, and having little knowledge, it perished. (481) Then the revered teacher Patañjali, who knew the traditions, composed a great commentary [*the Mahābhāṣya*], which was the basis of all principles of interpretation [used in the grammar] and their justifications.[14] (482) In it, those of imperfect intellect could find no

11. For a full discussion of these developments see David Carpenter, "Language, Ritual and Society: Reflections on the Authority of the Veda in India," *Journal of the American Academy of Religion* 60 (1992): 57–77.

12. See Vittore Pisani, "Sanskrit-Renaissance," *Zeitschrift der Deutschen Morgenländischen Gesellschaft* 105 (1955): 319–26.

13. These verses (*Vākyapadīya* 2.481–87) have traditionally been ascribed to Bhartṛhari himself. Recently, however, Ashok Aklujkar has suggested that they were actually written by one of Bhartṛhari's students. Even if this be the case, however, Aklujkar is quick to add that "the importance of 481–90 for the history of Sanskrit grammar is in no way diminished if they are not ascribed to Bhartṛhari. As the work of a junior contemporary of Bhartṛhari they remain almost as ancient and as reliable as they have so far been held to be." See his article "The Concluding Verses of Bhartṛhari's Vākya-kāṇḍa," *Annals of the Bhandarkar Oriental Research Institute* (Diamond Jubilee Volume) 58–59 (1977–78): 12.

14. I have here adopted George Cardona's translation of the phrase *sarveṣāṃ nyāya bījānām... nibandhane.* See his article, "Still Again on the History of the Mahābhāṣya," *Annals of the Bhandarkar Oriental Research Institute* 58–59 (1977–78): 92.

> foothold; it was bottomless in its profundity, yet seemingly shallow, by virtue of its skillfulness. (483) When that inspired [*ārṣa*] book, which was a counterpart[15] of the *Saṃgraha,* had been defiled by the grammarians Vaiji, Saubhava, and Haryakṣa, who depended upon dry reasoning, (484) then the tradition of grammar, which had fallen away from the students of Patañjali, eventually survived as a mere book in the south. (485) [Then,] after obtaining the tradition from the mountain, the teacher Candra and others, following the principles of [Patañjali's] commentary, again caused the tradition to flourish in many branches. (486) After studying both the traditions [*mārga-s*] based on those rules, and his own viewpoint, my teacher composed this collection of traditions. (487)[16]

Here Bhartṛhari's student clearly refers to a revival of Pāṇinian studies, Patañjali's *Mahābhāṣya* being by far the most important text of the Pāṇinian tradition next to Pāṇini's own *Aṣṭādhyāyī.* Candra is named as the primary figure in this revival, and this is undoubtedly to be taken as a reference to Candragomin, who is to be assigned to the middle of the fifth century C.E. This fits perfectly with the renewed prestige of Pāṇinian norms during the Gupta period. We thus have the witness of Bhartṛhari's own student to his teacher's role in this larger cultural movement. The *Vākyapadīya* is, in fact, a mature expression of this revival, in which the science of Sanskrit grammar is elevated to the status of an integral metaphysical system.

This transformation of a particular science into an integral philosophical viewpoint (or *darśana*) is not peculiar to grammar, but is witnessed

---

15. Here I follow Ashok Aklujkar's interpretation of the term *pratikañcuke,* "The Concluding Verses," pp. 19–23. It is interesting to note that Patañjali's work is here referred to as *ārṣa,* i.e., as belonging to or deriving from an *ṛṣi.* It would seem that both Pāṇini and Patañjali had been promoted to the rank of seers by the Gupta period and that Bhartṛhari himself viewed them as such. See also *Vākyapadīya* 1.23 *vṛtti,* where the great seers (*maharṣi-*s) are described as the authors of the grammatical *sūtra-*s and other treatises (*sūtrādīnāṃ praṇetṛbhiḥ*).

16. *Bhartṛharis Vākyapadīya: die Mūlakārikās nach den Handschriften herausgegeben und mit einem pāda-index,* ed. Wilhelm Rau (Wiesbaden: Kommissionsverlag Franz Steiner GMBH, 1977), 2.481–87.

This passage has been much discussed. See especially Paul Thieme, "Pāṇini and the Pāṇinīyas," *Kleine Schriften,* 2 vols. (Wiesbaden: Franz Steiner, 1971), 2:590–92; Aśok Aklujkar, "The Concluding Verses of Bhartṛhari's Vākya-kāṇḍa"; idem, "Interpreting Vākyapadīya 2.486 Historically (Part 1)," *Adyar Library Bulletin* 44–45 (1980–81): 581–601; idem, "Interpreting Vākyapadīya 2.486 Historically (Part 2)," L. A. Hercus et al., eds., *Indological and Buddhist Studies* (Canberra, Faculty of Asian Studies), (1982): 1–10; George Cardona, "Still Again on the History of the Mahābhāṣya," *Annals of the Bhandarkar Oriental Research Institute* 58–59 (1977–78): 79–99; and Hartmut Scharfe, "A Second 'Index Fossil' of Sanskrit Grammarians," *Journal of the American Oriental Society* 92 (1976): 276.

as well in the Nyāya and Mīmāṃsā, both of which developed specifically philosophical positions at about this same time, going beyond their more immediate and concrete concerns. Among these more general philosophical positions were specific theories of Vedic revelation. We saw how the theories of the Nyāya and Mīmāṃsā represented polar options, emphasizing either language or direct experience. While Bhartṛhari's transformation of grammar into a *darśana* must be viewed in the context of these more general developments, developments undoubtedly responding to the more pluralistic conditions of the Gupta period, his case is particularly interesting in that he represents an auxiliary Vedic science, namely, grammar (like Mīmāṃsā but *unlike* Nyāya, which rarely appeals to the Veda), which is nevertheless a science that attends to the direct experience of ordinary language (like Nyāya, which studies actual forms of argument, but *unlike* Mīmāṃsā, which recognizes only the canonical Vedic texts as subject matter). Bhartṛhari accordingly develops a quite distinctive view of Vedic revelation, which combines elements that the Nyāya and Mīmāṃsā tend to separate.

We will examine Bhartṛhari's doctrine of Vedic revelation in the next chapter. In concluding this introduction, it is worthwhile calling attention once more to the underlying structures that gave form to Bhartṛhari's age. On the one hand, as a *smārta* Brahmin educated as a boy in the traditional fashion, perhaps while residing at one of the many *agrahāra*-s that had become the sanctuaries of traditional Brahmanical learning, Bhartṛhari would have been deeply influenced by the structures of the Brahmanical social order. He would have memorized his family's Veda before going on to more advanced studies in grammar and thus would have imbibed some of the values and mentality of an earlier oral culture. He would have experienced at first hand the dynamic and pragmatic character of the language of his tradition, the language of ritual, *dharma,* and revelation.

On the other hand, there can be little doubt that Bhartṛhari also participated in the sophisticated intellectual life of a literate elite, which was composed of Buddhists and Jains, Vaiṣṇavas and Śaivas, as well as more traditional Brahmins. He was a master of the śāstraic, or "scholastic" style, and of the literary forms of the *kārikā* (verse) and the prose commentary, which were becoming the universally accepted genres of scholarly discourse, regardless of particular content. This implies a degree of participation in a common intellectual world, a common way of raising questions and presenting arguments, a degree of consensus on the form, if not the content, of knowledge. These points, shared by intellectuals of widely differing views, obviously owed much to the shared

Sanskritic culture: to the Sanskrit language itself, to a shared literacy, and to a shared position of privilege as members of a cultured ("Sanskritized") elite, dependent upon royal patronage.

As we shall see, the existence of these two worlds, and Bhartṛhari's participation in both of them, raised intellectual problems to which his *Vākyapadīya* must be seen as a response. Essentially, the co-existence of these two contexts brought into conflict two fundamentally opposed models of language and knowledge. On the one hand, there was the traditional Vedic view of language as Divine Speech, the language of the sacrifice that had become the language of *dharma,* the language of the learned, the *śiṣṭa*-s, who were the embodiment of Brahmanical orthopraxy. This was the view of language as a form of activity, as a source of merit and demerit. It was the view of Sanskrit as *saṃskāra,* a ritual means of purification, still available in the fifth century in the practice of the *svādhyāya,* or personal recitation of the Veda, by Brahmin householders.

On the other hand, there was the view of language as an instrument for the expression of subjective intentions and for the discursive representation of the world. This was a view that was presupposed by the very notion of a plurality of *pravāda*-s or *darśana*-s, the schools of thought or "viewpoints" that proliferated during the Gupta period. It was also a view encouraged by literacy and the existence of texts in a single language and genre that nevertheless represented opposing positions. It was fostered by the secular, urban, and pluralistic context made possible by Gupta rule.

We may conclude, therefore, that Bhartṛhari's position as a Pāṇinian grammarian in the late fifth century C.E. was determined not only by his education as a Brahmin, as a practitioner of a traditional *vedāṅga,* but also by his historical setting in the Gupta period and his participation in a Sanskritic culture and form of discourse that transcended a number of otherwise quite important religious differences. Given his situation, we may expect to find in Bhartṛhari some highly interesting insights into the manner of understanding and appropriating Vedic revelation in the midst of India's complex "Golden Age."

2

Bhartṛhari's Doctrine of Revelation

THE METAPHYSICAL FOUNDATION: THE TRUE WORD

Perhaps the best way to begin to understand Bhartṛhari's view of Vedic revelation is to begin as he does, with the ultimate ground of revelation, the absolute Brahman, which he characterizes as Word, *śabda*. In the opening verses of the Brahmakāṇḍa, which is the first book of his major work, the *Vākyapadīya*, the "Treatise on Sentences and Words,"[1] Bhartṛhari introduces us to the basic themes of his metaphysics:

1. While the *Vākyapadīya* is undoubtedly Bhartṛhari's most important work, it is not his only one. In addition to a commentary on Patañjali's *Mahābhāṣya*, which survives in only one incomplete manuscript, Bhartṛhari is also known to have composed a treatise on metaphysics entitled *Śabdadhātusamīkṣā*, which unfortunately has not survived. Nevertheless, the *Vākyapadīya* (hereafter VP) contains what was most probably Bhartṛhari's most complete formulation of his thought as a whole, ranging as it does from general metaphysical statements to the analysis of detailed points in Sanskrit grammar. The VP itself, perhaps more properly called the *Trikāṇḍī*, or "Work in Three Books," consists of three distinct books, the *Brahmakāṇḍa*, or "Book on Brahman," the *Vākyakāṇḍa*, or "Book on the Sentence," and the *Prakīrṇakāṇḍa*, or "Book on Miscellaneous Topics," also called the *Padakāṇḍa*, or "Book on Individual Words." The last book is further divided into fourteen separate *samuddeśa*-s, or "Discussions." The following chapter is based exclusively on a reading of these three books of the VP, hereafter referred to by the Arabic numerals 1, 2, and 3 respectively. In references to the first two books, the second Arabic numeral refers to the verse number. In references to the third book, the second Arabic numeral refers to the relevant *samuddeśa* and the third refers to the verse. In what follows, I have relied, where possible, on Wilhelm Rau's critical edition of the *kāraka*-s, or individual verses of the VP, *Bhartṛharis Vākyapadīya: die Mūlakārikās nach den Handschriften herausgegeben und mit einem pāda-index* (Wiesbaden: Kommissionsverlag Franz Steiner GMBH, 1977). I have also made use of Bhartṛhari's own commentary on the first two books of the VP, the *Brahmakāṇḍavṛtti*, or "Commentary on the Book on Brahman," and the *Vākyakāṇḍavṛtti*, or "Commentary on the Book on the Sentence." Through the kindness of Ashok Aklujkar, I have been able to consult his new critical edition of the *Brahmakāṇḍavṛtti*, which unfortunately still remains unpublished. An earlier edition of this portion of Bhartṛhari's commentary is that of K. A. Subramania Iyer, *Vākyapadīya*

> Brahman, the True Word, which is without beginning or end, which is the imperishable Syllable, manifests itself in the form of objects; from it the production of the world [proceeds]. (1) Although it is proclaimed to be one, it is divided[2] through having recourse to its powers. Although it is not different from its powers, it exists as if it were different from them. (2) The six transformations, beginning with birth, which are the source of the differentiation of beings, are dependent upon its power of time, to which parts have been attributed. (3) Of that One, which is the seed of all things, there is this state of multiplicity, having the form of the enjoyer, the object to be enjoyed, and the enjoyment. (4)[3]

Bhartṛhari presents us with the most distinctive aspects of his metaphysics at the very outset, and in doing so locates himself firmly within the Vedic tradition while at the same time giving that tradition a particular emphasis. Bhartṛhari accepts the identification of ultimate reality with the eternal Brahman, an identification that had been established much earlier in the classical Upaniṣads. What is distinctive about his opening verse is his use of the word *śabdatattva.* The exact meaning of this term has been a matter of some debate. It is a Sanskrit compound combining the word *śabda,* literally "sound," "speech," or "word," with the

---

of Bhartṛhari with the Vṛtti and the Paddhati of Vṛṣabhadeva (Poona: Deccan College Postgraduate and Research Institute, 1966). For Bhartṛhari's commentary on his second book, the *Vākyakāṇḍavṛtti,* I have used Iyer's recent critical edition *The Vākyapadīya of Bhartṛhari, Kāṇḍa II, with the commentary of Puṇyarāja and the ancient Vṛtti* (Delhi: Motilal Banarsidass, 1983). Bhartṛhari's authorship of the commentary on the first two books of the VP has been disputed, most especially by Madeleine Biardeau, in the introduction to her French translation of the Brahmakāṇḍa, *Vākyapadīya Brahmakāṇḍa, avec la Vṛtti de Harivṛṣabha* (Paris: Institut de Civilisation Indienne, 1964). Biardeau's objections to Bhartṛhari's authorship have been discussed by K. A. Subramania Iyer, *Bhartṛhari: A Study of the Vākyapadīya in the Light of the Ancient Commentaries* (Poona: Deccan College, 1969): 33–36, and more recently by Aklujkar, "The Authorship of Vākyapadīya-vṛtti," *Wiener Zeitschrift für die Kunde Südasians* 16 (1972): 181–98. Biardeau's caution led me initially to restrict my study of the *Vākyapadīya* to the *kārika*-s, or verses of his text. Returning at last to the text of Bhartṛhari's *vṛtti,* I was unable to find any significant divergence in meaning between the main text and Bhartṛhari's auto-commentary. Consequently I have come to accept what is now the dominant scholarly opinion, represented by Aklujkar, that the *vṛtti* is indeed Bhartṛhari's own. This has always been the traditional view among Indian grammarians themselves. The following interpretation of Bhartṛhari's theory of Vedic revelation is accordingly based on both the *kārika*-s and the *vṛtti.*

2. Here I have accepted a variant recorded by Rau, according to which one reads *bhinnaṃ śaktivyapāśrayāt.* In doing so, I am following the precedent set by Paul Hacker in his *Vivarta: Studien zur Geschichte der illusionistischen Kosmologie und Erkenntnistheorie der Inder* (Wiesbaden: Franz Steiner Verlag, 1953), p. 14. K. A. Subramania Iyer, in his *Vākyapadīya of Bhartṛhari with the Vṛtti* (Poona: Deccan College, 1965), p. 4, admits *bhinnaṃ* to be the better reading, although he does not follow it in his translation.

3. VP 1.1–4. In what follows the translations are my own.

word *tattva,* which refers to the true essence or ultimate reality of something. In Bhartṛhari's opening verse the term can be taken as an adjective meaning either that Brahman has speech as its essence or that Brahman is the essence of speech. Both of these interpretations have merit, depending upon whether we take *śabda* to refer to actual speech or to the expressiveness that underlies all speech. The term can also be taken nominally, however, and this is how I have translated it, as the true or ultimate Reality (*tattva*) that is Speech or Word (*śabda*), or more simply, and somewhat freely, the True Word. This identification of the absolute with the word (*śabda*) is noteworthy. While it was not uncommon in the tradition deriving from the Upaniṣads to separate *śabdabrahman,* or the "Word-Brahman," understood as the Vedic corpus, from the supreme (*para*) Brahman, here the absolute itself is directly described as the True Word, which Bhartṛhari also refers to as *śabdabrahman.* It is true that in continuity with the earlier Vedic tradition of a transcendent or hidden aspect of Speech, Bhartṛhari too will speak of a supreme Brahman (*para brahma*) and of a supreme source or origin (*parā prakṛti*), there is no sense of a fundamental opposition between the latter and Brahman as the True Word. Thus when he further describes Brahman here as *akṣara,* we should undoubtedly take this as a reference, not only to the well-known Upanishadic meaning of "imperishable" (though this sense is certainly to be included), but also to its early meaning in the Ṛg Veda, the divine Syllable, the transcendent source of the world order.[4] Bhartṛhari in fact explicitly tells us, in this same verse, that this True Word, the imperishable Syllable, is the origin of the world order.

Elsewhere Bhartṛhari supports this claim through a direct appeal to the Veda: "Those who know the Veda know that this universe is a transformation [*pariṇāma*] of the Word. This universe first came forth from the hymns (of the Veda)."[5] Unlike the Vedic texts, however, Bhartṛhari goes on to explain how this is possible. The next three verses (2–4) present the most characteristic and fundamental feature of his metaphysics, the notion of the *śakti*-s, the powers or capacities of Brahman. This notion allows Bhartṛhari to develop an essentially non-dualist metaphysics that is nevertheless thoroughly dynamic. As we will see below, for Bhartṛhari the world order is a dynamic system of interconnecting forces or actions that are the actualizations and self-manifestations of Brahman's own intrinsic capacities. The changing world as we experience it is the condition (*sthiti*)

4. See J. A. B. van Buitenen, "Akṣara," *Journal of the American Oriental Society* 79 (1959): 176–87.
5. VP 1.124.

that Brahman assumes through its power of self-veiling (*avidyāśakti*) and its power of Time (*kālaśakti*). The world is understood less as a world of substantial things than as a process of action and experience, having a dynamic triadic structure. Rather than a world of things, the world is primarily a world of actions and relations, the actualizations of Brahman's expressive potentialities.

The concept of *śakti* is the key to Bhartṛhari's metaphysics, which could perhaps best be described as a metaphysics of identity-in-difference (*bhedābheda*), though Bhartṛhari himself does not use this term. As capacities of Brahman, the *śakti*-s are identical with the ultimate Reality, which Bhartṛhari also refers to as *tattva.* Accordingly, they are in themselves quite real. And yet, paradoxically, to the extent that they are taken to be multiple, they are unreal. Brahman is transcendent in relation to the world precisely to the extent that the latter is (wrongly) viewed as multiple. The *śakti*-s may appear to be multiple, but as capacities of the unique Brahman they are identical with it. Brahman is the unitary Reality that is endowed with the capacity to manifest itself under the apparent form of diversity while remaining one.

Bhartṛhari is careful to point out that Brahman's unity is not of a numerical sort. Thus in the *Sādhanasamuddeśa,* or the "Discussion of Means," in the third book of the VP, the *Padakāṇḍa,* the "Book on Words" (VP 3.7.39), he tells us that although identity (*ekatva*) and difference (*pṛthaktva*) are commonly considered to be different, in the ultimate sense (*paramārthe*) they are not. Rather, it is the ultimate Reality (*tattva*) that shines forth (*prakāśate*) under the form of identity and difference.[6] The unity that characterizes the ultimate Reality is clearly different from the mere numerical or quantitative unity that characterizes our ordinary experience of the world. The latter is merely the logical correlate of plurality and belongs to the same level as it. This notion of a "transcendental" unity is required to understand Bhartṛhari's doctrine of Brahman as endowed with a multiplicity of powers that are nonetheless "identical" with it. There is a "coincidence of opposites" in Brahman that transcends the mundane categories of identity and difference. Our understanding of the *śakti*-s must follow different lines from our understanding based on the categories that characterize the world of objects. Like Brahman, with which they are identified, the powers transcend such categories.[7]

6. See also VP 3.7.40: "What is undoubtedly difference, that is not different from unity. What is undoubtedly unity, that is not different from difference."

7. See especially the concluding verses of the *Diksamuddeśa* of the third *kāṇḍa,* VP 3.6.24–28.

They are endowed with a dynamism and a relationality that the latter lack. Borrowing a Western term, one could say that the *śakti*-s are more "dialectical."

One of Bhartṛhari's most important discussions of the relation of the manifest world to its ground is found in the *Dravyasamuddeśa,* the "Discussion of Substance," in the third book. In the following passage, Bhartṛhari emphasizes the transcendental status of *tattva* and relates it to the nature of language:

> The tradition of the ancients is that there is no difference between Ultimate Reality and non-ultimate reality. What some take for non-ultimate is in fact the Ultimate which has not been carefully examined. (7) The Ultimate Reality which is not divided by any artificial construct takes on the form of such constructs. Here [in the Ultimate Reality] there is no temporal division; and [yet] the division of time is perceived. (8) Just as there is no possibility whatsoever for the attributes of objects to exist in [pure] knowledge, and yet knowledge, which is completely different from an object nevertheless is established as if it were identified with an object, so too, while there is no possibility whatsoever of diversified objects within the Ultimate Reality, this Ultimate Reality, which is completely different from diversified objects, nevertheless seems to be identified with such objects. (9–10) The Reality which remains after the final withdrawal of the forms [of the universe at the end of a world cycle] is the Eternal which is expressed in speech and is not separate from speech. (11) That [Reality] neither exists nor does not exist; it is neither one nor different; it is neither connected nor divided; it is not made manifold nor is it otherwise [than manifold]. (12) That [Reality] is not, and it is; it is one, and it is multiple; it is connected and it is divided; it is made manifold and it is otherwise [than manifold]. (13) That One [Reality] is seen in the form of the relation of the word and its object; that [One Reality] is what is seen, seeing itself, the one who sees, and the purpose of seeing. (14) Just as, in the case of a bracelet, gold remains as what is real after the form [of the bracelet] has perished, so too, upon the perishing of [all] forms, they say that what [remains] as real is the highest original Nature. (15) That [original Nature] is that which is expressed by all spoken words; and these words are not different from it; and even though there is no difference [between this original Nature as the ultimate object of words and the words that express it], there is

> a relation between them as if they were essentially different. (16) Just as in sleep there are contrary forms of one and the same mind, such as the forms of self and other, friend and enemy, speaker and the purpose to be expressed, so too in the unborn, eternal, Ultimate Reality, devoid of all temporal sequence, the contradictory forms of birth [and death, etc.] are perceived. (17–18)[8]

These verses make it clear that the paradoxical nature that characterizes Brahman characterizes language as well. This should not surprise us, since, for Bhartṛhari, Brahman is precisely the *True Word.* This True Word is endowed with the capacity to appear in a state of multiplicity, as so many "words," while at the same time remaining essentially one.

Before turning to Bhartṛhari's description of the Veda itself, it is worth making one additional observation on the above verses. One cannot help but notice the close similarity between verses 11–12 above and the last two propositions of Nāgārjuna's *tetralemma.* This is but one indication of the Buddhist influence evident in many aspects of Bhartṛhari's thought. Other striking instances are his uses of the term *vikalpa* in the sense of "mental construction" and his distinction between an ordinary, mundane level of reality (*vyavahāra*) and a higher, ultimate level (*paramārtha*). In addition, there are structural parallels between elements of Bhartṛhari's thought and a number of Yogācāra Buddhist ideas (as represented, for example, by Vasubandhu), which, as Chr. Lindtner has noted, are "too striking to be purely coincidental."[9] Such instances provide ample evidence of Bhartṛhari's attempt to accommodate his thought to some fundamental Buddhist notions even while trying to maintain an essentially orthodox, Vedic perspective. Like the later Vedāntin philosopher Śaṅkara, Bhartṛhari's attempt to defend his tradition against the Buddhist challenge in many cases entailed appropriating key insights from his opponents. We will return to this point in a later chapter.

The Veda as **Anukāra** *of Brahman*

After describing the metaphysical foundation of Vedic revelation, Bhartṛhari turns to the Veda itself:

> The Veda is the means for attaining [*prāptyupāya*] that [Brahman] and is its imitative resemblance [*anukāra*]. Although it is one, it

8. VP 3.2.7–18.
9. Chr. Lindtner, "Linking up Bhartṛhari and the Bauddhas," *Asiatische Studien* 47 (1993): 197.

is proclaimed again and again by the great seers as having, as it were, many paths. (5) There are many paths to its divisions; it is the accessory in one rite. The fixity of the powers of its words is seen in its branches. (6)[10]

For our purposes, verse 1.5 is one of the most important in the VP, and we must examine it closely. Here Bhartṛhari tells us that the Veda is the *prāptyupāya* and the *anukāra* of Brahman, that it is in reality one, although the great seers proclaim it "as if" (*iva*) it had many paths. The apparent multiplicity involved here would seem to refer to the differentiation of the Ṛg, Yajur, Sāma and Atharva Vedas rather than the various branches (*śākhā*-s) of each of these, since these branches are dealt with separately in 1.6. The unity that Bhartṛhari has in mind here thus precedes or underlies the fourfold division with which we are familiar. In fact, 1.5 bears comparison with the description of Brahman, the True Word, in 1.2: both the True Word and the Veda are described as one and yet as existing in a diverse state. One presumes that the Veda, prior to its fourfold division by the *ṛṣi*-s, is identical with that True Word itself.

Most important in 1.5, however, are the two terms that Bhartṛhari uses to describe the Veda directly: it is the means for the attainment of Brahman (*prāptyupāya*) as well as the "imitation" of Brahman (*anukāra*). What Bhartṛhari means by calling the Veda the means for the attainment of Brahman will best be considered when we examine the role that he attributes to the discipline of grammar in this process. For the moment, we will restrict our attention to the term *anukāra,* which is not a particularly common term in classical Sanskrit.

The term *anukāra* is formed as a primary derivative of the verbal root *anukṛ,* which is composed of the root *kṛ,* to do or to make, and the preverb *anu-,* meaning after, following, near to, subordinate to, with. As a primary derivation *anukāra* would normally indicate either the action expressed by the verbal root or the agent of such action.[11] On the basis of its etymology, therefore, *anukāra* could mean either a doing or making after or with or the agent of such activity.

The occurrence at 1.5 is not the only use Bhartṛhari makes of this term. It appears, for instance, at 1.88: "The constant defect of knowledge and speech is the imitating of difference [*bhedānukāra*]; speech has a form affected by sequence; knowledge has recourse to the object

10. VP 1.5–6.

11. See William D. Whitney, *Sanskrit Grammar* (London: Oxford University Press, 1960), p. 421.

of knowledge."[12] The term also occurs at 2.7: "Just as light, which is one and (illumines) all objects, is divided by imitating the differences [*bhedānukāreṇa*] of visible objects, so too is the understanding of the meaning of the sentence."[13] Bhartṛhari uses the term on three other occasions, at VP 2.135, 3.9.100, and 3.14.570. In all three cases *anukāra,* twice in the instrumental as in 2.7 above, is compounded with the term *pratyaya,* meaning an idea or conception in the mind, with the meaning of imitating, following upon, being dependent upon or conformed to such an idea.

It is interesting to note the uses of the closely related term *anukaraṇa* in the grammatical tradition itself. In his glossary of grammatical terms, Louis Renou defines *anukaraṇa* as an "imitation," "a word or element which imitates an original called *prakṛti,*" and refers to the following *paribhāṣā* or "interpretative principle" of the tradition: *prakṛtivad anukaraṇam bhavati,* "an imitation is like (its) original."[14] He continues: "More specifically, *anukaraṇam* designates an 'equivalent' by which one seeks to reproduce a form such as one has understood."[15] That Bhartṛhari knew the *paribhāṣā* referred to by Renou is certain, since it is given in the *Mahābhāṣya* of his undisputed master, Patañjali.[16]

The grammarians' use of the term *anukaraṇa* points to another aspect of the meaning of *anukāra* as we find it in 1.5: the notion of resemblance. The imitation is "like" its original (*prakṛtivad*). The concept of *prakṛti* resonates deeply both with Bhartṛhari's grammatical method and with the metaphysics that underlies it. Bhartṛhari uses the term *prakṛti* to refer to ultimate Reality, or Brahman,[17] as well as to the original linguistic form from which all grammatical derivation proceeds. This commonality of usage is not fortuitous but rather is a consequence of Bhartṛhari's metaphysics. As we have seen, Brahman is *Śabdatattva,* the True Word from which the "production" or "derivation" (*prakriyā*) of the world proceeds. Bhartṛhari uses the same term, *prakriyā,* to describe both the production of the world (1.1) and the production of the finished verbal form from its stem. *Brahma śabdatattvam* is thus the "stem" or "root" that underlies the "inflected" forms of the world, the *vikāra*-s, the modified forms

12. VP 1.88.

13. VP 1.7.

14. See Nāgojibhaṭṭa, *Paribhāṣenduśekhara, paribhāṣā* 36, ed. Kielhorn (Poona: Bhandarkar Oriental Research Institute, 1960), pt. 2, p. 175.

15. Louis Renou, *Terminologie grammaticale du Sanskrit,* 2 vols. (Paris: E. Champion, 1942), 1:24.

16. MBh 1.1.2, *Śivasūtra* 3. On Bhartṛhari's relationship to Patañjali, see VP 2.481–87.

17. See VP 3.2.11; 15–16. See also VP 1.136, 3.1.43, and 3.6.18.

that are the end products of the transformations of the Word.[18] The Veda, as the *anukāra* of Brahman, standing in a relation of conformity to and dependence upon its source, occupies a mediating position between this source and the diverse forms of the world. It presents, within the dynamic framework of the world as a whole, a level of expression and action that is directly related to the unitary ground of that world. It thus presents the established order of dharma in contrast to the often disorderly world of everyday activity (*vyavahāra*).

To say that the Veda as *anukāra* is the "imitative resemblance" of Brahman should not be taken to mean, however, that the Veda somehow offers us a "description" of Brahman. For Bhartṛhari, the function of Vedic revelation is not to provide us with a representation of the "object" Brahman. Rather, the Veda functions as an imitative "presentation," or *Darstellung,* of the unity of Brahman, mediating Brahman directly through the dynamic idiom of language and action in their inseparable interrelationship. In its concrete linguistic form, the Veda mediates the unity of the True Word by manifesting the original order through which the world is related back to its unitary source. Like the Mīmāṃsakas, Bhartṛhari maintains that there is an eternal relationship between language and the world, and for him this relationship is grounded in the unity of the True Word.[19] The language of the Veda, as well as all correct language derived from it, preserves these relations and thereby makes available a traditional world that makes manifest, by its relational structures, the unity of its ground.

But, to repeat, this making manifest is not of a merely cognitive nature. For Bhartṛhari, language functions primarily to mediate action, not ideas: "All that which is to be done in the world is based on language."[20] Thus the Veda as the *anukāra* of Brahman serves as the original source of *dharma,* since *dharma* is that mode of action which conforms to or "imitates" the ultimate order of things, the order originally imposed on things by the Veda as the arranger of the worlds.

The Role of the Seers

To return to VP 1.5, Bhartṛhari there refers to the seers, or *ṛṣi*-s, as the "proclaimers" of the Veda. He examines the role of these *ṛṣi*-s in some detail in two different sections of his commentary on the Brahmakāṇḍa. His first remarks form part of the commentary on this verse. In explaining

18. *Śabdapariṇāmaḥ.* See VP 1.124.
19. See VP 1.23.
20. VP 1.129ab: *itikartavyatā loke sarvā śabdavyapāśrayā.*

what it means to refer to the Veda as the *anukāra* of Brahman he describes the role of the seers in the manifestation of the Veda:

> The seers who have directly seen the ritual ordinances, who see the mantras, see the subtle, eternal Word which is beyond the senses. Desiring to make it known to others who have not directly seen the ritual ordinances, they proclaim [literally, repeat from memory] an image [*bilma*] [of it], desiring to relate what they have directly seen, heard, or experienced, as if in a dream.[21]

Bhartṛhari follows this with a passage taken word for word from an earlier text, Yāska's *Nirukta* (1.20):

> The seers saw the ritual ordinances directly. To others who had not seen the ritual ordinances directly they proclaimed the mantras by way of instruction.[22]

It is obvious that what Bhartṛhari has done is to rework the passage from Yāska to give prominence to the seers' vision of the subtle Word. All that Yāska says is that the seers saw the ritual ordinances directly and then proclaimed the mantras. Bhartṛhari, however, quotes Yāska's description only after himself providing a significantly modified version. Although he accepts Yāska's language and says that the seers saw the ritual ordinances directly, he goes on to specify what this means. According to him, to see the *dharman*-s, the ritual ordinances, is actually to "see" (*paśyanti*) the Word that is eternal and beyond the senses. He identifies the vision of the ritual structure of the world order with the vision of the Word. This identification, linking as it does *dharman* (the Ṛg Vedic term) or *dharma* (the classical term) with visionary experience, lies at the very heart of Bhartṛhari's interpretation of Vedic revelation.

Bhartṛhari further specifies the seers' experience by referring to it indifferently as what they "saw," "heard," and "directly experienced, as if in a dream." This description, coupled with Bhartṛhari's description of the Word as beyond the senses, prevents us from interpreting the seers' vision in any simplistic way. Its inwardness is expressed by the comparison with dream experience, while its "objectivity" is no less certain, since it is unthinkable that Bhartṛhari would have understood the Word and *dharma* as merely psychological realities.

21. VP 1.5 vṛtti.
22. VP 1.5 vṛtti (continued).

Bhartṛhari's *vṛtti,* or commentary, on 1.5 contains one more description of the role of the seers, which describes the process in more detail:

> What is called the Veda is a single object of vision established in vision itself [*darśanātmani sthito dṛśyo 'rthaḥ*]. Because it is impossible to explain that which is [thus] undifferentiated, the great seers caused that essential form of speech to acquire sequence, for the sake of [its] manifestation in a differentiated form. Then, without overstepping its unity, [the Veda] was proclaimed in different paths because of its different [modes of recitation]: *saṃhitā, pada,* and *krama,* by the great seers who established schools for the Vedic study of the students.[23]

Once again Bhartṛhari insists on the unity of the Veda and underlines its origin in a unitive vision. It is noteworthy that the transition from vision to actual utterance is conceived of as the manifestation of the essential form of speech itself rather than the use of speech to express what is beyond it. The primary function of the seers is to cause that essential Word to attain the sequential, temporal form of actual utterance. They do not "compose" the Veda; they "enact" it. They "translate" or "transform" it from its unitary visionary state to its temporal, manifested state as a form of dharmic *activity,* originally the sacred speech employed as an integral component of the ritual action of the sacrifice.

The function of a seer is thus first to *see* and then to *act,* to speak and thereby to "repeat" (as is implied in the verb *sam-ā-mnā-)* or "imitate" (as is implied in the term *anukāra)* the unitary Word in the medium of actually spoken sounds, in the activity of speech. They function merely to bring about *a change in state* in the Veda: they are not its "authors."[24] They are rather its "agents." They "act-ualize" or "en-act" the potencies immanent within the True Word itself.

The function of the seers is also the topic of Bhartṛhari's commentary on 1.173. This verse actually forms a pair with 1.172. Both deal with the nature of revelation (*śruti*) and tradition (*smṛti*). Verse 1.172 presents what is most probably the Mīmāṃsā view, and in 1.173 Bhartṛhari presents his own view.

---

23. VP 1.5 vṛtti (continued).

24. Bhartṛhari says this explicitly at 1.148, where he contrasts the Veda with tradition by describing the former as being like consciousness itself (*caitaṇyavat*) and as *apauruṣeya,* literally "non-human."

The fundamental point of contrast between the two positions is the question of whether or not the differentiated state of the world (and by implication, the Veda) is permanent or not. The Mīmāṃsaka denies the existence of world-cycles and thus accepts the present differentiated condition of the world as permanent. As a correlate of this, the division of the Veda into its various branches is believed to be a permanent state of affairs.

By contrast, Bhartṛhari accepts the existence of world-cycles. Accordingly, the Veda itself goes through the process of manifestation, which we have already examined in some detail. In 1.173 the cosmogonic side of this process is emphasized, and this helps us better understand Bhartṛhari's view of the seers and their function. The verse itself presents a summary statement: "Insight into *śruti* [or Veda] belongs to those who become manifest out of the undifferentiated. The *smṛti* is composed on the basis of indications [found in the *śruti*] after the nature of existent things has been examined."[25] Bhartṛhari's commentary on this verse, though rather long, bears quoting in full:

> Some people believe that this present differentiated condition of the world is eternal. For them there is no such thing as a *yuga* or a *manvantara* [i.e., various periods within a developing cosmic cycle], nor do they recognize any extraordinary division such as the day and night of Brahmā [corresponding to a complete cosmic cycle]. Their viewpoint on the function of *śruti* and *smṛti* has been given in the previous verse.
>
> But those who believe that the eternal cause develops by an activity of sleeping and waking that imitates [the sleeping and waking] of an individual man [understand *śruti* and *smṛti* this way]: Some seers become manifest in intuition [*pratibhā*] itself. Seeing the great Self that is defined as Being and that is the source of Nescience, they become identified with it through direct insight. Some, however, become manifest in knowledge [*vidyā*]. They become identified with the Self [which has acquired the form of the] mind-knot, which is free from the elements such as the ether, whether individually or collectively, and which has an unbounded power of imaginative construction. In their case, whatever is adventitious, being the activity of Nescience, is all secondary. But whatever is knowledge per se, eternal and non-adventitious, is primary. Through their intuitive

25. VP 1.173.

> knowledge [*prajñā*] they see the entire Veda [*āmnāyam*], joined with the capacity for every differentiation and with the capacity for indifferentiation, like a word that cannot be approached through hearing. Some, however, after examining the nature of those objects that relate to the welfare and harm of man, and having seen indications relating to them in the Vedas, composed the tradition with its visible and invisible purposes. *Śruti,* however, is proclaimed first in an undivided state, according to vision, with words that are without deviation, and then again, divided into schools.[26]

Bhartṛhari describes three types of seers here, which can be ranked according to the intensity of their vision and their stage in cosmic evolution. The first type, being the first to become manifest at the beginning of a "day of Brahmā," is identified with pure vision. Here knowledge and being are identified. Though they see the source of the Nescience (*avidyā*) that will soon cast a veil over Being's luminosity, there is no indication that this Nescience itself is as yet actual. The picture is one of perfect self-conscious unity.

At the next stage, and among the seers of the second type, the power of Nescience becomes active and we now have a less perfect vision, mixed with what is adventitious, but still inward, independent of the subtle elements from which the material world will evolve. These seers see the Veda that is still one, but that already displays its capacity for differentiation, for becoming the Veda as actually proclaimed in human speech.

Finally, Bhartṛhari describes the third type of seer, which is really to be identified with the *śiṣṭa*-s, the learned authors of the various traditional texts that derive their authority from the Veda, but are also based on the experience of their authors.

It is the second type of seer described here that helps us understand the manner in which the Veda as unitary, visionary Word takes on the form of actually uttered words, for it is clearly this type that actually "proclaims" the Veda. Both here and in the text cited earlier, Bhartṛhari describes a crucial intermediary stage at which the unity of direct vision intersects with the multiplicity of spoken words. This is the stage which Bhartṛhari elsewhere describes as the *madhyamā* stage of speech, lying between the stage of vision (*paśyantī*) and actual utterance (*vaikṛtī*). It is a stage that corresponds neither to pure consciousness (*citi, caitaṇya*) nor

26. VP 1.173 vṛtti.

to pure exteriority and difference (*vikāra, vyavahāra*), but to the *buddhi* or intellect, and the image (*pratibimba*) that becomes the basis for the use of language.[27] Conceived of in terms of psychology, this intermediate stage mediates between pure consciousness and the world of objects. It appears to be what we would call the imagination. But here the context is not purely individual and psychological but cosmogonic, and the role of the imagination is assimilated to the creative activity of the True Word in its self-manifestation. It is the True Word itself that introduces the factor of diversification, the power of Nescience or self-veiling (*avidyā-śakti*) that makes possible the manifestation of the world of multiplicity. For Bhartṛhari this process remains mysterious. He refers to it only as an *adbhutavṛtti,* a "marvelous activity."[28] It is the fundamental mystery of the True Word's intrinsic capacity to manifest itself while never overstepping its own unity. For Bhartṛhari, this fundamental cosmic mystery is likewise the fundamental mystery of language and consciousness.

As regards the role of the seers, finally, consideration of this cosmogonic context in which their role is described, a context in which the True Word's intrinsic capacity for self-manifestation is to the fore, leads us to the conclusion that even in their limited role of proclaiming or "enacting" the Veda, "translating" it from its visionary to its uttered state, the seers function not purely as individuals but also as vehicles of the True Word's own intrinsic dynamism. In introducing diversity and temporal differentiation into the essential form of Speech, they are merely imitating the True Word itself in its move to self-manifestation. Indeed, they are themselves perhaps best understood as symbols of this process. It is a process that ends not with the *vikāra*-s, or manifold forms of the world of ordinary experience and action (*vyavahāra*), but with the Veda as the *anukāra,* the True Word, with the world revealed as language and the order that that language reveals, the *dharma.* This order, the order of *dharma,* entails an element of interiority, the interiority first of the seer's inner vision and then of his speech based upon this vision. It is not a private, merely "subjective" interiority, however. It is essentially intersubjective, since it is mediated by language experienced as a form of *action,* action that structures a *common* social world. Vedic revelation is thus not merely cosmic; it belongs to the human, social world, the world of conscious agents. Yet

27. See Bhartṛhari's commentary on VP 2.31, as well as 3.14.326cd: "That which exists as an image is the basis of language." In his discussion of relation (3.3), Bhartṛhari describes this intermediate mental stage as possessed of "secondary" or "metaphorical" being (*aupacārika*-sattā).

28. VP 3.3.81.

neither is it strictly speaking a human product. Rather it is the Veda that produces the human, since the human exists properly only through the mediation of Vedic society and its *dharma,* and thus through the language that makes this *dharma* known. Human identity and human agency are thus deeply involved in the True Word and its self-manifestation. As we shall see, the True Word is in fact the human being's deepest Self.

The notion of *anukāra,* as the imitative enactment of the seer's direct vision of the True Word, thus contains elements of order and interiority that set it apart from the mere diversity and exteriority of the *vikāra*-s, the objects of ordinary experience. Within the dynamic world brought into being by the actualization of the *śakti*-s, therefore, the Veda as Brahman's *anukāra* constitutes a world of ordered and interrelated actions, an integral world of *dharma* that mediates the unity of the True Word and provides the necessary means for the attainment of a vision of its transcendental unity, a vision that, as we shall see, constitutes deliverance.

BHARTṚHARI AND THE TRADITION: THE MEDIATION OF REVELATION

In the verses that immediately follow his description of the Veda, Bhartṛhari takes up this topic of tradition:

> Having based themselves upon [the Veda], and on [various other] indications, those who know the Veda have created the traditions, that have many forms and have both visible and invisible purposes. (7) The doctrines of the monists and the dualists, which have been variously received, are based upon those of its passages which have the form of [merely] commendatory remarks [intended to encourage one in the performance of one's duty]; [these doctrines] are born of [their authors'] own opinions. (8) The true purity is also expressed there, the truth contained in [only] one word; connected with the syllable *Oṃ,* it is compatible with all doctrines. (9)[29]

By "traditions" (*smṛti*-s) here Bhartṛhari means texts, such as the famous *Laws of Manu* and other Dharma Śāstras, or didactic texts on *dharma,* that claimed to extend the principles of *dharma* revealed in the Vedas to spheres of activity to which they were not explicitly applied in

29. VP 1.6–9.

the Vedic texts themselves. More will be said about this notion of tradition below. Here Bhartṛhari describes the authors of these texts as basing themselves partly on the Veda itself and partly on "other indications," i.e., whatever non-Vedic evidence is relevant to the tradition concerned. In the case of the Dharma Śāstras, this evidence included the correct behavior of those knowledgeable of the Veda (*śiṣṭācāra*).

The next two verses in Bhartṛhari's text are significant because of the position they take in regard to the two main trajectories within the developing Vedic tradition, namely, the concentration on ritual, as represented by the Śrauta and Gṛhya Sūtras, the Dharma Sūtras and Śāstras, and eventually by the Mīmāṃsā school of ritual exegesis, and by the speculative interest in the nature of ultimate reality, found in the Brāhmaṇa-s, Āraṇyaka-s and Upaniṣads, and later the Vedānta. In verse 8, Bhartṛhari uses the term *arthavāda,* which I have translated as "commendatory remarks." This term derives from the ritualist milieu and refers to those non-injunctive descriptive statements in the Vedic texts that have no direct ritual significance: they do not enjoin ritual activity. In the Mīmāṃsā school they are explained as significant only inasmuch as they encourage one in the performance of the ritual. They thus have a practical significance, even if a derived one. Their direct descriptive value is not recognized. By contrast, it is precisely the descriptive use of language that gains ascendency in the Upaniṣads, in their doctrines concerning the identity of Brahman and Ātman. Statements in the Upaniṣads do not enjoin actions; they make statements such as the *mahāvākya,* or "great saying," *tat tvam asi,* "that (Brahman) you are," which affirms in propositional form the identity of the Ātman with Brahman. The Mīmāṃsakas viewed all such doctrinal statements as *arthavāda*-s and rejected the Upanishadic and later the Vedāntic notion that they bore the main weight of Vedic revelation. It is this attitude toward the descriptive use of language that Bhartṛhari evokes in verse 8. Many doctrines (*pravāda-s*) have been elaborated on the basis of these *arthavāda*-s, whether by monists or by dualists. All such conflicting doctrines have, according to Bhartṛhari, been born of the mental constructions (*vikalpa*-s) of their authors. In contrast to such doctrinal positions, but also in contrast to the strictly ritualist interpretation of the Mīmāṃsā, Bhartṛhari finds the heart of Vedic revelation, the "true purity," to be that knowledge (*vidyā*) which is connected with *praṇava,* namely, the sacred syllable *Oṃ*. In contrast to mutually exclusive doctrinal positions, this knowledge is *sarvavādāvirodhinā,* literally, "not opposing any doctrine." As Bhartṛhari will make abundantly clear, this knowledge is the knowledge of the True Word itself, which in the expressed form of the Divine Speech of the Veda, as Brahman's *anukāra,* is the subject matter of Bhartṛhari's chosen discipline, the *vedāṅga* of *vyākaraṇa,* or grammar.

These verses thus help us to understand how Bhartṛhari sought to locate himself among the developing intellectual traditions of Brahmanical culture. With the Mīmāṃsakas, and as the practitioner of a *vedāṅga,* Bhartṛhari adopts a positive attitude toward Vedic *dharma.* As we shall see below, grammar is first and foremost in Bhartṛhari's mind a science of *dharma,* a science of the activity of correct or dharmic speech, which he conceives of as a form of meritorious action, analogous to sacrificial action. In this he follows Patañjali, as noted earlier. On the other hand, Bhartṛhari shares the concern with Brahman and with spiritual liberation that was eventually to typify the Vedāntin. But unlike the doctrinal reception of Vedic revelation that one finds in the later Vedānta, for Bhartṛhari the Veda is not disclosive so much by virtue of what it *says,* the propositions it contains, as by virtue of what it *is* and what it *does.* Bhartṛhari is interested in the Divine Speech itself as a form of activity, as the *anukāra,* or imitation of Brahman, the self-mediation of the intrinsic dynamism of the True Word itself.

Bhartṛhari and the Smarta Tradition

Bhartṛhari's thought, as expressed in the verses discussed above (VP 1.7–9), reflects the world of the so-called *smārta* Brahmins, those who lived in accordance with the *dharma,* the socio-religious norms, as codified in the traditional (*smṛti*) texts such as *Laws of Manu.* These texts place a high value on study and teaching and indeed present the social function of religious education (rather than ritual priesthood) as the vocation best suited to a Brahmin in post-Vedic society.[30] It is to this *smārta* tradition that Patañjali belonged, and it is the *smārta* attitude toward the authority of correct dharmic speech that he presented in his *Mahābhāṣya.* Such *smārta* Brahmins were undoubtedly the frequent recipients of the *agrahāra*-s, or royal land-grants, that were probably the setting for Bhartṛhari's early formative years as a student. Bhartṛhari's experience of Vedic revelation seems to have been nourished by this traditional world of the Brahmin householder, even as it reached out to the broader, more pluralistic world of Gupta society. If Bhartṛhari's scepticism regarding doctrinal controversy reflects the cosmopolitan setting of

30. On the social dimensions of Vedic study, see Charles Malamond, *Le Svādhyāya: Récitation Personnelle du Veda,* Taittirīya Āraṇyaka 2 (Paris: Institut de Civilisation Indienne), p. 61.

the Gupta court, his appeal to the purity of the Divine Speech reflects a deeper foundation of his thought, by virtue of which he rightly viewed himself as a man of tradition.

What exactly did Bhartṛhari understand his tradition to be? First of all, he accepted the standard view that tradition, or *smṛti,* mediates between Vedic *dharma* and broader realms of experience. This view was shared by the Mīmāṃsakas, who emphasized the dependence of tradition on actual Vedic texts, going so far as to hypothesize "lost" Vedic texts to account for traditions for which scriptural support was lacking in the Vedic texts then extant. For Bhartṛhari, however, the tradition's rootedness in the Veda (*vedamūlatva*) has a deeper significance than mere dependence on Vedic texts. It signifies rootedness in the True Word itself, through the mediation of Vedic *dharma.*

It is precisely this mediation of *dharma* that is the defining characteristic of tradition. *Dharma* constitutes that *upāya,* or means, that is indispensable for happiness and ultimately for spiritual liberation. Tradition must undertake the continuing task of applying and adapting the dharmic norms inherited from the past to the conditions of the present. *Dharma* is a form of action, and action insists on being "practical": it *must* be appropriate to the conditions of the times if it is to happen at all. As noted in the previous chapter, with the decline of Brahmanical hegemony in India, in the wake of Aśoka and the Mauryan Empire, the elaborate *śrauta* sacrifices became "impractical" in a way that the ritual use of language did not. The use of the Divine Speech was more easily adapted to the changed post-Vedic conditions. Language too could be a form of *dharma,* provided it was "correctly" used. Increasingly, therefore, the "medium" of tradition, namely, the Sanskrit language, became the "message" of tradition, namely, *dharma.* It is this view of the language of revelation as itself a form of *dharma* that Bhartṛhari accepted from his predecessor Patañjali and that he makes central to his own understanding of tradition.

Traditional Knowledge and the Critique of Reason

Bhartṛhari's most complete discussion of tradition occurs at VP 1.27–43, where he makes his commitment to it quite clear. Although the immediate purpose of these verses is to defend the traditional value of the study of grammar as a study of *dharma,* it contains some of Bhartṛhari's clearest statements on the importance of tradition generally and on the nature of knowledge in its relation to tradition. Although we will save a discussion of grammar per se for the next chapter, the more general import of these verses makes a full discussion of them appropriate here:

> The correct forms of words, which are means for attaining merit, are established by the learned on the basis of tradition. Incorrect words, although no different than correct words in their capacity to convey meaning, are of an opposite character [as regards merit]. (27) Whether eternal or produced, words have no beginning. This constancy [of words], which is like [the constancy] of living creatures, is called permanence. (28) No one can render this constancy [of words] useless. Therefore this tradition [of grammar], which has the correctness [of words] as its subject matter, has been composed by the learned. (29) *Dharma* cannot be established by reason [alone] without tradition. Even the knowledge of seers is dependent upon tradition. (30) The unbroken paths of *dharma* that have been established cannot be set aside by anyone by means of reasoning. (31) A clear understanding of things is extremely difficult to attain on the basis of inference, because the powers of those things [upon which such inference would have to be based] differ according to differences of circumstances, place, and time. (32) The power of a substance, which is well-known in regard to such and such an action, can be blocked by coming into relation with some other particular substance. (33) What is inferred with effort by talented reasoners is argued to be otherwise by other, more talented reasoners. (34) Experts' knowledge of jewels, coins, and the like is born of repeated experience and cannot be communicated to others. It is not derived by inference. (35) The extraordinary powers of Rakṣasas, Pitṛs, and Piśācas go beyond perception and inference. They are born of *karma*. (36) The knowledge of the past and future, which is possessed by those whose minds are undefiled and for whom the light has become manifest, is not to be distinguished [as regards its immediacy] from perception. (37) The words of those who, by means of the eye of the seers, see things that are beyond the senses and unknowable [by ordinary means] cannot be set aside by inference. (38) One who does not doubt the vision [of such men], looking upon it as if it were his own knowledge, has placed himself on the side of direct perception; how can someone divert him? (39) In determining what is good and bad, people from the outcastes on up make little use of learned treatises [but rather depend upon the words of such men of vision]. (40) One who depends upon tradition,

which continues without a break like consciousness itself, cannot be obstructed by logicians. (41) Like a blind man feeling his way as he runs along a rough path, one who relies primarily upon inference is likely to fall. (42) Therefore, basing themselves on the instruction that is without author [i.e., the Veda] and on the tradition with its auxiliaries, the learned composed this instruction concerning words. (43)[31]

The basic argument of these verses, which, let it be noted, is fundamentally rhetorical, is that the *śiṣṭa*-s, the "traditional experts" (in the case of grammar, primarily Pāṇini and Patañjali), have composed the grammar as a science of *dharma* and that it is from its connection with this subject matter that the discipline derives its importance. Bhartṛhari supports this claim by invoking various examples of the contingency of merely rational knowledge and of the irreducible priority both of knowledge derived from the tradition and of the vision that that tradition makes possible. The contingency of knowledge based on empirical observation and inference based on it is merely the epistemological consequence of Bhartṛhari's metaphysics, which we saw to be based on the concept of the *śakti*-s. In Bhartṛhari's view, there are ultimately no stable substances accessible to direct inspection that could provide a solid foundation for the rational elaboration of a body of objective knowledge. The world is relational to its very core, and what constitutes adequate knowledge varies with time and place. All worldly entities, as well as the arguments that would be based on them, are thus context-dependent. True knowledge must focus on this context, on the structural relations that pattern the dynamic process of worldly activity. True knowledge must be knowledge based on *dharma,* on the constitutive order of the world, rather than on the individual things ordered. It is a knowledge of a thing's place in the dharmic order, a place that is subject to change. In the final analysis, the only reliable source of this knowledge is the *śiṣṭa,* the expert who embodies *dharma* and by virtue of this has access to an intuitive insight into its workings. The *śiṣṭa* is endowed with a practical wisdom that is intuitive in character. His mastery of the principles of *dharma* gives him a spontaneity in their application, an application adjusted to the demands of the season. This is brought out well in Bhartṛhari's commentary on 1.171. In the *kārikā* itself he states that the powers of words (and hence their capacity to produce merit) are seen (*dṛśyante*) by those who know the essential

31. VP 1.27–43.

nature of things. In his commentary he emphasizes the "timeliness" of tradition:

> This tradition is established according to the times, with reference to the capacities of men. The learned are recognized only by inference from their usage of correct [speech]; they possess an inner light (*antaḥprakāśa*) that is unobstructed with regard to all things knowable. According to the times, they see without error (*paśyanti*) the powers of words that are divided according to the limits of different times, as associated with the means for producing *dharma* and *adharma.*[32]

It is the "inner light" of the *śiṣṭa,* his vision, that gives him the capacity to faithfully apply the received Vedic tradition to his present context.

Toward the end of the Brahmakāṇḍa, Bhartṛhari presents another somewhat briefer discussion of tradition in its relation to the Veda and to human reason:

> No one admits the existence of a tradition that was not produced [by some author]. If all traditions were to perish, the threefold Veda would remain as a seed [from which new traditions could grow]. (148) If the doctrines perished and even if there were no one else to make new ones, the world would not stray from the *dharma* that is taught in the *śruti* and the *smṛti.* [149] As long as knowledge is based on one's own [dharmic] nature, there is no point to learned treatises. If *dharma* is the cause of knowledge, the Vedic tradition is the basis of *dharma.* (150) Reasoning that does not contradict the Veda and the traditional disciplines is the eye of those who do not see. For the purpose of a sentence is not established by its form alone. (151) Through reasoning many different principles of interpretation are developed.[33] For instance, a word that is actually present [in the text] may not be meaningful, or it may mean something different [from what it actually says], or its meaning may become clear from indications [found elsewhere in the text]. (152) Human reasoning is in fact only the power of words. [Reasoning] that is in accord with the words [of the text] is [acceptable as] a

32. VP 1.171 vṛtti.

33. On this translation of *nyāya* as "rule of interpretation," and on the translation of VP 1.127–29 generally, see the remarks of George Cardona, "Still Again on the History of the Mahābhāṣya," p. 93, note 29.

principle of interpretation. Outside its traditional context, however, [reasoning] is baseless. (153)[34]

The first two verses quoted here may seem contradictory at first sight. In 150 Bhartṛhari tells us that knowledge is based on *dharma* and that the latter is based on the Veda. All knowledge, therefore, derives from the Veda. But in 149, Bhartṛhari says that even if all the traditions perished, people would still continue to live by *dharma.* The apparent contradiction here disappears when one recalls what was said above about the *śiṣṭa,* the "traditional expert." The *śiṣṭa*-s embody this tradition. Indeed, to the extent that they perfect *dharma* themselves, they *are* the tradition. Their textual productions are strictly secondary. Their practice is firmly established in the form of the life of the community and especially, as we have seen, in the form of correct speech. In these verses, Bhartṛhari calls attention not only to the necessity of the traditional mediation of *dharma,* but to the further necessity that this mediation lead to *realization.*

We have seen that this realization ideally ends in vision, in an immediate and intuitive understanding of *dharma* and its source, the True Word. Reasoning cannot overrule this intuitive understanding, but it can be of use where such insight is lacking. It can serve, as Bhartṛhari says in 151, as the "eye" of those who do not see, provided of course that it not contradict the Veda. In his commentary Bhartṛhari explains that reasoning such as that employed in grammar or in the ritual exegesis of the Mīmāṃsā school is intended to aid those of "lower vision" (*arvāgdarśanānām anugrahe*). The reasons are the same as those that he gave in his earlier defense of tradition. Just as the objects of the world are essentially mutable and can be adequately known only through a contextualized insight, appropriate to their time and place, so too the sentences of the Veda must be understood in context. Two sentences having exactly the same form may convey different purposes. Their power (*śakti*) can vary with their context (*prakaraṇa*) even when their form (*rūpa*) remains the same. Reasoning can help establish this context, but as Bhartṛhari goes on to say in 153, this reasoning itself is ultimately the power of words and is valid only if it acknowledges this dependence. Reasoning used against the text is baseless. Such reasoning tries to set itself up in independence of language, following the characteristics of objects rather than the powers of words. Bhartṛhari calls this type of reasoning "dry reasoning" (*śuṣkas tarkaḥ*) and warns that it is destructive of tradition and ultimately ground-

34. VP 1.148–53.

less.[35] Bhartṛhari in fact blames the decline of the grammatical tradition precisely on such dry reasoning.[36]

Such are the basic outlines of Bhartṛhari's understanding of tradition. Not surprisingly, the central category is language: language as *dharma,* as the bond of a much broader social praxis, an "orthopraxis." However, this language, the Divine Speech, is not merely an extrinsic instrument of social order. It is also an inner reality, the very foundation of human rationality and of consciousness itself. Language's indirect mediation of vision through *dharma* is in reality a form of *self-mediation.* But to see this one needs the eyes of a grammarian, a grammarian who, like Bhartṛhari, knows the path that leads from words to the Word.

35. VP 1.153 vṛtti.
36. See VP 2.484.

3

The Reception of the Language of Revelation: From Words to the Word

Those within the Vedic and Brahmanical traditions experienced revelation most concretely as a form of powerful language, the origin and support of the dharmic order. Bhartṛhari's doctrine of the True Word and of the tradition of *dharma* dependent upon it clearly represents a speculative development of this fundamental experience of the language of revelation, of the Vedic *bráhman,* symbolized in Bhartṛhari's time by the sacred syllable *Oṃ*. Bhartṛhari's own reception of Vedic revelation in the fifth century was framed by his views of the Veda as *anukāra* of the True Word, of the seers, or *ṛṣi*-s, as cosmic beings, and of the Vedic tradition as mediating their original visions. But on the most concrete level, his reception of Vedic revelation was inseparable from his reception of its *language,* his experience of this language as a grammarian and as a *smarta* Brahmin living amid the intellectual ferment of the fifth century. He resisted the temptation to reduce this experience to the experience of "mere" words, whether these be the injunctive words required for the performance of the sacrifice or the descriptive words that try and inevitably fail to describe the unity of Brahman and Ātman. Rather he was able to encompass both of these perspectives within the more fundamental perspective of a metaphysics of language that underlay a dialectics of spiritual transformation.

In this chapter we will examine Bhartṛhari's views on the reception of Vedic revelation. We will begin with his critique of the representational use of this language, which is closely connected with the "critique of reason" that we reviewed in the previous chapter and with his more positive description of the essential nature of language. We will then move on to consider his description of the actual experience of language, which will lead us in turn to the dialectic of language and vision, to the process of spiritual transformation that lies at the heart of his own reception of Vedic revelation in his own historical context.

THE NATURE OF LANGUAGE[1]

In presenting Bhartṛhari's view of tradition, we have already had occasion to refer to his use of the term *vikalpa,* which we translated as "mental construction." This term is perhaps more familiar from Buddhist sources, but in fact Bhartṛhari makes wide use of it in order to describe the basic functioning of representational language. Its use is closely connected with a distinction that Bhartṛhari has probably taken over from Buddhist sources, namely, the distinction between the *vyavahāra,* or "worldly," and the *paramārtha,* or "ultimate," levels of truth. Representative language functions only at the former level, which is essentially the level of *avidyā,* ignorance. *Paramārtha* or ultimate truth, on the other hand, applies only at the level of *tattva,* or ultimate Reality.[2] *At the vyavahāra* level, all language use is based upon various limiting conditions (*upādhi-s*) that are devoid of ultimate reality: "The real is named by means of words that have unreal limiting factors."[3] These *upādhi*-s are the linguistic counterparts of the differentiated forms (*ākāra-s*) of the world:

> As gold, even though pure, becomes expressible by words such as "bracelet" when it is joined with its own perishable forms, [and] just as the power of the eye, for instance, [to see all possible objects] is restricted by [looking through a] narrow tube, so the power [of the word] is restricted by the division created by forms.[4]

These *upādhi*-s and *ākāra*-s, as the differentiating factors of the phenomenal world, are what Bhartṛhari calls, in the context of his ontology,

1. Portions of this section originally appeared in my article "Bhartṛhari and the Veda," in Jeffrey Timm, ed., *Texts in Context: Traditional Hermeneutics in South Asia* (Albany: SUNY Press, 1992), pp. 17–32.

2. Bhartṛhari's uses of the term *vyavahāra* are far too numerous to require specific references. For the term *paramārtha,* which is much less common, see 2.22; 3.6.26; and 3.7.39. In all these cases, the term clearly refers to a level of truth that transcends "worldly" antinomies such as identity and difference conceived in a quantitative fashion. At 3.7.39, the *paramārtha* level is explicitly connected with the level of *tattva,* which we have discussed above, p. 37.

3. VP 3.2.2cd.

4. VP 3.2.4–5.

the *śakti*-s. Both words and objects are endowed with a multitude of such "powers" or "capacities" to enter into relation with one another, and their indeterminate nature accounts for the indeterminate nature of the worldly knowledge based on them. We have already seen Bhartṛhari draw this consequence from his doctrine of the *śakti*-s in the critique of knowledge that he developed in the context of his defense of tradition. There he focused on the objective pole, emphasizing the dependence of the potencies of objects on specific relations of time and place. In the Vākyakāṇḍa, he calls attention to the "subjective" pole, to the indeterminacy of the speaker's intention and to the resulting relativity that characterizes the referential use of language:

> Just as a sense organ, being directed to [an object], can present it in various ways, so too the understanding of a meaning [is presented] in many ways by language. (134) The meaning of a word, intended in one sense by the speaker, is divided up among different speakers according to their own ideas. (135) In regard to one and the same visible object, the viewpoint is variously divided; and one and the same person views it differently at different times. (136) The meaning of one and the same word is construed variously by one [person] and by many. Due to the indeterminate bases [for the employment] of one and the same word, an object is construed in many ways by one person or by many. (137) Therefore the viewpoint and speech of those who have not seen the ultimate nature of things is faulty and very delusive. It is forever indeterminate. (138) And the vision of the seers, to the extent that it is established in the Ultimate, is of no use for ordinary worldly transactions; it is not a basis for the [representational use] of words. (139)[5]

These verses do not need a great deal of commentary. They merely draw the consequences of an ontology that admits no ultimately fixed, determinate, substantial entities. All entities encountered in ordinary experience are, according to Bhartṛhari, merely "bundles" of potencies (*śaktimātrāsamūha,* 3.7.2) that are actualized only in specific (and fleeting) contexts. The potencies are never actualized in such a determinate, permanent way as to give rise to a "substance" that would have a reality distinct from its potencies. The potencies, as reducible to the dynamic aspect of the True Word, are real; but their momentary configurations

5. VP 2.134–39.

are strictly that: momentary. They exist as "entities" only by virtue of the larger context in which they find themselves. And when this context changes, so do they. Words, and their capacities to signify, are equally mutable. Meaning here is a function of the whole context, the entire configuration of "powers" that obtains at a given moment. The individual word-meanings, to the extent that they can be isolated, are merely temporary manifestations of the self-expressiveness of the True Word.

What is most interesting about these verses is their context within the Vākyakāṇḍa. They conclude a longer section that had set out twelve possible views of word-meaning. The twelfth and final view is given above and can be taken as Bhartṛhari's conclusion, namely, that word-meanings per se are indeterminate. In fact, he had already argued earlier in this same book that words are merely abstract entities, abstracted from the unity of the sentence.[6] For the sake of instruction, the grammarian may construct such artificial entities as words and present the sentence as a product of their interconnections. In reality, however, each sentence is an irreducible unity of expression, quite devoid of parts.

In the verses immediately following those given above, Bhartṛhari returns to this theme of the primacy of the sentence and of sentence meaning. In verses 1.143–52, he develops his notion of *pratibhā,* "insight" or "intuition," as the meaning of the sentence. We will consider this notion of *pratibhā* carefully below, along with the closely associated notion of *sphoṭa.* These two notions will bring us into contact with the full fact of language as Bhartṛhari experienced it, as a dynamic mediator of visionary experience. We will better understand his view of the synthetic actuality of language, however, if we first consider the analysis that he makes of it in his role as a grammarian.

As a Pāṇinian grammarian, Bhartṛhari inherited the system of analysis and description employed by Pāṇini in his *Aṣṭādhyāyī.* Whereas Pāṇini is usually viewed as focusing on the derivation of words, however, Bhartṛhari is often presented as a semanticist, concerned more with "meaning" than with grammatical derivation of forms. While there is a grain of truth in this characterization, it is a bit misleading. In the first place, Bhartṛhari is not interested primarily in what we would call semantics, but in what we should rather call pragmatics. Furthermore, for Bhartṛhari, the deepest "meaning" of language is inseparable from its form. This form is primarily the *kāraka* structure of the sentence, and

6. See, for instance, 2.10 and 14.

this theory of the *kāraka*-s, which we shall discuss presently, was in fact first introduced by Pāṇini.

What is characteristic about Bhartṛhari is his explicit insistence that the sole genuine unit of language is the *sentence,* not the word. People do not utter words, they utter sentences. And they utter these not because they wish to *name* things, but because they wish to *do* things. Language is intended to mediate action, and this means that the heart of language is the sentence centered on the verb. Nouns and the objects they name are merely accessories of the action expressed by the verb.

This emphasis on the dynamic "verbal" character of language, which is perfectly consistent with Bhartṛhari's thought as a whole, means that his understanding of the nature of language will become most apparent in his analysis of the sentence rather than in his analysis of individual words. In fact, Bhartṛhari analyzes the sentence into a dynamic relational structure composed of what he calls *kāraka*-s, literally, "doers." These *kāraka*-s correspond, at the level of language, to the more general ontology of the *śakti*-s. It is only through the mediation of language at the level of the sentence that the world's dynamic potential becomes actual, since only the sentence transcends the level of static, named "substances" in order to present them as *sādhana*-s, "means" for the accomplishment of action.[7] Since we know from Bhartṛhari's ontology that it is precisely the act, i.e., the actualization of the *śakti*-s of Brahman, that is ultimately real, we may say that language, through its dynamic *kāraka* structure, discloses a truth about the world that is inaccessible to the naive immediacy of sense perception, focused on separate entities, as well as to the inferential reasoning based upon it, what Bhartṛhari called "dry reasoning."

Bhartṛhari develops his theory of the *kāraka*-s in the *Sādhanasamuddeśa,* or "Discussion of Means," located in the third book of the VP. According to Bhartṛhari, the entire world, as it is presented by language, is divided up into that which is *sādhya,* or "to be accomplished," and that which is *sādhana,* or the means for accomplishing something. Whatever language presents as being *sādhya* is an action (*kriyā*). Everything else is subordinated to this action as a *sādhana,* or means for its actualization. In the sentence, what is *sādhya,* namely, the action to be performed, is expressed by the verb, while the various *sādhana*-s required for the action are expressed by nouns. Verbs and nouns are never found in an isolated state, however, as mere "words." We have already seen that such

7. Language is capable of this feat because it does not exist in the mode of an object, but rather is endowed with a "secondary" or "metaphorical" (*aupacārika*) mode of being. See VP 3.3.39–51 for Bhartṛhari's discussion of this concept.

words are mere abstractions. In fact, verbs and nouns are always found in an inflected state, always provided with a suffix or declensional ending (*pratyāya* or *vibhakti*) that integrates them into the single relational whole of the sentence. Only the whole is real, since only there are the potentials of the verbal and nominal stems actualized in a single relational unit capable of expressing an action.

The conjugational and declensional endings are thus the key morphological features that display the intrinsic relational structure of language. This relational structure itself, which is *expressed* by but not *identical* with these morphological features, is represented by the system of the *kāraka*-s, of which there are six: *kartṛ* (agent), *karma* (object), *karaṇa* (instrument), *saṃpradāna* (recipient), *apādāna* (origin, point of departure), and *adhikaraṇa* (locus). These relations may be expressed in many different ways at the morphological level, but however expressed they provide the fundamental structure of the sentence. The sentence with this *kāraka* structure in turn provides for the ordered expression of the myriad *śakti*-s, which compose our world in the form of discrete actions. Although the *śakti*-s seem innumerable, they can be subsumed under the structure of the six *kāraka*-s, which Bhartṛhari actually refers to as six *śakti*-s (3.7.35), and these six in turn ultimately express only the one *śakti,* the dynamism of the True Word as ontological ground of the phenomenal world.

There is, therefore, an impressive fit between Bhartṛhari's general ontology and his analysis of language. This should not be surprising, in the light of his avowal, along with his tradition, that the manifest universe is a transformation of the Word. But what is impressive is that Bhartṛhari does not leave this traditional belief at the level of a mere assertion but explicates it through the minutiae of his grammatical analysis, which shows at the level of specific morphology and syntax that language and action are two sides of a single reality, or, more precisely, that they together make manifest the dynamic potential of that Reality.

It is interesting, indeed crucial, to note that Bhartṛhari's understanding of the sentence as a structure of *kāraka* relations stands in marked contrast to classical Western views. Beginning with Aristotle's *De Interpretatione,* Western thinkers have accepted a subject-predicate analysis of the sentence or "proposition," along with the table of substance-related categories associated with it. Sentences or propositions are intended primarily to attach names to objects. The comparison with Bhartṛhari is illuminating. The sentence is not interpreted as a subject-object proposition, and it is not associated with a table of categories focused on substance. On the contrary, Bhartṛhari's "table of categories" is the system of the *kāraka*-s, the set of ideal relations that together characterize *action* rather than substance. The sentence is focused on the mediation of action, not on predication. As we shall see, the sentence as a whole does not signify a synthesizing act of the intellect so much as the manifestation of the intrinsic order or relatedness of the world.

THE EXPERIENCE OF LANGUAGE: PRATIBHĀ

So far we have been discussing language in terms of the analyzed structure of the sentence. But Bhartṛhari tells us explicitly[8] that such analysis, while useful as an *upāya,* a means, is itself ultimately false and based on ignorance (*avidyā*), since it requires mentally dividing what is in fact undivided. Let us now return to Bhartṛhari's description of the "full fact" of language, as it is experienced whole, free from the arbitrary divisions introduced by grammarians. His description of this experience focuses on the notion of *pratibhā,* which he describes, following the verses on word-meaning discussed above, at 2.143–52:

> When the meanings [of the words] have been grasped separately, then an intuition arises as different from them. That, they say, is the meaning of the sentence, produced by the meanings of the words. (143) It cannot in any way be described to others as this or that; it is established as an activity proper to each individual; it cannot even be described by the agent [who experiences it]. (144) It spontaneously effects the integration, as it were, of the [word] meanings; when it has assumed the form of the whole, it exists as an object, so to speak, [of knowledge]. (145) Whether it is born immediately from the word, or following upon [its] residual traces, no one goes beyond it in matters of action. (146) The entire world recognizes its validity; the undertakings, even of animals, proceed by its power. (147) Just as various visible powers, such as those of liquor, are born without effort [solely] by the ripeness of particular substances, the same is true of the intuitions of those possessing them. (148) Who changes the song of the male cuckoo bird in the spring? How are the various creatures taught to build their nests? (149) Who impels the birds and beasts in their various activities —

8. At 2.233: "In the [grammatical] treatises, only ignorance is described by the different derivations [employed by the various grammatical schools]. Knowledge, however, arises by itself, without the [various] constructions [imposed upon it by the various grammatical] traditions."

> eating, loving, hating, swimming—well-known among the descendants of their species? (150) This [intuition] comes from tradition alone, accompanied by previously inherited dispositions. Tradition is distinguished as both proximate and remote. (151) Six types of intuition are recognized: those that arise by nature, from one's Vedic school,[9] from repetition, from *yoga,* from an unseen [cause], or from some particular [cause]. (152)[10]

I have translated *pratibhā* here as "intuition." Literally *pratibhā* means "shining back," from the root *bhā-* meaning to shine, be luminous. The sense that Bhartṛhari gives it here is that of a spontaneous insight that shows one how to act in a particular situation, a kind of practical sense or virtue. The thoroughly practical nature of this insight should not seem so strange, in view of all we have said up to now. What may still strike one as odd is Bhartṛhari's mention of what we would call animal instinct in this connection and his further statement that even the intuition of animals comes from tradition. This sense of oddness comes both from the context, a discussion of language, and from our assumption that language is an exclusively human phenomenon. In order to escape our perplexity we need not assume that Bhartṛhari is seriously suggesting that animals speak well-formed Sanskrit sentences. Rather we need only recall that language, in the sense of spoken words, is in Bhartṛhari's view only one aspect of the manifestation of the True Word. The world as a whole is a transformation of the Word (1.124), and is sustained by it (1.122). *Pratibhā* is accordingly far more than the "meaning" of the sentence, the specific intuitive insight mediated by articulate speech. It is more fundamentally the luminosity of the True Word itself, as the principle of world order. Thus at 1.122, the world with its many forms is said to have *pratibhā* as its essence (*pratibhātmāyaṃ bhedarūpaḥ*). We further saw, in our discussion of Bhartṛhari's description of the origin of the Veda in his commentary on 1.173, that the original seers were believed to become manifest in *pratibhā* and while in that condition to see (*paśyanti*) the great Self (*ātmā*), which is itself described as Being (*sattā*). In his commentary on 1.144, he goes so far as to identify *pratibhā,* and *sattā,* Being, and to describe the former as "derived from ultimate Reality, the source of the transformations of beings, and possessed of the capacity of being both the end

9. Here I have adopted a variant reading reported by Rau, substituting his *vivaraṇaḥ* with *caraṇaḥ*.
10. VP 2.143–52.

and the means."[11] Bhartṛhari clearly believes that Being, or ultimate Reality itself, inasmuch as it is oriented toward its own self-manifestation, is essentially self-luminous. He is fond of describing the self-manifestation of Brahman or the True Word as a "shining forth" (using forms of the verb *pra-kāś-*, to shine forth).[12] The True Word is itself described as light (*jyotiṣ*), as at 1.12 and its commentary, and the highest stage of the Word is called *Paśyantī,* literally, the Seeing One. It is this light that is experienced by the Vedic seers, by ordinary humans in their experience of language, and by the animals in their instinctive behaviors. The intensity of the experience varies, hence the need for the explicit teaching of *dharma* through the tradition. But the ultimate basis of all these various levels of intuitive knowledge is one and the same light. Differences in level are differences in degree, not in kind.

Bhartṛhari also stresses the unique quality of *pratibhā.* In the case of the sentence, intuition arises spontaneously. It is not the result of effort. It cannot be understood in terms of the "parts" of the sentence, which merely occasion its appearance. The sentence, conceived as a sequence of uttered sounds, merely manifests *pratibhā*; it does not create it.

Whether Bhartṛhari describes the full fact of language, the "speech event" with its practical intent, from the perspective of language itself or from the perspective of one's experience of language, it retains the character of a disclosive event, always concrete and particular, yet disclosive of the True Word itself, as delimited by that particular situation. Understanding is something that *happens,* both in the sense that it breaks forth spontaneously, without a how or a why, and in the sense that it has a practical import, that it culminates in action. In both of these ways, it transcends the individual subject. *Pratibhā* is not properly a synthesizing act of the individual intellect. It is rather the *manifestation* of the luminosity, the intelligibility, that underlies the world order itself, and it therefore determines and situates the subject in a concrete and practical situation. This is most apparent in the case of the *pratibhā* that guides animal behavior. Here *pratibhā* is a kind of instinct that integrates animals into an entire world of patterned behaviors. The *pratibhā* experienced by humans is in principle not so different. Ideally, as experienced by the seers and the *śiṣṭa*-s, it should guide one in the performance of *dharma,* in action that is attuned to the traditional order established by the Veda. As it is the *dharma* of birds to build nests, so it is the *dharma* of human beings to

11. VP 1.144 vṛtti.
12. See for instance 2.30–33; 3.3.87; and 3.7.39.

offer sacrifice. The human being as actor is a participant in a complex, interconnecting world of *dharma,* a world of dynamic relations that actualize the myriad potentialities of the True Word. It is the fundamental unity of the whole that shines forth as *pratibhā,* at whatever level.

THE DIALECTIC OF LANGUAGE AND VISION

Bhartṛhari's description of language, and particularly his description of *pratibhā,* seems to grow out of an experience of a deep, underlying reciprocity between vision and action, a reciprocity that is grounded by the luminosity and dynamism of the True Word. Vision is both the origin and goal of action, but in between lie the mediating paths of *dharma.* Just as dharmic action originated in the seers' "enactment" of their original visions, so the re-enactment of *dharma* leads ultimately back to that original immediacy. Bhartṛhari tells us directly that *dharma* is the cause (*hetu*) of knowledge (*jñāna,* 1.150). This claim makes sense only in light of the ontology of action that he has developed through his doctrine of the *śakti*-s and their basis in the True Word. Action is not understood to be something that remains extrinsic to the actor. On the contrary, it is *constitutive* of the actor. In a very real sense, a person *is* what a person *does.* It is this fundamental principle that underlies the classical Indian doctrine of *karma,* a word that literally means merely "action." It is the quality of one's action, the degree of its conformity to the norms of *dharma,* that determines the quality of one's being, the degree of one's purity. And it is precisely the degree of one's purity that determines the degree of one's vision. Thus *acting* in accord with the Word is the necessary pre-condition for *seeing* the Word.

Bhartṛhari's doctrine of the luminous and dynamic Word thus provides the principles necessary to mediate between what one might call the active and the contemplative lives. The mediation itself, however, is a long dialectical process. The reciprocity of dharmic action and visionary experience might be clear to Bhartṛhari himself. But what of the ordinary "worldly" (*laukika*) person? It is true that Bhartṛhari's description of *pratibhā* is intended to be phenomenological: everyone competent to use language should properly experience it as Bhartṛhari has described it. Such at least is the implicit claim. But this cannot be said about the further claim that this common experience of *pratibhā* is merely the tip of the iceberg, merely a remote glimmer of the luminosity of the Word itself. Nor is it true that the ordinary person "sees" that the relationality implicit in the most common action, the very fact that action is possible at all, is a distant reflection of the dynamic unity of the True Word with its *śakti*-s. These are rather the insights of Bhartṛhari the grammarian *cum* metaphysician, for whom "the light has become manifest" (1.37). Not everyone is able to see so clearly. In addition to the seers and the *śiṣṭa*-s, those who can see directly, who have *already* perfected *dharma,* there are also those "of lower visions" (1.171 *vṛtti: arvāgdarśanānāṃ puruṣāṇām)* who need the teachings of the tradition and the "eye of reason" in order to stay on the right path. The *dharma* is not perfectly realized by all, nor even by the majority. Indeed, in Bhartṛhari's day, the elaborate *śrauta* sacrifices of earlier times had been replaced by smaller rites, easier to perform. Vedic *dharma* increasingly took the form of correct or dharmic speech rather than ritual sacrifice, yet even here there were problems. Bhartṛhari complains that incompetent speakers have "mixed up" the Divine Speech.[13] It is for precisely this reason that the science of grammar is necessary: to teach those who cannot see, who have not perfected (*saṃskṛta*) themselves sufficiently to be able to perform *dharma* spontaneously and gain insight into its luminous source.

There is thus a considerable distance between Bhartṛhari's vision of the world and language as the self-manifestations of the True Word on the one hand and the ordinary person's experience on the other. When Bhartṛhari says that Vedic *dharma* is the cause of knowledge, he certainly includes in this knowledge all the traditional teachings about correct behavior, the teaching of the *varṇāśramadharma,* the socio-religious structure of the *smārta* society of his day. But this is not all that he has in mind. For Bhartṛhari, *dharma* is not only a matter of external observance. *Dharma* is also an attribute of language. Language, however, is more than a social reality. It is at the same time an inner reality. The practice of *dharma* is thus led, by way of Bhartṛhari's emphasis on the *dharma* of language, into the person's inner life. The practice of *dharma* leads one finally to a deeper knowledge of the *foundations* of *dharma* in the True Word itself, as the common ground of both self and society. For Bhartṛhari, the practice of *dharma* thus reaches its ultimate fulfillment in a vision of the Word.

The *dharma* of language is of course the special province of grammar. It is thus not surprising to find that Bhartṛhari describes the discipline of grammar as a path leading ultimately to the Light of the Word: "The wise say that grammar, near to Brahman, is the highest of austerities; it is the

13. VP 1.182. Here the idea of "mixture" includes the idea of impurity, as in the "mixture" of castes.

first of the auxiliary sciences of the Vedas. This is the direct path to that highest essence of the Word that has taken on the divisions of form, to that most pure Light."[14] At 1.14–22, Bhartṛhari continues this high praise of grammar and then provides a description of its ultimate goal:

> "That [i.e., grammar] is the door to salvation, the remedy for all the impurities of speech. It is the purifier of all sciences and appears in each one. (14) Just as the universals of objects are all based upon the universals of words, so in the world this is the foremost of the sciences. (15) This is the first step on the ladder leading to attainment. This is the straight royal road for those desiring liberation. (16) Here the self that has gone beyond error and that has taken on the form of the hymns, sees the sole source of the [Vedic] hymns, the body made of hymns. (17) That which is the highest form of undifferentiated speech, that which is the pure Light, which becomes manifest even in this darkness, (18) that Light which those approach who have gone beyond the differentiated view of forms and operations, beyond light and darkness, (19) that in which the causes of speech, like the signs of the alphabet, shine like a reflected image, by means of a yoga preceded by words, (20) that in which the various syllables of the Atharva, the Aṅgiras, the Sāman, Ṛg, and Yajur (Vedas) are encompassed in their distinct condition, (21) that which is one and which is variously divided by differences of production, that is the supreme Brahman, which is attained through the mastery of grammar. (22)[15]

The precise meaning of these verses is difficult to determine, and we will have to supplement them with statements made elsewhere in the VP. It is immediately apparent however that Bhartṛhari is describing the culmination of a peculiar type of yogic experience, a yoga "preceded by words" that entails an inner transformation of the practitioner and leads to a visionary experience of a Light "beyond light and darkness." We must be cautious, however, and resist the temptation to immediately identify this yoga with the type taught in the *Yogasūtra*-s. Here the practitioner is said to "take on the form" of Vedic hymns, and this evocation of a Vedic context provides our best clue as to what Bhartṛhari has in mind. The term used here is *chandasya,* which according to Monier-Williams

14. VP 1.11–12.
15. VP 1.14–22.

can mean "taking the form of hymns."[16] Monier-Williams himself refers to Taittirīya Saṃhitā 1.6.11.4, where this term is used to describe the god Prajāpati. This entire verse recalls the passage in the Śatapatha Brāhmaṇa (10.4.2.21–22), where Prajāpati sees all beings "in the Veda" and decides to construct for himself a body "made of hymns." The sacrificer too, imitating the example of Prajāpati, constructs for himself a body made of hymns through his performance of the sacrifice. With this "sacramental body" he will reach the heavenly world after his death. What is involved here is actually a homology that developed out of the early speculations on the sacrifice. Prajāpati is homologized to the sacrifice that he created as his "image" or "counterform" (*pratirūpa*), as his body "made of hymns." The sacrificer conforms himself to the divine Prajāpati through conforming to or "appropriating" his "counterform." Since this "counterform," which is the sacrifice, exists pre-eminently in the form of hymns [*chandas*], one who has been thoroughly conformed to it is described as *chandasya,* "conformed" to the Vedic hymns.

Bhartṛhari explicitly mentions Prajāpati at 1.125–26 in order to further explain his claim that the world is a transformation of the Word, having developed out of the Vedic hymns (1.124): "Having divided his body in many ways, Prajāpati, in the form of hymns (*chandasya*) entered it in many ways, by means of the parts [of himself which were] composed of hymns. [For this reason], the sacred form of Prajāpati exists pre-eminently within those in whom abundant, virtuous speech is established."[17] Through these verses Bhartṛhari links his own thought with the Vedic cosmogonic myths that describe Prajāpati's dismemberment, which brought the world into existence, and the subsequent reuniting of his *membra disiecta* by means of the sacrifice. These myths, which in fact complement the myths describing Prajāpati's creation of the sacrifice as a "counterform" of himself, emphasize the initial, inchoate form of the universe prior to its "re-formation" or reintegration by means of the sacrifice. The manifest world is presented as the dismembered body of Prajāpati. Even as such, however, the divine is immanent within it. In Bhartṛhari's language, this multiple world, though afflicted with difference (*bheda*), is nevertheless a "condition" (*sthiti*) of Brahman (1.4). The mode of Prajāpati's presence in the world is defective, however. In

16. Monier-Williams, *Sanskrit-English Dictionary* (Oxford: Clarendon Press, 1899), p. 405, col. 1.

17. VP 1.125–26. Although Rau accepts these verses as Bhartṛhari's own, Iyer treats them as quotations given in the *vṛtti.* Whichever is the case, they may safely be taken as representing a tradition that Bhartṛhari approved.

fact, the unity of the transcendent (*anirukta*) and the immanent (*nirukta*) Prajāpati, or of the Brahman and the Ātman, is only potential. It must be realized through sacrificial action. The scattered limbs of Prajāpati must be reassembled in the form of the sacrifice. Prajāpati must receive a "body made of hymns," and so must the individual sacrificer, who is also afflicted by the "fallen" or dispersed condition of the world. The second verse given above makes this same point through an appeal to the connection between the sacrifice and the Divine Speech: the divine presence of the transcendent (*anirukta*) Prajāpati within individual persons is a function of their participation in the correct or "virtuous" (*sādhvī*) speech of the sacrifice, the Divine Speech that is also the subject matter of the discipline of grammar. Bhartṛhari thus believes that the divine as immanent, as the *ātman,* is present within all human beings, minimally as the capacity for speech, and that this latent presence must be realized. He says this most clearly at 1.143: "They say that the self [*ātman*] of the speaker, the word established within, is the great Bull with whom one desires union."[18] The mention of the "great Bull" here is a reference to Ṛg Veda 4.58.3, where this great Bull is said to be the great God (*maho devaḥ*) who entered mortal beings. Here Bhartṛhari identifies this great God with the inner Word present within each individual. In this he follows his master Patañjali, who also referred to the great God as *śabda,* the Word.[19] Bhartṛhari is thus appealing to a long tradition of identifying the divine or the Ultimate with the Word, the Ṛg Vedic *vāk* or *bráhman,* which he has reformulated in his doctrine of the True Word. We are already familiar with the "cosmic" aspect of this tradition and Bhartṛhari's appropriation of it. Here, however, he calls attention to the *inner* Word as the very foundation of the human subject. It is this additional doctrine of an inner Word that makes his "yoga preceded by words" intelligible. Whereas the earlier Vedic tradition had focused on the performance of the sacrifice as the means of reintegrating the performer into the encompassing divine order, Bhartṛhari is here building upon the rethinking of the earlier tradition that had taken place in the centuries that preceded him.[20] By the fifth century that tradition had found a new form that placed much greater emphasis on individual householders with their simplified rites and keener interest in spiritual liberation. Vedic *language,* however, remained crucial as a highly adaptive link with the

18. VP 1.143.
19. See MBh 1.3.21.
20. For a discussion of this rethinking, particularly with regard to the status of the language of Vedic revelation, see Carpenter, "Language, Ritual, and Society."

ancient *dharma.* Here Bhartṛhari unites the concerns for Vedic *dharma* mediated by the Divine Speech with the concern for spiritual liberation, which had originally arisen outside Vedic circles. His "yoga preceded by words" was well adapted to the religious practice of the Brahmin householder and to the Brahmin's practice of *svādhyāya,* or the independent study of Vedic texts.

The *svādhyāya* was one of the five "great sacrifices" of the Brahmin householder. These "sacrifices," only one of which actually involved an oblation (of milk) into fire, had come virtually to replace the earlier, more elaborate system of sacrifice laid down in the Vedic texts during the post-Vedic period. The *svādhyāya* itself was presented as a *brahmayajña,* or "sacrifice of and to *bráhman,*" *bráhman* here referring primarily to the Veda itself, though for Bhartṛhari it could just as well refer to the True Word. It was a highly ritualized form of recitation, one clearly assimilated to the practice of ritual sacrifice and one in which the formality of the *practice* of recitation virtually overshadowed the *content* of the recitation.

As one of the five "great sacrifices" that slowly displaced the earlier *śrauta* cult, this practice of the daily *svādhyāya* became one of the central religious duties of the learned Brahmin, or *śiṣṭa,* in the post-Vedic period. As already noted, it is likely that Bhartṛhari would have practiced something like it, perhaps in a modified form, though there is no way of knowing for sure. It nevertheless represents the concrete practical form in which the language of revelation was received on the part of many individual Brahmins, and something like it probably provided the ritual context for the performance of the "yoga preceded by words" described here. Through it Bhartṛhari would have been able to preserve *dharma* in a quite concrete form as a necessary form of mediation leading to vision. The true Self was to be realized *through* the tradition and its rites, and not in spite of them. Still, this process of realization was possible as a genuinely spiritual process only because the Self to be realized through the objective mediation of the traditional language was already present in a more or less obscure form within each individual, providing the ground for the appropriation of that tradition.

This process of appropriation is a process of the gradual transformation and purification of the individual through the progressive perfection of *dharma.* In the verse immediately following VP 1.143, Bhartṛhari draws this connection between the perfection of *dharma* and the attainment of Brahman: "Therefore the purification of speech is the attainment of the highest Self; one who knows the ultimate nature of (this process of purification) attains the immortal Brahman."[21] Significantly the word that I have translated as "purification" is *saṃskāra,* a term common in the ritual literature denoting a "perfecting" or transformation of the individual by ritual means, by virtue of which he is integrated into the full sacramental life of the community. The word itself is derived from the root *kṛ-,* to do or make, as was the term *anukāra.* With the preverb *sam-* it denotes perfective action that alters the ontological and social status of the actor. The Sanskrit language is, as the name itself indicates, the *saṃskṛta,* or "perfected" language. It is, as we have been told all along, the "correct" or "virtuous" (*sādhu*) speech, the use of which is a form of *dharma.* Bhartṛhari's use of the term *saṃskāra* here makes this connection with *dharma* even more apparent.

Bhartṛhari's commentary on VP 1.143–44 further elaborates the basic themes of these verses. The *vṛtti* on 1.143 begins — again following Patañjali — by distinguishing the eternal Word from the produced word, the word as effect (*kārya*). The latter is to be understood as the image (*pratibimba*) of the former, which alone is the true or essential Word (*vāgātman*). Bhartṛhari then describes the eternal Word:

> The eternal Word, however, is the source of all everyday usage; [in it] all sequence is suppressed, it dwells within everyone, it is the origin of all transformations, the support of all actions, the foundation of both happiness and suffering; it has the unrestricted power of producing effects everywhere [but] is like a light that is obstructed by things like pots [being placed over it]; its boundary encompasses the entire field of enjoyable objects; it is the source of all corporeal objects, having the appearance of eternal activity through all forms of consciousness and all forms of differentiation, imitating the process of sleep and waking, possessing the power of generation and destruction through activity and the cessation of activity, like rain and forest-fire [create and destroy a forest]; [it is the] Lord of all, endowed with all power, the great Word-Bull. Those who know the yoga of speech, having broken through the knot of ego-consciousness, are united with it, completely without separation.[22]

This passage leaves no doubt as to the identity of the inner Word and the True Word that is the origin of the manifest universe. Bhartṛhari

21. VP 1.144.
22. VP 1.143 vṛtti.

clearly accepts the Brahmanic and Upanishadic identification of Ātman and Brahman, yet while insisting that this identity is mediated through language, since the latter, properly understood, is in fact the *self-mediation* of the True Word. From the human perspective, this identity is not merely given but must be *achieved* through a process of purification. Bhartṛhari's commentary on VP 1.144 describes this process in more detail:

> When the True Word [as existing within a person in its obscured state] is purified through receiving a form that is fully established in its correctness, and when a particular merit has become manifest, due to the removal of defective forms, well-being is established [for that person]. When one has achieved the yoga preceded by words by the repeated practice [of this process of purification], and when one has correctly experienced the intuition (*pratibhā*) that derives from ultimate Reality, which is the origin of the transformations of beings, [and is] Being [itself], endowed with the capacity [for taking on the form of both] the end and the means, then complete rest is achieved.[23]

This same process is also described in the *vṛtti* on VP 1.14, which refers to grammar as the "door to salvation":

> The grammarian who has acquired particular merit through the use of correct speech, being united with the great Word-Ātman, attains freedom from the senses. Having arrived at the unmixed stage of the Word, he seeks the intuition which is the source of the transformations of the Word. From there, from that intuition which is suitable only for Being, he reaches the Supreme Origin, in which all differentiation has ceased, by means of a withdrawal from the activity of the impulses [which are left over from the effort involved in] the yoga preceded by words.[24]

Several points in these passages merit comment. First of all, as we saw in Bhartṛhari's discussion of tradition generally, so here the practice of *dharma,* specifically the *dharma* of correct speech, leads ultimately to vision, to the experience of intuition, or *pratibhā,* here not merely the insight into the meaning of a sentence but a more intense experience of the

23. VP 1.144 vṛtti.
24. VP 1.14 vṛtti.

luminosity of Being itself. Through the purification of words and the repeated use of words so purified one arrives finally at a vision of the Word. This final outcome is affirmed in a verse that Bhartṛhari quotes with approval: "When, by the repetition of the Veda, this boundless darkness has departed, the supreme, bright, undying inner Light becomes manifest."[25]

Second, this process entails a transformation of the person. Specifically, it requires that one break through a false sense of self, the "knot" of the ego. Bhartṛhari repeats this in his commentary on VP 1.5: "The attainment of Brahman is nothing other than going beyond the knot of the ego that says 'mine' and 'I.' "[26] We may thus conclude from these two points that the process of purification that Bhartṛhari has in mind assimilates the individual subject to the objective Self, or Ātman — equally the True Word — through the mediation of the latter. The individual subject is thus caught up in the movement of the True Word's own process of self-manifestation. Ultimately, it is discovered that the individual subject has its true reality precisely as a particular moment within this process. Bhartṛhari does not admit substantial souls any more than he admits external, substantial objects. Like the actions that ultimately constitute its being, the subject, or better, the *agent,* is no more — but also no *less* — than the self-veiling and self-manifestation of the True Word. Viewed from the perspective of the highest truth, therefore, revelation is the self-revelation of the Word to itself. But this process of the self-revelation of the Word, for some "marvelous" (*adbhuta*) and finally inexplicable reason, a reason ultimately to be sought in the luminous and dynamic nature of the True Word itself, occurs only through the mediation of the world that it itself brings into being. Viewed from the perspective of this world, the level that Bhartṛhari calls *vyavahāra,* however, revelation has a certain kind of necessity. This is the "contingent necessity" of the individual person, who, while being ultimately a concrete moment in the self-mediation of the Self, can come to such genuine self-knowledge only through the long "detour" of *dharma* and the language of Vedic revelation upon which it is based.

CONCLUSION

With this brief examination of the linguistically mediated transformation of the human subject through the "yoga preceded by words," we

25. VP 1.5 vṛtti.
26. VP 1.5 vṛtti.

bring our study of Bhartṛhari to a close. Looking back over the ground that we have just covered we see that the centrality of the language of revelation in Bhartṛhari's thought stands out quite clearly. Grounded in the True Word and proclaimed in its differentiated state by the seers of the Veda, as *anukāra,* or "imitative resemblance" of this Word, the language of revelation in turn provides the ground for the social, religious and linguistic practices of the learned Brahmins, or *śiṣṭa*-s, of the post-Vedic Brahmanical tradition. Bhartṛhari's traditionalism thus comes through quite clearly, but no more clearly than does his keen interest in the *experience* of revelation through the dialectic of language and vision just described. These two poles of objective mediation and individual experience are inseparable in Bhartṛhari's thought. One who would see the Word must first master the words.

In this respect, despite Bhartṛhari's emphasis on the spiritual experience of the individual in the appropriation of the language of revelation, his assimilation of this language, following his master Patañjali, to the "correct speech" of the grammarians makes his model for the reception of revelation quite restrictive. Bhartṛhari was a member of a very exclusive club, the learned Brahmanical elite, and his view of revelation makes its mediation inseparable from the linguistic and social practices of the members of that elite group. One who has been able to master the subtleties of Pāṇini's description of the "divine speech" and then proceed to the contemplation of its structure and ultimate ground, as envisioned here, might well attain to an experience of the Light "beyond light and darkness." For most, however, it would be the objective and external forms of mediation that would remain most apparent, and these forms were part and parcel of a hierarchically arranged society that carefully controlled access to them and that, as Norvin Hein has argued, was particularly in the Gupta period experienced as increasingly oppressive by many of its members.[27] It is not surprising, then, that the new theistic models of revelation, such as Krishna's self-revelation to Arjuna, as presented in the Bhagavad Gitā, models that Bhartṛhari nowhere mentions, were increasingly popular and have remained so down to the present. What makes Bhartṛhari's insights into the nature of revelation so valuable, namely, his faithfulness to the basic Vedic paradigm centered on the power of sacred speech, also proves a liability in a historical context where it is precisely this sacred speech that has been appropriated as the badge of orthopraxy by a very

27. See Norvin Hein, "A Revolution in Kṛṣṇaism: The Cult of Gopāla," *History of Religions* 25 (1986): 296–317.

restricted and dominant social group. While the presence of revelation as a dynamic, living experience in India would increasingly come to be associated with the "incorrect" vernacular languages, first in the south and later in the north, Bhartṛhari wedded it inseparably to the language of a social and intellectual elite.

On the other hand this emphasis on the form of correct speech as the form of *dharma* makes Bhartṛhari's view of the reception of revelation in some respects potentially somewhat more expansive. For if one links Vedic *dharma* to a form of speech, then presumably anyone who can attain mastery of this form can find access to *dharma.* As noted in an earlier chapter, Sanskrit by this time had become a *lingua franca* serving not merely Brahmanical intellectuals but intellectuals generally, Buddhists included. Correct Pāṇinian Sanskrit became the norm for the expression of serious intellectual ideas, whatever their particular content. Indeed, the "Candra" credited in the *Vākyapadīya* itself with the revival of the study of Patañjali's *Mahābhāṣya*[28] is probably correctly identified with the *Buddhist* grammarian Candragomin.[29] Does this mean that for Bhartṛhari even non-Brahmins who had mastered the form of the divine speech could gain some access to its ultimate ground? Unfortunately it is impossible to know whether Bhartṛhari himself saw or indeed intended this more liberal implication of his doctrine, just as it is impossible to know whether, on the contrary, he consciously intended his ideas to serve as an ideological justification of the Brahmanical establishment. All we can say is that the potential for both seems to be present in his view of revelation. Either way, the reception of revelation remains tied to an elite form of culture. The ideological potential of such a theory of revelation is something that deserves notice, and it is something to which we will return at a later point. At present we must move on to our study of Bonaventure.

---

28. See above, p. 32.

29. On the identity of Candragomin, see the introduction to Michael Hahn's *Candragomins Lokānandanāṭaka* (Wiesbaden: Otto Harrassowitz, 1974). On the grammatical work of Candragomin, see Louis Renou, "Les 'innovations' de la grammaire de Candragomin," *Études de Grammaire Sanskrite* (Paris: Adrien-Maisonneuve, 1936), 88–143.

PART II

Bonaventure

4

Bonaventure on Christian Revelation: Introduction

St. Bonaventure, the thirteenth-century Christian theologian, believed in a divine Word that, though divine, eternal, and beyond all limitations of time and space, nevertheless became incarnate in human form in a small town in Palestine at the very beginning of what we today call the Christian era. For Bonaventure, the incarnation, death, and resurrection of Jesus of Nazareth was the central event that gave meaning to a long series of revelations that both preceded this event and continued after it. The incarnation marked the center of time, the midpoint of human history, a history that was — and for Bonaventure continued to be — a history of revelation.

Living in thirteenth-century France, Bonaventure acknowledged revelation as a historical event in the past, as the source of the church's authoritative text, the Bible, and as a continuing reality in the communities to which he belonged: the church itself and the order of the Friars Minor, founded by a man whom Bonaventure believed to have been a prophet, St. Francis of Assisi. Bonaventure's conception of revelation is thus multifaceted. Revelation is at once historical, experiential, textual, and communal. In the following chapters, we will have to try to sort out these distinct elements and also try to discover their underlying unity. But we must begin by locating Bonaventure in his historical context.

BONAVENTURE'S HISTORICAL CONTEXT

Like the fifth century in India, the thirteenth century in the medieval West has often been viewed as a kind of "golden age," in this case, the golden age of Christian scholasticism and of medieval Christendom generally. It was a time of florescence, built upon the extraordinary century that preceded it. Born John Fidanza in 1221, in the small town of Bagnorea, Italy, near present-day Orvieto, Bonaventure's life spanned the century.[1] Living at Paris for most of his adult life, a contemporary of Thomas Aquinas and friend of the French king, Louis IX, and toward the end of his life a cardinal of the church and a confidant of the pope, he was at the center of some of the most important developments of the high Middle Ages. His career was remarkable by virtue of its variety. He was at once a scholastic, a mystic, an administrator, a pastor and respected preacher, and a papal advisor. What is even more remarkable is that he was able to synthesize these various regions of experience and give them a coherent expression in his written works.

No reliable record remains of Bonaventure's earliest years, but possibly as early as 1236 and certainly by 1242 he was a student of arts at Paris. In 1243 he became a Franciscan and a student in theology of Alexander of Hales.

From 1243 to 1248, Bonaventure studied theology, and in the latter year began his commentary on Peter Lombard's *Sentences,* which by this time had become the recognized textbook of theology at Paris. Bonaventure's commentary on the *Sentences* was his most extensive work of scholastic theology and will be an important source for the study of his "metaphysics of revelation" below.

In 1253 Bonaventure became a master of theology and over the next few years produced some of his most important theological treatises, including his brief theological textbook, the *Breviloquium,* and his series of *Disputed Questions.* These years marked the highpoint of Bonaventure's career as a scholastic theologian at the University of Paris.

In 1257 Bonaventure was elected the Minister General of the Franciscan order, and the character of his writings became more pastoral in orientation as he assumed the responsibilities of his new office. He also

---

1. The most accessible life of Bonaventure is the one by Etienne Gilson, included as the first chapter of his study, *The Philosophy of St. Bonaventure,* trans. Illtyd Trethowan and Frank J. Sheed (Paterson, N.J.: St. Anthony Guild Press, 1965), pp. 1–78. A detailed chronology of his life is presented by J. Guy Bougerol, *Introduction to the Works of Bonaventure,* trans. José de Vinck (Paterson, N.J.: St. Anthony Guild Press, 1964), pp. 171–77. In addition, there is the lengthy entry on Bonaventure, written by E. Longpré, in the *Dictionnaire d'Histoire et de Géographie Ecclésiastiques* (Paris: Librairie Letouzey et Ané, 1937), 9:741–88; and the biography included by the Quaracchi editors in the final volume of their critical edition of Bonaventure's works, *Doctoris Seraphici S. Bonaventurae Opera Omnia,* 10 vols. (Quaracchi: Collegia S. Bonaventurae, 1882–1902), 10:39–73. Further references to Bonaventure's works will be to this edition and will be given in parentheses according to volume and page number, following the title of the particular work.

began to compose mystical and devotional treatises, under the influence of the saint whose disciples he had now been called upon to lead. In 1259, Bonaventure paid a visit to La Verna, Italy, where Francis had had his famous vision of the six-winged seraph. The result of this visit was Bonaventure's best-known work, *The Soul's Journey into God,* a mystical treatise organized on the basis of Francis's vision. Other devotional works also date from this period, such as *The Tree of Life* and *The Triple Way.*

In 1260 Bonaventure oversaw the revision of the constitutions of the Franciscan order at the General Chapter at Narbonne and was also asked to write an official life of St. Francis for the order, which he completed the following year. In 1267–68, he undertook the revision of some of his earlier sermons in order to produce a collection of model sermons, an expression of his concern for the friars' vocation of preaching.[2] It was probably also at this time that Bonaventure made the final revisions on his commentary on the gospel of Luke, which was also intended to aid the task of preaching.[3] In these works one can see him applying his theological expertise, gained during his years as a student and master at Paris, to the practical concerns of the church and to the more personal concerns of the individual in search of God.

In the late 1260s Bonaventure grew more polemical as he became involved in a number of controversies. In 1267–68 he presented a series of collations, the *Collations on the Ten Commandments* (1267) and the *Collations on the Gifts of the Holy Spirit* (1268), in which he defended a Christocentric view of reality against the radical Aristotelians. In 1269 his *Apology for the Mendicants* appeared, a defense of the Franciscan doctrine of absolute poverty. Finally, in 1273, Bonaventure gave another series of collations, the *Collations on the Six Days,* one of his most important works, in which he combined a metaphysics of exemplarism with a prophetic view of history, influenced by both Joachim of Fiore and the figure of St. Francis, all within the framework of a radically Christocentric vision of reality. In many ways this last work was to be his greatest, and we will have occasion to return to it. It is unfortunate that it still remained incomplete when, in 1273, Bonaventure was made a cardinal by Gregory X and called upon to help in the preparation for the Sec-

---

2. See *Sancti Bonaventurae Sermones Dominicales,* ed. J. Guy Bougerol (Grottaferrata: Collegio S. Bonaventurae, 1977), esp. Bougerol's lengthy introductory study, where he argues for this collection's status as a collection of model sermons.

3. See Dominic V. Monti, "Bonaventure's Interpretation of Scripture in the Exegetical Works," Ph.D. dissertation, University of Chicago, 1979, pp. 149–221, esp. p. 154.

ond Council of Lyon. It was while Bonaventure was in attendance at the council that he died, on July 15, 1274.

BONAVENTURE'S INTELLECTUAL CONTEXT

Like Bhartṛhari, Bonaventure inherited a tradition that had grown quite sophisticated. Both men operated in scholastic environments in which many facets of their respective traditions were coming under intense intellectual scrutiny. Unlike the situation in classical India, however, in the medieval West there had been nothing like Buddhism, a successful rival that had succeeded in calling the very foundations of the tradition into question. Such was not to be the case in the West until the Enlightenment. It is true that Bonaventure himself viewed Aristotelian metaphysics as in some ways a threat to the revealed truth of the Christian tradition, but even if they had constituted a rival religious movement (which they did not), it is unlikely that the Aristotelians, without their own Aśoka, would have been in a position to shake the foundations of Christian certitude in the way that the Buddhists had shaken the old Brahmanical system of India. As a consequence it is not until the Enlightenment that revelation is thematized as a central theological issue in the West. In the Middle Ages the issue of the nature of Christian revelation was not thematized as such but was rather dealt with in a variety of more indirect ways. One way to do this was to examine what one might call the theological presuppositions of revelation, something that Bonaventure did *via* his trinitarian theology of the threefold Word. In more concrete terms, one could focus on the nature of scripture, and more importantly on the proper methods of its interpretation. But there was also a good deal of interest in the phenomenon of prophecy, especially in the thirteenth century, perhaps stimulated by a growing consciousness of the rival claims of "the" Prophet, Muhammad. Closely associated with both of these specific forms of revelation was the central practice of preaching, which at times could itself border on prophecy. Bonaventure had a good deal to say about each of these, and in each case he was taking up a discussion with a long tradition behind it. In order to appreciate Bonaventure's intellectual context we need to know something of this background.

Martin Dibelius once noted that, as far as Christianity is concerned, "in the beginning was preaching."[4] Not only do we first encounter Jesus him-

4. Martin Dibelius, "Die alttestamentlichen Motive in der Leidensgeschichte des Petrus- und des Johannes-Evangeliums," *Zeitschrift für die alttestamentliche Wissenschaft* 33 (1918):

self, at the beginning of Mark's gospel,[5] as a preacher proclaiming the Kingdom of God, but the Christian tradition itself was born of preaching, the preaching of the risen Christ by the preachers *par excellence* of the early church, the apostles. An apostle was essentially a "messenger" (from *apostellein,* "to send"), sent by Christ to proclaim the gospel. He was one who had seen the resurrected Christ and who had been commissioned by him to preach.[6] Apostolic preaching thus originated in the direct experience of the risen Christ by an individual apostle.

Closely related to apostolic preaching was a second form of speech that was often accepted as revelatory of the divine will, namely, prophecy. Prophecy was understood as a gift of the Spirit, given to the early Christian community as a sign of the imminence of the Kingdom.

The importance of the apostolic preachers and charismatic prophets as church leaders did not last, however. The apostolic function of preaching gradually passed to the president or bishop of the community. And after the second century, Christian prophets no longer occupied an important place in the church. The development of formal structures of authority and the move toward greater uniformity in what soon begins to be called a "catholic" church left less room for the spontaneous guidance provided by the inspired speech of the prophet. Although preaching in the primitive church had probably not originally been limited to specific persons, the challenges of various heretical movements in the second century and the emergence of the office of the bishop as "first among equals" led to its becoming a specifically episcopal function. From this time on, preaching was understood as an official function of the church, incumbent upon the bishop or on whomever the bishop might delegate for the task.[7]

We find a similar restriction or reinterpretation of Christian prophecy.[8] For the first Christian century, the recipients of this gift, the Christian

---

146, quoted by Krister Stendahl, *The School of St. Matthew and Its Use of the Old Testament* (Philadelphia: Fortress Press, 1968), p. 13.

5. Mark 1:14–15.

6. Mark 16:15; Matthew 28:19–20; Luke 24:47–48; John 20:21. See also Raymond E. Brown, "The Twelve and the Apostolate" in *The Jerome Biblical Commentary* (Englewood Cliffs, N.J.: Prentice-Hall, 1968), p. 798; and Hans von Campenhausen, *Ecclesiastical Authority and Spiritual Power in the Church of the First Three Centuries* (London: Adam & Charles Black, 1969), pp. 17–23.

7. This was to remain the case in the West, with some exceptions, until the Council of Vaison (529) recognized the right of regular clergy to preach. See Jean Longère, *La prédication médiévale* (Paris: Études Augustiniennes, 1983), pp. 30–31.

8. James Ash has argued that it is to the emergence of the office of the monarchial bishop that we must attribute the disappearance of spontaneous, "unofficial" Christian prophecy. See James L. Ash, Jr., "The Decline of Ecstatic Prophecy in the Early Church," *Theological Studies* 37 (1976): 227–52.

prophets, played an important role in the early communities.[9] By the second century, though Christian prophets had begun to disappear, their authority transferred to the monarchial bishop,[10] who exercised the "gift of prophecy" primarily through the interpretation of the Christian scriptures. Prophecy thus came to be viewed through the lense of scripture, as either the prediction of the future, in the manner of the classical prophets who foretold the coming of Christ, or as the revelation of the hidden meaning of scripture on the part of Christian preachers, primarily the bishops.[11] Both tendencies can be seen clearly in Gregory the Great, who assimilated the classical prophets mentioned in scripture to the great preachers of the church, such as himself.

In the early Middle Ages the interpretation of prophecy as the spiritual interpretation of scripture became a commonplace. This interpretation of prophecy seems to have been inspired by St. Paul's discussion of prophecy as intended for the edification of the church, at 1 Corinthians 14:1–5. Medieval commentators on this passage invariably interpret it as a reference to scriptural interpretation.[12] Running parallel to this tradition of prophecy as interpretation was another tradition of prophecy as the form of inspiration that allows one to predict the future. The *locus classicus* for this view, which stressed as well the nature of prophecy as a form of inspiration, was the definition of prophecy given by Cassiodorus: "Prophecy is a divine inspiration that announces the outcome of certain things, either through actions or through words, with an unshakeable truth."[13] Implicit

9. On early Christian prophecy, see David E. Aune, *Prophecy in Early Christianity and the Ancient Mediterranean World* (Grand Rapids: Eerdmans, 1983). Other recent studies include E. Earle Ellis, *Prophecy and Hermeneutic in Early Christianity: New Testament Essays* (Tübingen: J. C. B. Mohr, 1978); *Prophetic Vocation in the New Testament and Today,* ed. J. Panagopoulos (Leiden: E. J. Brill, 1977); and J. Reiling, *Hermes and Christian Prophecy: A Study of the Eleventh Mandate* (Leiden: E. J. Brill, 1973).

10. See Ash, "The Decline of Ecstatic Prophecy in the Early Church," 227–52.

11. See for instance Ambrosiaster's definition of prophecy in the fourth century, *In primam epistolam ad Corinthios* 12:28 (PL 17:263b): Prophetas duplici genere intelligamus, et futura dicentes, et scripturas revelantes.

12. In the ninth century, for instance, Rabanus Maurus, in his *Expositio in Epistolam I ad Corinthios* c. 12 (PL 112.116), comments on 1 Corinthians 14 by distinguishing two types of prophets: those who predict the future and those who reveal the meaning of scripture. In the twelfth century, Peter Abelard continues this tradition, describing prophecy as the "grace of interpretation, i.e., of expounding scripture," in his *Expositio in Epistolam ad Romanos* Bk. 4, on Rom. 12:6 (PL 178.939). For William of St. Thierry, too, prophecy is the "knowledge of the hidden meanings of scripture," as well as the *discretio spirituum,* the discernment of spirits. See his *Expositio in Epistolam ad Romanos* Bk. 7, on Rom. 12:6 (PL 180.673). And for Peter Lombard, St. Paul's *qui prophetat* (1 Cor. 14:3) means *qui exponit scripturas* (*In Primam Epistolam ad Corinthios* [PL 191.1664]).

13. Cassiodorus, *In Psalterium Praefatio* c. 1 [PL 70.12]. This definition was to have a long and varied history. It was later quoted in the *Glossa ordinaria,* although in a slightly altered form, changing Cassiodorus's *aspiratio divina* to *inspiratio vel revelatio divina,* and

in both of these views of prophecy was the idea that prophecy involved some kind of special inspiration by the Spirit. The first attempt to develop an explicit theory of prophetic inspiration was made by Augustine, who applied ideas of Neoplatonic origin to the description of prophecy, and in doing so cast the problem of prophetic inspiration in terms of vision and illumination, an approach that was to be central for Bonaventure as well.[14]

Central to the narrowing of scope of both preaching and prophecy as media of revelation in the early history of the church was the development of specifically Christian "scriptures." If the church was born out of the kerygmatic preaching of the apostles and sustained by the inspired utterances of its prophets, its survival as an institution and as an "orthodoxy" amid the religious controversies of the early centuries seems to have required not only the centralized authority of the bishop, but also the mediation of canonical texts that could provide the basis for the bishop's authoritative instruction.

An important step toward constructing a new, specifically Christian book, a "New Testament," seems to have been taken by the church father Irenaeus.[15] In his polemics against the gnostics, Irenaeus broke with the earlier reliance on the Hebrew scriptures as the source of "proof texts" and appealed more frequently to the new Christian writings. At a time when the fact of the plurality of gospels in the church was causing real concern,[16] Irenaeus argued for the authoritative status of four of them, taken as a whole: "Since God made all things in good and fitting order, it was necessary also that the form of the gospel should be well designed and put together."[17] The four individual gospels, the products of diverse

---

adding that prophecy is therefore a form of vision, and the prophet a seer (*Glossa ordinaria, Prothemata in Psalterium* [PL 113.842]). Perhaps it is not by accident that the mention of vision in the *Glossa* is accompanied by the introduction of the term *revelatio,* a more "visual" term than *inspiratio.* Peter Lombard repeated Cassiodorus's definition in his commentary on the Psalms, more or less as it appears in the *Glossa,* although somewhat shortened (Peter Lombard, *Comm. in Psalmos, Praefatio* [PL 191.58]). In Lombard's shortened form, the definition was then quoted widely by the scholastics of the thirteenth century.

14. See Augustine, *De Genesi ad Litteram,* Bk. 12, trans. John Hammond Taylor, S.J., *The Literal Meaning of Genesis,* 2 vols. (New York: Newman Press, 1982), 1:178–231; and the discussion of Wolfgang Wieland, *Offenbarung bei Augustinus* (Mainz: Grünewald, 1978), pp. 39–106.

15. In what follows, I am drawing upon Hans von Campenhausen's discussion of Irenaeus, in his *The Formation of the Christian Bible* (Philadelphia: Fortress, 1972), pp. 182–209. See esp. p. 186: "Irenaeus, so far as we can tell, was the first catholic theologian who dared to adopt the Marcionite principle of a new 'scripture' in order to use it in his turn against Marcion and all heretics."

16. On this matter, see Oscar Cullmann, "The Plurality of the Gospels as a Theological Problem in Antiquity," in his *The Early Church: Studies in Early Christian History and Theology* (Philadelphia: Westminster Press, 1956), pp. 39–54.

17. Irenaeus, *Against Heresies* 3.11.9, quoted by von Campenhausen, *Formation,* p. 200.

local communities over several decades, each with its distinctive image of the life and teachings of Jesus, are here identified as "the" gospel, with a fourfold form that is the result, not of historical chance, but of divine necessity. Irenaeus writes that "the Scriptures are indeed perfect, since they were spoken by the Word of God and his Spirit."[18] Here he is not speaking of an inspired author, but of a divine author, the Word of God. The origin of the scriptures is assimilated to the divine act of creation: "The Word, the Artificer of all . . . has given us the gospel under four aspects, but bound together by one Spirit."[19] As the "creation" of the Word, the gospels take on a cosmic aspect: "It is not possible that the gospels can be either more or fewer in number than they are. For, since there are four zones of the world in which we live, and four principal winds . . . it is fitting that she [the church] should have four pillars, breathing out immortality on every side."[20]

Even more than Irenaeus, however, it was Origen who, as von Campenhausen has noted, made Christianity into a "religion of the Book."[21] For Origen, the entirety of the Bible is verbally inspired in all its parts.[22] Everywhere in scripture "the same eternal Logos holds sway, making of scripture a single, miraculous, unified divine instrument for teaching salvation."[23] Origen went so far as to argue, in his *Commentary on Matthew,* that the Word "is as it were incarnate in the Bible." As Hanson notes, "nothing could assure us more eloquently of Origen's conviction of the divine status and authorship of the Bible than this startling doctrine of the Bible as the extension of the Incarnation."[24] By the time of Origen, then, we have a new Christian Bible, a Christian *sacra scriptura* in the strongest sense of a unified, verbally inspired document.

Thus within a few centuries of the apostles' original proclamation of their experience of the risen Lord Christian revelation had become the possession of a settled institution — the church and its bishops — and this possession in turn provided the institution with its legitimacy. It was this institutionalized form of revelation as a sacred text that nevertheless remained open to interpretation through both prophecy and preaching that

18. Irenaeus, *Against Heresies* 2.28.2, trans. Alexander Roberts and James Donaldson, in *The Ante-Nicene Fathers,* 10 vols. (Edinburgh, 1867; U.S. reprint ed., Grand Rapids: Eerdmans Publishing Co., 1977), 1:399.

19. Ibid., 3.9.8, *Ante-Nicene Fathers,* 1:428.

20. Ibid.

21. Von Campenhausen, *Formation,* p. 325.

22. See R. P. C. Hanson, *Allegory and Event: A Study of the Sources and Significance of Origen's Interpretation of Scripture* (London: SCM Press, 1959), pp. 187–209.

23. Von Campenhausen, *Formation,* p. 319.

24. Hanson, *Allegory and Event,* pp. 193–94; *Comm. on Matt.* 15.3.

Bonaventure inherited. In coming to grips with each of these concrete aspects of revelation as he received it from his tradition, Bonaventure tapped the resources of the early medieval tradition that had preceded him, most particularly in its Neoplatonic form as found for instance in the twelfth-century school of St. Victor, but most importantly in the highly influential writings of pseudo-Dionysius, the sixth-century Christian Neoplatonist. But perhaps the most pervasive influence on Bonaventure's thinking, especially as regards his understanding of preaching and prophecy, was St. Francis and Bonaventure's involvement in the order of Friars Minor that Francis had founded.

BONAVENTURE THE FRANCISCAN

Francis of Assisi (c. 1181–1226), one of the most famous and most beloved of Christian mystics, had an enormous impact on St. Bonaventure. Though Francis died while Bonaventure was still a young boy, Bonaventure joined the order that Francis had founded while he was still a young student in Paris, and his involvement with the Franciscans shaped the rest of his life.

Francis himself had been a charismatic preacher who was part of a larger movement of itinerant preachers in the twelfth century who traveled the countryside preaching repentance and extolling the life of "evangelical perfection," a life lived in accordance with the life of the apostles, as portrayed in the Christian gospels. The Franciscan order that Bonaventure knew, however, was as much a product of papal attempts to enlist the early Franciscans in the cause of church reform as it was an expression of Francis's own ideal of a simple life of poverty. By the time Bonaventure joined the order in 1243, the Franciscans had become a major presence at the University of Paris. In 1231 the man who was to be Bonaventure's teacher, Alexander of Hales, an established master at the university, had created a stir by entering the order and transferring his chair in theology to the Franciscans. The Franciscans had first arrived in Paris in 1219, and the story of the Franciscan and Dominican friars at the University of Paris throughout the thirteenth century is in part the story of their struggle to establish themselves as the dominant force against the opposition of the secular masters already in place there. Their eventual success was due in large part to continued papal and royal support of their cause.[25]

25. On the friars and the French monarchy, see Lester K. Little, "Saint Louis' Involvement with the Friars," *Church History* 33 (1964): 125–48.

The friars' relations with the secular masters at the university were complicated by the involvement of some of the Franciscans in the prophetic ideas of Joachim of Fiore (1135–1202). In 1254, a radical Joachite treatise, entitled *An Introduction to the Eternal Gospel,* was published by the Franciscan Gerardo di Borgo San Donnino. In this work Gerardo claimed that the writings of Joachim of Fiore, the twelfth-century prophet of a coming "age of the Spirit," constituted a new "eternal gospel" that was destined to replace the canonical New Testament. Although such radical views were not typical of the Franciscans as a group, their most outspoken critic, William of Saint-Amour, used the scandal created by Gerardo's work to launch an all-out attack, not only on the friars' position within the university, but on their religious ideals as mendicants vowed to a life of poverty. In his *Treatise on the Dangers of Modern Times (Tractatus de Periculis Novissimorum Temporum),* published in 1256, William rejected this ideal as unbiblical and accused the friars of being false apostles.[26] In the midst of this controversy, John of Parma, who in 1256 was Minister General of the Franciscans and who was known to be sympathetic to Joachim's prophecies of a coming third age, was forced to resign, in spite of the fact that he was widely respected for his exemplary sanctity and commitment to the order. Given the privilege of recommending his own successor, John nominated Bonaventure, who was thus elected Minister General in 1257. This ended his brief career as master of theology at the university, and he inherited a controversy that was to shape some of his most significant reflections on the nature of revelation.

Another controversy was also brewing, fueled by the rising enthusiasm for the works of Aristotle, especially as interpreted by his twelfth-century Muslim commentator Ibn Rushd, better known in the West as Averroes (1126–98) and represented at Paris by Siger of Brabant. Bonaventure was one of those who felt that Aristotelian doctrines, especially in the uncompromising form in which they were presented by the radical Aristotelians like Siger, were incompatible with Christian faith. Although Bonaventure was no longer a master at Paris, in 1267–68 he took to the pulpit to present his *Collations on the Ten Commandments* (1267) and his *Collations on the Gifts of the Holy Spirit* (1268), in which he attacked the doctrines of the radical Aristotelians and advocated in their stead a thoroughly Christocentric view of reality. This line of defense reached its culmination in 1273, in his final series of collations, the *Collations on*

26. On William of Saint-Amour's views, see James Doyne Dawson, "William of Saint-Amour and the Apostolic Tradition," *Mediaeval Studies* 40 (1978): 223–38.

the Six Days, already mentioned above, which were heavily influenced by Joachim's view of history and by the figure of St. Francis.

These controversies provided the intellectual context in which Bonaventure put the final touches on both his exemplaristic metaphysics of revelation, and his view of the history of revelation and applied each to the interpretation of the significance of revelation in his own age. In the following chapters we will examine some of the ways in which he pursued these questions, both at the level of theoretical reflection — as a scholastic theologian and speculative mystic — and at the level of practice — as preacher, religious leader, and, in some sense at least, prophet. In the next two chapters we will examine what I shall call his metaphysics of revelation and the conception of the history of revelation that is closely related to it. This will be followed by a closer look at Bonaventure's own reception of revelation, in the three forms of scripture, preaching, and prophecy, and in the context of the thirteenth century.

5

The Metaphysics of Revelation

PROLOGUE IN HEAVEN: BONAVENTURE'S THEOLOGY OF THE TRINITY

In the theology of St. Bonaventure, to understand revelation means, in the deepest sense, to understand the Trinity. According to traditional Christian belief, God exists as both One and Three. The simple divine nature subsists as three distinct Persons, the Father, the Son, and the Holy Spirit. This doctrine of the triune God, together with the doctrine of the incarnation of the second Person of the Son in Jesus of Nazareth, expressed for Bonaventure the central mystery of the Christian faith and, indeed, the mystery of existence itself. This mystery is for him, in an important sense, a mystery of revelation. The entire universe, together with its history, is conceived as a revelation of the Trinity, and this revelation, in all its breadth and variety, is grounded in the three Persons of the Trinity.

Bonaventure's discussion of God the Father presents us with a God who is supremely self-communicative. From all eternity, the Father's plenitude of being naturally overflows in the generation of a Son, his Word and Image, together with whom he further breathes forth the Holy Spirit, in an eternal act of perfect mutual love. This generation or emanation of the Son and "spiration" of the Spirit provide the divine prototype for all subsequent creation and revelation, and both are ultimately rooted in the primal fecundity of the Father, what Bonaventure calls his *fontalis plenitudo,* or "fountain fullness." How are we to understand this supreme, self-giving plenitude that lies at the heart of reality and is the root of all revelation?

In his well-known work *The Soul's Journey into God* Bonaventure tells us that the most fitting name for God is not Being, but the Good, and that the Good is the principal foundation for the contemplation of the emanations of the divine Persons within the Trinity.[1] Following his teacher Alexander of Hales,[2] Bonaventure invokes a metaphysical principle that derives from pseudo-Dionysius, the sixth-century Christian Neoplatonist: *bonum est diffusivum sui,* the Good is self-diffusive.[3] It is a consequence of God's nature as the Good that it continually overflows itself, and it is this overflowing of the divine being that produces a plurality of persons in God.

In his earliest account of the Trinity in his commentary on Peter Lombard's *Sentences,* Bonaventure links this fundamental self-communicative nature of God with the Person of the Father, through a discussion of God's primacy, appealing to yet another Neoplatonic principle. There is in God, he says, the highest primacy:

> But to the extent something is more prior, to that extent it is more fecund and the principle of others. Therefore, just as the divine essence is the principle of other [created] essences because it is first, so the Person of the Father, since it is first, originating from no one else, is the principle and is endowed with fecundity in respect to [the other] Persons.[4]

The Father is absolutely first, and is therefore absolutely fecund, powerful, self-communicative. The Father is first because he is unbegotten, without origin. Bonaventure refers to this characteristic of the Father as his *innascibilitas,* his "unbegottenness," and employs the Neoplatonic principle to give this essentially negative concept a profoundly positive meaning. In Bonaventure's view reality itself is characterized by its tendency to communicate or express itself. This is true of all things, and the divine being is no exception. Indeed it is most true of the divine: "We must admit that there is generation in the divine Being. And I believe

1. *Itin.* 6.1 (5:310b). See also *Itin.* 5.2 (5:308).

2. On Alexander's use of the concept of the Good, see the prolegomena to the critical edition of his *Summa Theologica* (Quaracchi, 1924), pp. xxxv–xxxviii.

3. Bonaventure makes frequent use of this principle. See, for instance, I *Sent.* d. 19, p. 1, art. unic., q. 2, arg. 3 (1:344); d. 45, a. 2, q. 1, resp. (1:804b); II *Sent.* d. 1, p. 2, q. 2, f. 3 (2:41); d. 7, p. 2, art. unic., q. 1, arg. 5 (2:190); IV *Sent.* d. 8, p. 1, dubia 2 (4:188); *De Myst. Trin.* q. 2, a. 1, ad 7 (5:60). See also pseudo-Dionysius, *Celestial Hierarchies,* 4, 1 and *On the Divine Names,* 4, 1ff.

4. I *Sent.* d. 2, art. unic., q. 2, f. 4.

that the most important reason for this is the fact that every nature is communicable."[5]

According to Bonaventure, the "fountain fullness" or fecundity of God the Father has two aspects, a fecundity of nature and a fecundity of will, and thus gives rise *in divinis* to two processions or emanations. The natural fecundity of the Father gives rise to the emanation of a second Person, the Son, *per modum naturae*. The Father's fecundity of will gives rise to the emanation of a third Person, the Holy Spirit, *per modum voluntatis*.[6]

Bonaventure uses three principal titles to refer to the second Person — Son, Image, and Word, each of which adds an important dimension to his understanding of the second Person as the ground of revelation. The title of Son most directly expresses the natural emanation that is referred to as generation. Bonaventure defines generation as an emanation according to a conformity of nature or as the production of something that is similar to the producer in substance and nature.[7] Thus the natural emanation of the second Person from the Father as his Son has as its consequence the Son's perfect likeness to the Father: "The Son emanates by nature, and because he emanates by nature, he emanates as a perfect express similitude. For nature produces what is similar and equal to itself."[8] The metaphor of generation in God is thus intended to underscore the substantial unity and equality of the Father and Son.

The title of Image stresses the second Person's likeness or similitude to the Father. As the perfect and express similitude of the Father, the Son is indeed his most precise Image.[9] In addition, the notion of image brings with it the related notions of representation and imitation. Whenever a product represents something in a precise manner, it is called an image.[10] And image, by its very nature, implies imitation.[11] Thus the title of Image points us in two directions, so to speak. As associated with the idea of imitation, it implies the return of the Son to the Father, his assimilation (*assimilatio*) to his Source, which, being a perfect adequation, gives the second Person the additional character of Truth.[12] As associated with the idea of representation, on the other hand, the notion of image points to the

5. I *Sent.* d. 9, art. unic., q. 1, resp. (1:181b).
6. See I *Sent.* d. 13, art. unic., q. 3, resp. (1:236a).
7. I *Sent.* d. 9, art. unic., q. 1, resp. (1:181a).
8. I *Sent.* d. 31, p. 2, a. 1, q. 3, ad 1 (1:544a).
9. I *Sent.* d. 7, art. unic., q. 2, ad 4 (1:140b). See also *Brev.* p. 1, c. 3, n. 8 (5:212a).
10. See I *Sent.* d. 6, art. unic., q. 3, arg. 3 (1:129a).
11. I *Sent.* d. 31, p. 2, a. 1, q. 1, f. 4 (1:540a).
12. See I *Sent.* d. 8, p. 1, a. 1, q. 1 (1:151a).

key concept of expression (*expressio*), which will be the primary character of the second Person as Word and Exemplar. These two "directions" are hardly to be opposed, however, for as Bonaventure himself says, expression itself is a kind of assimilation.[13] The image, like the word, is expressive or representative only because it is fully assimilated or conformed to that which it expresses. The likeness that is found in the image is a *similitudo imitativa.*

The third title of the second Person that Bonaventure employs is that of the Word. Viewed both from the perspective of his work as a whole and from our own specific interests in his theory of revelation, it is this title that holds the central place. The primary importance of the title of Word is that it makes explicit the expressiveness that underlies the consubstantiality and similitude expressed respectively by the titles of Son and Image. In addition to being the similitude *expressa,* as was the Image, the Word is also a similitude *expressiva,* an expressive similitude.[14] The divine Word expresses all that the Father is and all that he can create and thus becomes the principle *in divinis* of all expression or manifestation *ad extra* in creation. The title of Word thus includes the significance of the other two titles and goes beyond them.[15] It brings us to the threshold of Bonaventure's notion of exemplarism and the closely related schema of the "threefold Word," the *verbum increatum,* the *verbum incarnatum,* and the *verbum inspiratum,* which lies at the root of his doctrine of revelation and which consequently will be the primary concern of the present chapter. Before turning to a consideration of this threefold Word, however, it is necessary to add a few remarks on Bonaventure's theology of the third Person, the Holy Spirit.

The essential likeness of the Father and the Son has a further aspect. As consubstantial they share a common will (*voluntas*).[16] This common will, being divine, is inseparable from *liberalitas,* which is freedom, but also generosity, the fecundity of the will. Liberality or freedom is the perfection proper to the will and is thus found in the highest degree in God, where, being identical with the divine being, it is perfect.[17] The most perfect act of the will, however, is love, and thus the Father and the Son are to be united with one another not only by a common will, but also

13. *De Sci. Christi* q. 2, resp. (5:9a).
14. See I *Sent.* d. 27, p. 2, art. unic., q. 2, resp. (1:485b).
15. Ibid., q. 3, resp. (1:488a).
16. I *Sent.* d. 11, art. unic., q. 2, resp. (1:215b).
17. I *Sent.* d. 10, a. 1, q. 1, f. 3 (1:195a). See also II *Sent.* d. 25, p. 1, dubia 3 (2:609a), and ibid., d. 37, a. 1, q. 1, ad 2 (2:863a).

by a perfectly free and generous act of mutual love. This free act of love is the source of the Holy Spirit, which is its recipient. Proceeding from the Father and the Son as pure liberality, as pure love, He is the supreme Gift, or better the principle of liberality (*ratio liberalitatis*), in whom all possible gifts are given.

Just as Bonaventure discussed three primary titles of the second Person, namely, Son, Image, and Word, he mentions three titles of the Holy Spirit: Spirit, Love, and Gift. In each series of titles, the first two refer to the respective Person primarily in terms of its role within the Trinity as such, whereas the last title in each case names the respective Person in terms of its potential relations with the world. Thus the Son as Word is the ground of all possible divine self-expression in creation, while the Spirit as Gift is similarly the ground of every possible supernatural gift.[18] As we shall see below, Bonaventure attributes all revelation not to the activity of the Word per se, but to the activity of the *verbum inspiratum,* the *inspired* Word. It is the emanation of the Holy Spirit as free and generous love that provides the foundation in God for revelatory activity of the Word as inspired, as a divine gift of grace.

Thus, as we said at the outset, revelation for Bonaventure is deeply trinitarian. It is the self-manifestation of the Trinity *by* the Trinity. As he makes clear in his discussion of the temporal missions of the Son and Holy Spirit, the appearances of the Word and Spirit in history are to be understood as manifestations of their respective emanations within the Trinity.[19] Revelation will be of Truth, since of the Word; but it will also come as a gratuitous act, as an event rooted in the liberality and spontaneity of the Spirit.

Nevertheless, although Bonaventure's theology of revelation is essentially trinitarian, i.e., involves all three Persons of the Trinity, we noted above that the second Person as Word holds a privileged place. We must now consider this Word more closely, and specifically in its relationship to creation, redemption, and revelation as the threefold Word, the *verbum increatum, incarnatum,* and *inspiratum,* always keeping in mind, however, their common trinitarian background.

---

18. Bonaventure points out this parallel himself, at I *Sent.* d. 18, art. unic., q. 5, ad 4 (1:331b).

19. See I *Sent.* d. 15, p. 1, art. unic., q. 4, resp. (1:265b). Bonaventure explains that to say that the Father sends the Son means that the Father "declares" or "manifests" the emanation of the Son. See also I *Sent.* d. 15, p. 2, art. unic., q. 2, arg. 3 (1:271b).

THE DOCTRINE OF THE THREEFOLD WORD

We have already identified several fundamental themes of Bonaventure's metaphysics of revelation. These include the key notion of emanation or expression, rooted in the primacy of the Father and the self-diffusiveness of the Good, and the notion of similitude, which results from emanation as expressive act, inasmuch as this act is simultaneously an act of expression and an act of assimilation: that which is expressed, that which emanates, is by this very fact also assimilated, conformed to its source, and is thus the latter's *similitudo expressa* or image. These themes, and with them the theme of revelation, come together in Bonaventure's doctrine of the Word, which is, according to him, "nothing other than an express and expressive similitude."[20] One will notice that Bonaventure's definition of the Word as *similitudo expressa et expressiva* contains within it his definition of the image as *similitudo expressa,* and at the same time shares in the mode of emanation of the Son, namely, emanation *per modum naturae.*[21] In the Word the mystery of the second Person comes to its fullest expression, as expression itself. Here the two fundamental notions of emanation and similitude, stressed respectively by the titles of Son and Image, are united in the single notion of expression, understood both passively (*expressa*) and actively (*expressiva*). The original expressiveness of the Father that is the ground of possibility of the second Person as Son and Image is brought forth precisely as such in the Word. The Word is the expression that expresses; its reality as expression lies precisely in its expressiveness, in its relation to the Father, to that of which it is the expression. We have already noted Bonaventure's preference for the title of Word, as the most adequate name for the second Person, and it should now be clear that his is a preference well founded. It is essential to remember, however, that the expressiveness of the Word, which looks forward to creation, revelation, and redemption, is inseparable from the primal fecundity of the Father and the natural mode of emanation of the Son. Bonaventure's understanding of the expressiveness of the Word remains rooted in his understanding of the self-diffusiveness of the Good.

The centrality of the Word in Bonaventure's thought is brought out clearly by his schema of the threefold Word. As we shall see, this schema allows him to bring the entirety of creation, both in its structure and in

20. I *Sent.* d. 27, art. unic., q. 3, resp. (1:488a).
21. I *Sent.* d. 12, art. unic., q. 4, resp. (1:225b). See also I *Sent.* d. 27, p. 2, art. unic., q. 4, resp. (1:490a).

its history, under the sign of the Word, and thereby under the sign of revelation. The created order is understood as a text, as the *liber naturae,* the book of nature, in which the divine Word is to be read. Rooted in the divine Word as its Exemplar, the universe is itself a word, an image, an expression of the Divine. It is God's Word, the *verbum increatum,* spoken *ad extra* in the act of creation which is equally an act of self-disclosure, a theophany. Against the backdrop of this book of nature, the drama of human freedom will be played out, under the guidance of the *verbum inspiratum,* the inspired Word, and centered on the event of the *verbum incarnatum,* the Word as incarnate in Jesus of Nazareth. It is this drama that will provide the subject matter of the book of scripture. The schema of the threefold Word and its expression in creation and human history is thus a powerful unifying theme in Bonaventure's thought. In addition, his discussion of the *verbum inspiratum* provides one of the best introductions to his theology of revelation, which is an integral part of his trinitarian theology of the Word. A closer examination of this threefold Word will thus round out our examination of Bonaventure's metaphysics of revelation and prepare the way for the more specific investigations of the next chapter.

THE *VERBUM INCREATUM:* THE WORD AS EXEMPLAR

Bonaventure develops his theme of the threefold Word most fully in his *Collations on the Six Days,* given near the end of his life at Paris. There he presents the threefold Word as the key to contemplation:

> The key to contemplation is a threefold understanding: the understanding of the uncreated Word, through whom all things are produced; the understanding of the incarnate Word, through whom all things are restored; and the understanding of the inspired Word, through whom all things are revealed. For unless one can consider how things arise, how they are led back to their end, and how God shines forth in them, it is not possible to have understanding.[22]

Just as the general title of Word brings out the intrinsic expressiveness of the divine and presents the possibility of divine self-expression *ad*

22. *Coll. in Hex.* 3.2 (5:343a). Further references to the threefold Word include *Coll. in Hex* 9.1–8 (5:373–74); *Brev.* 4.1 (5:242a); *Itin.* 4.3 (5:306b); *Lig. Vitae* 12.46 (8, 84ff.); *Sermones de Tempore:* Feria quinta in coena Domini, *Sermo* I (9:249a), and *Dominica* II *Post Pascha, Sermo* III (9:301).

extra, so this further development of the doctrine of the Word as threefold presents in summary form this same capacity for self-expression as an actuality. The threefold Word is the Word as related to creation and to human history, and an understanding of this relationship is the key to a proper understanding of the world. Thus while the doctrine of the Word as the second Person of the Trinity is an "immanent" doctrine, a doctrine of the Word *in divinis,* the doctrine of the threefold Word is an "economic" doctrine, a doctrine of the Word as active in creation. The bridge between the two is the uncreated Word, the second Person as the expressive divine reality that we have examined in the previous sections, but now considered specifically as the Exemplar of creation. It is through the uncreated Word that all created things come into existence as "expressions" of that Word.[23] The expressiveness that we have found immanent within the Trinity does not end there. As a created participation in the Word, every aspect of creation expresses its Creator, more or less clearly as it is more or less directly related back to the Exemplar that is both origin and goal. Like the emanation of the divine Image in eternity, the creation of the created image in time is simultaneously an expression and an assimilation. The existence of the creature is the result of a divine act of creation *ex nihilo,* but as an expressive act of the creative Word, creation is also an assimilation or appropriation of the creature to its uncreated Archetype. The creature, precisely as created, is a similitude of its Creator. In the case of the human person, who concerns us here as the recipient of revelation, this creative expression and assimilation is so intimate as to make possible a direct relationship with the divine Exemplar and consequently has the status of a *similitudo expressa:* the human being is the *imago Dei,* the image of the Image. As such, the human being is capable of receiving the direct illumination of the divine Light and in particular can become the recipient of divine revelation.[24]

Bonaventure's doctrine of the uncreated Word as Exemplar thus provides the metaphysical foundation of his cosmology, his anthropology —

23. The creative role of the uncreated Word is mentioned repeatedly. Through it all things are created. See, in addition to *Coll. in Hex.* 3.2, quoted above, *Brev.* 4.1 (5:241a). Through the uncreated Word the human race comes into existence. See for instance *Brev.* 4.1 (5:242a).

24. The theme of creation is brought together with the theme of illumination in a passage from one of Bonaventure's sermons, which brings out the "theophanic" character of creation through the Word. The uncreated Word is said to support the universe and nourish it wisely on intellectual illuminations (*splendores*), which come together in the soul through the reflection of the threefold mirror of the universe: the archetypal mirror of the world *machina,* the hierarchical mirror of the created intelligences, and the monarchical mirror of the Eternal Art, which is to say, the Word as Exemplar. See *Sermones de Tempore:* Dominica II *Post Pascha, Sermo* III (9:301).

the human being as *imago Dei* — and his theory of knowledge as illumination, each of which is a further elaboration of the key notions of *expressio* and *assimilatio.*

As an act of divine self-expression or self-manifestation, Bonaventure conceives of the entire created universe as a hierarchically ordered series of expressions of and participations in the divine Exemplar. The world is the "book of creation" (*liber creaturae, liber mundi*), a system of signs that expresses its divine author. And in the midst of this world of signs stands the human person, created as the image of God, the intended reader and interpreter of the world text. The importance of revelation in Bonaventure's thought cannot be fully appreciated unless one first understands this notion of the human person as the created image of God, the interpreter of the book of creation, and later of the book of scripture. Bonaventure's metaphysics of revelation is here directly connected with his anthropology. The created image must be understood in terms of its dependence upon the uncreated Image.

Like all creation, the human being as *imago Dei* was brought into being *ex nihilo,* out of nothing. Bonaventure's interpretation of the traditional Christian doctrine of creation *ex nihilo* provides a key to his understanding of created existence as such and of the human being in particular. For Bonaventure, the act of creation brings about an ontological mutation, the emergence into existence of that which had no prior existence.[25] The creature's passage from non-existence to existence is an ontological trauma from which it will never fully recover. Created existence, precisely because it is created and not self-subsistent, is radically unstable and hence deeply dependent upon the continual conserving influence of its Creator. In responding to the question of whether God is present in all things, Bonaventure expands upon the fragile condition of the creature:

> The creature is essentially mutable and empty, and both for the reason that it is produced out of nothing. Because the creature is, and received its being, from another, who caused that to be which earlier had no being, it is not its own being, and thus is not pure act, but is mutable. For this reason it is changeable and variable, and lacks stability. Thus it can exist only through the presence of that which gave it being. A clear illustration of this is the impression that a

25. See *III Sent.* d. 1, p. 1, a. 3, q. 1 (3:30–33): Utrum creatio mutationem dicat, a question that receives a positive answer.

seal makes in water: it cannot last for a moment unless the seal is present.[26]

A more vivid image of absolute dependence would be hard to find. Only the continual conservation of the creature by its Creator prevents the waters of non-being from rushing in and overwhelming the creature's fragile existence.

In the case of the human being in particular, this mutability at the heart of all existence leads to the all-important distinction that Bonaventure draws between the human being as image and the human being as likeness. The human being as image is created as a temporal being, directly and consciously related to God by nature, but, being mutable, free to turn away. One becomes *like* God, one is transformed from image to similitude, through the free acceptance of the divine influence or illumination that initiates a process of active imitation through which one is progressively assimilated or conformed to one's divine Exemplar, which one consequently expresses through a progressively higher degree of similitude. Revelation as an actual experience, as a divine-human encounter or event, must be understood in the context of this free yet divinely initiated activity of *imitatio,* the dialectical assimilation of image to Image, of created expression to divine Exemplar, in which the mystery of divine self-expression and the human labor of its reception, interpretation, and assimilation are united in a moment of illumination and grace.

Bonaventure's view of the radical mutability and dependence of the creature is, so to speak, the shadowy side of his view of creation as a theophany, or self-manifestation of the divine. Viewed in itself, the creature is the perfect picture of dependence. The contingency of its existence is a continual witness to its origin from non-being. But what appears dark when viewed in isolation becomes suddenly luminous when properly oriented. It is in turning toward the Creator that the emptiness of the creature is filled by an influx of divine light. The creature's relation of dependence is but the necessary pre-condition for the relation of an image to its exemplar. Herein lies the key to Bonaventure's hierarchical view of creation. The dignity of the human being within this hierarchy is to be directly and consciously related to the divine Exemplar, to have been made in its image and to be capable of its free and conscious imitation. Here again we see the intimate connection between human contingency, experienced as freedom, and the human's privileged status as the *imago Dei:* only

26. I *Sent.* d. 37, p. 1, a. 1, q. 1, resp. (1:639a).

a human being, created in the image of God, can freely choose either likeness or unlikeness, either participation or isolation. Thus, while for Bonaventure the human soul is by nature ordered to God in an immediate way, this natural endowment is continually threatened by its intrinsic mutability. Nevertheless, the soul is capable of higher degrees of conformity to the Word: it can become a more perfect expression and likeness through a greater assimilation under the influence of grace. Implied in this anthropology is thus a *process,* of assimilation through imitation, a potential *itinerarium in Deum,* the first stage of which is conferred by nature, but which continues under the influence of grace. Bonaventure's doctrine of the image, therefore, points beyond itself to his doctrine of the soul as the potential likeness and similitude of God, as well as to his doctrine of grace. This leads us beyond the creative activity of the uncreated Word, however, and on to the Word as incarnate and inspired.

THE *VERBUM INCARNATUM:* THE WORD AS REDEEMER

Bonaventure's doctrine of the human being as the *imago Dei* is properly a part of his doctrine of creation, and we have now examined it in connection with his understanding of the uncreated Word as Exemplar. His notion of likeness or similitude, however, properly belongs to his theology of grace. As we move from the creative activity of the *verbum increatum* to the redemptive and revelatory activity of the *verbum incarnatum* and the *verbum inspiratum,* we enter into the drama of human freedom and its history, as understood through the myth of humanity's creation, fall, and redemption. A few words about this general context will be helpful before we proceed.

As a Christian, Bonaventure accepted the belief that the first man and woman were created in both the image and likeness of God and were thus in a state of grace, enjoying a greater degree of intimacy with their Creator than their own nature as image would have made possible. However, they soon lost this additional gift of likeness by disobeying their Maker. This well-known story of Adam and Eve's first disobedience is important because it sets up the dramatic tension that will be resolved in the incarnation of the Word. According to Christian belief, the Fall created a barrier between humans and God that humans themselves were incapable of removing.

Bonaventure describes the original human condition in terms of two books and two modes of perception: a book written within, which is the eternal Art and Wisdom of God, or the uncreated Word, as we have seen, and a book written without, which is the sensible world.[27] In their original state, reading the outer book led the first couple on to the inner book, but through the Fall, brought on by an excessive interest in the external book of the world, they lost the eye of contemplation needed to read the inner book, the divine Wisdom of the uncreated Word. Henceforth they were to remain partially blind, unable to read between the lines of the text of creation and grasp its deeper meaning. It is this background of human frailty, of blindness and loss, that gives a dramatic quality to the Christian notion of redemption through the incarnate Word and to the central notion of grace. Human helplessness and guilt are met by divine redemption and forgiveness. Through the free initiative of a loving Father, the Word becomes flesh, and the inner and outer books are reunited through a new, more readable text, the book of scripture.

Although this decisive event of the incarnation of the Word can justly be viewed as the central focus of the entirety of Bonaventure's theology, our own immediate interests do not require that we discuss his Christology in great detail. The significance of the *verbum incarnatum* as the subject matter of revelation will become clearer when we examine Bonaventure's understanding of prophecy and scripture. Despite the central role of the incarnation in Bonaventure's theology, we shall see that he actually ascribes all revelation, not to the Word as incarnate, but to the Word as inspired. For this reason it is difficult to discuss the revelatory function of the former until one has discussed the latter. Although Bonaventure believed that the fullness of revelation was reached only in the incarnation of the Word, he saw this crucial event, both in its long preparation throughout human history and in the event itself, as incomprehensible without the witness provided by the inspired Word. This is so primarily because the revelatory function of the incarnate Word itself cannot be separated from the function of the inspired Word, any more than either can be separated from the original creative work of the uncreated Word. They are, after all, three functions of one and the same Word.

The interrelatedness of the inspired Word and the incarnate Word is indicated by Bonaventure in his sermon entitled "Christ, the One Teacher of All." There he describes Christ as the "principle of all revelation by his coming into the mind" and adds that "he comes into the mind as the revelatory light of all prophetic vision." Further, he states that "without this light, which is Christ, no one can penetrate the mysteries of faith."[28]

---

27. See *Brev.* 2.11 (5:229a).
28. *Sermo* IV, n. 2–3 (5:568a).

Christ is thus the inner Word that inspires the prophets, as well as the "light of faith." The inner illumination of the inspired Word is therefore operative both in prophecies of Christ's coming, prior to the incarnation, and in the act of faith in Christ after his coming in the flesh.

As the incarnate Word, Christ the human being is the most perfect expression of God in creation. Through him, the text of creation once again becomes legible. However, the revelation of God in Christ is by no means a totally direct, undialectical manifestation of the divine splendor. This would be impossible in a world that has lost its resemblance to its Creator. The presence of God in such a world can only be indirect, through humility and ultimately through suffering and death. Although Christ is the perfect similitude of the Father, revealing him in his signs, words, and deeds,[29] he is known as such only through faith, that is, through the inner workings of the inspired Word. The outer life of Jesus by itself is not strictly speaking revelatory. It becomes so only when viewed with the eyes of faith. Like the outer word of sense, which is spoken to reveal the thought that remains hidden within, so too "the flesh was manifested externally while the divinity was hidden within."[30] While the outer word truly expresses the inner divine Word, it is understood only by those whose understanding is inwardly illuminated by the light of the inspired Word, by Christ's coming into the mind. Even in the incarnation, the revelation of the Word retains an inner dimension. But the interiority here should not be understood as an unmediated subjectivity. It is founded rather on the Word's own inner witness to itself, to its own objective presence as the incarnate Word. Our customary language of subject and object fails to express the true character of the actual experience that Bonaventure is trying to describe through his language of a Word that is both threefold and one, present both "objectively" in history and "subjectively" within the mind.

Bonaventure thus understands the revelation of the incarnate Word in the larger context of the revelations of the uncreated Word and the inspired Word. The revelation of the one Word of God displays a complex structure which is at once metaphysical, historical, and psychological. A metaphysics of expression, a historical dialectic of creation, fall, and redemption, and an anthropology of image and likeness are combined in an attempt to express the mediated immediacy of the experience of revelation. In all this, however, it is the mediation effected by the inspired

29. See *Collationes in Evangelium S. Joannis,* n. 3 (6:536a).
30. *In Nativitate Domini, Sermo* II, n. 1 (9:107ab).

Word that remains central. It is to this *verbum inspiratum* that we must now turn.

THE *VERBUM INSPIRATUM:* THE WORD AS REVEALER

It is in Bonaventure's theory of the inspired Word that the metaphysics of expressionism, the history of salvation, and the anthropology of the human being as the *imago Dei* are brought together in a metaphysics of revelation. Here we must distinguish between actual revelatory events, such as the giving of the Law to Moses or the preaching of Jesus of Nazareth, and the fundamental structure of all such events as revelatory. In his theory of the inspired Word, Bonaventure developed a theory of the event of revelation per se, which goes beyond a Neoplatonic metaphysics of emanation or expression by affirming the utter gratuitousness of all such events and thereby stops short of undermining their spontaneity and historical singularity. The central elements of this metaphysics of revelation are Bonaventure's notions of a spiritual influence (*influentia*) or illumination (*illuminatio, illustratio*), which builds upon the exemplarism or expressionism that we have already examined; a metaphysics of light, again drawn from the Neoplatonists; and a concept of hierarchy borrowed from pseudo-Dionysius. The metaphysics that results is best encapsulated in Bonaventure's notion of the inspired Word. In the previous section we noted the interdependence of the incarnate Word and the inspired Word in the process of revelation. The distinction between the two has traditionally been referred to as that between "objective" revelation and "subjective" revelation. The danger of such language is that it introduces a modern dichotomy that obscures the fundamental unity of the trinitarian *experience* of revelation as Bonaventure describes it. By contrast, Bonaventure's notion of the threefold Word as truly one Word preserves the dialectical complexities of the actual experience of revelation, while his notions of spiritual influence and hierarchy preserve its historical and social character.

We have already noted that Bonaventure understands the entirety of the created world as a hierarchically ordered series of created participations in the divine. This participation is in the divine not only as Word or Exemplar, but also as Light, as *summa lux.* These two modes of participation are really not different, since for Bonaventure the creature participates in being through its form or essence, and this formal participation is a participation in the Light as much as in the Word — the two ultimately being the same. However, Bonaventure's use of a metaphysics of light tends to bring out the *dynamic* nature of this formal participation, whereas an exclusive use of exemplarism could run the risk of suggesting a static essentialism foreign to his understanding of human existence. For Bonaventure, to participate in the Light is not merely to participate in knowledge, but also in being. Similarly, what is involved in being a similitude of God is not merely a structural resemblance (*convenientia proportionis*), but also, and primarily, an active, intentional, or "existential" participation (*convenientia ordinis*). Thus the use of a metaphysics of light allows Bonaventure to focus on the dynamic mode of being involved in similitude per se, which is also the mode of being of grace.

In the first book of his *Sentence Commentary,*[31] Bonaventure specifies the mode of being of light as that of an *influentia,* and then adds that spiritual light, which he identifies with grace, has this same mode of being.[32] He begins by listing three possible modes of being: that of a permanent substance with its own principle of being, that of change per se, and that of an *influentia,* midway between permanence and change.[33] The mode of being of an influence is one of total dependence. It subsists precisely in becoming — it is being continually produced, and this is its being. Further, in view of its total dependence on its producing principle, its mode of being is the same as the being of its principle or cause; one finds in both a similar mode of actuality (*consimilis modus actualitatis*).

Referring to Augustine, Bonaventure specifies that light has the mode of being of an *influentia* (*lumen semper nascitur*), of being *semper in fieri,* always coming into being. He then concludes his response with what is for us a crucial extension of its significance: "Similarly, he [Augustine] in general says of spiritual light, that it is grace."[34] The being of the spiritual light of grace is also to be understood as an *influentia,* which has its being *semper in fieri.*

In another place, Bonaventure expands on what he means by referring to grace as an influence: "Grace is not in the soul as something independent, but as an influence coming from another principle which is completely different from it."[35] He then attempts to clarify his meaning

31. I *Sent.* d. 9, art. unic., q. 4, resp. (1:186b).
32. On the following, see also Johann Auer's discussion of Bonaventure's use of the metaphysics of light in his theology of grace in his study, *Die Entwicklung der Gnadenlehre in der Hochscholastik, Erster Teil: Das Wesen der Gnade* (Freiburg im Breisgau: Herder, 1942), pp. 196–99.
33. On this threefold division of the modes of being, see Joseph Ratzinger, "Licht und Erleuchtung: Erwägungen zu Stellung und Entwicklung des Themas in der abendländischen Geistesgeschichte," *Studium Generale* 13 (1960): 368–78, esp. pp. 371–72.
34. I *Sent.* d. 9, art. unic., q. 4, resp. (1:186b).
35. II *Sent.* d. 26, a. 1, q. 5, f. 7 (2:642b).

by a comparison with light: "Grace is like a certain influence proceeding from a supernal light, which is always in contact with its source, like light [is in continual contact] with the sun."[36]

Grace, then, is a spiritual *lumen* that stands in continual dependence upon its source, the divine *lux,* as the latter's influence. Its continual dependence, or *coniunctio* with its origin, the *lux superna,* makes it similar to its source. Grace is similitude *essentialiter.*[37] Thus Bonaventure is identifying grace, similitude, and spiritual light, all belonging to the order of grace and sharing this quality with the divine by virtue of a relation of absolute dependence, founded on a mode of being as *semper in fieri.* Grace is thus ultimately pre-figured in the divine itself, in the Son as the *lumen* and *similitudo* of God the Father as *summa lux,* and pre-eminently in the Holy Spirit, as the wholly gratuitous product of their mutual love.

Returning now to the theme of image and similitude (taken in the strict sense), it will be clear that, while the human being is the image of God by nature, because it exists as an independent being through composition with matter, it is the similitude through grace, through the influence of spiritual light, that instills in the soul a new, immaterial quality or habit and relates it directly to the divine life of the Trinity that it now resembles. This is the "illumination of grace" that begins in the sacrament of baptism and culminates in the light of glory. Here the dynamic potential of the image is realized through the influence of grace, which is understood in terms of the mode of being of light. It is this dynamic influence of the light of grace in the soul that facilitates the existential conversion from image to similitude through the free act of the will.

Bonaventure's application of his metaphysics of light to his explanations of grace and similitude, and the resultant theme of a spiritual illumination, insures that his understanding of this illumination will be in primarily ontological rather than epistemological terms. Just as it is human *being* as image that constitutes one's openness to the influence of general or common illumination, so it is the transformation of this being from image to similitude, under the higher influence of the spiritual illumination of grace, that constitutes the most perfect actualization of this openness. This emphasis on the ontological is a consequence of the basic premise of a metaphysics of light, namely, that being *is* light.[38] Degrees of being are also degrees of illumination.

---

36. Ibid., q. 6, resp. (2:646a).

37. I *Sent.* d. 48, a. 1, q. 1, ad 3 (1:852b).

38. For a history of the metaphysics of light in Western thought, see Clemens Baeumker, *Witelo, Ein Philosoph und Naturforscher des XIII. Jahrhunderts,* Beiträge zur Geschichte der

With the material now before us — material concerning God's self-expression as Word and Light, especially as these are manifest in creation through the human being as the image and similitude of God and as they give rise respectively to Bonaventure's metaphysics of exemplarism and of light — we are in a position to understand the distinction that he makes between two types of illumination. In his *Disputed Questions on the Mystery of the Trinity,* he says that the divine Wisdom, which he calls the Book of Life, gives testimony of the eternal Trinity to people in this life through the influence of light. Quoting from the prologue to St. John's gospel, he says that the Book of Life is the light of men and women because it is the "true light which illumines everyone coming into this world." He continues to specify, however, that this Light illumines in a twofold manner, namely, through an innate light (*lumen inditum*) and through an infused light (*lumen infusum*).[39] Here we have a reference to the much discussed doctrine of illumination, conceived as an account of the possibility of the certainty of human knowledge (i.e., through the *lumen inditum),* and the much less discussed doctrine of spiritual illumination, which is none other than revelation in the strict sense, considered, however, in a most general way, and not specified as either prophetic, scriptural, private, or whatever.

If we are to understand this twofold process of spiritual influence or illumination, and the assimilation of the soul to the Trinity, a process that lies at the heart of Bonaventure's metaphysics of revelation, we must look more closely at an element of his thought that we have so far mentioned only in passing. This is his fundamental notion of hierarchy, which he borrowed from pseudo-Dionysius. We are already familiar with many of the ideas that underlie it: the ideas of expression, illumination, and influence; the ideas of image and similitude, and of their progressive assimilation to their Exemplar. Through the key notion of hierarchy, these ideas are shown to be interdependent elements of a single, structured process, a process that is for all intents and purposes identical with the process of revelation that Bonaventure ascribes to the illuminations of the inspired Word. A brief look at Bonaventure's understanding of hierarchy will thus help us to put the elements discussed so far in proper perspective. In particular, it will allow us to relate the anthropological and metaphysical elements of his theory of revelation through what we may call a social ontology.

Philosophie des Mittelalters, Bd. 3, Heft 2 (Münster: Aschendorffschen Buchhandlung, 1908), pp. 357–426. Bonaventure is a major representative of this tradition.

39. *De Myst. Trin.,* q. 1, a. 2, resp. (5:55).

Bonaventure, following pseudo-Dionysius, defines hierarchy as "a divine order, knowledge, and action, assimilated as much as possible to the divine form, and ascending to the likeness of God in proportion to the divine illuminations given to it."[40] As this definition makes clear, a hierarchy combines the elements of illumination, knowledge, and assimilation that we have found to be essential to Bonaventure's understanding of revelation. It is the additional elements of order and action that will hold our attention here.

In discussing this definition, René Roques explains that the Dionysian concept of order, which Bonaventure here adopts, has three essential constituents. Hierarchical order is objective, it is interior, and it comes from God.[41] As objective, a hierarchy is endowed with definite structures and laws. Hierarchies are ordered arrangements of spiritual beings, whether the latter be pure spirits (angels) or embodied spirits (humans). Bonaventure distinguished four such hierarchies: the Trinity itself; the celestial hierarchy composed of nine orders of angels; the ecclesiastical hierarchy composed of the members of the church; and the hierarchy that is to be found within the human soul, when the latter is assimilated to God, to the divine Hierarchy of the Trinity.

As ordered arrangements of spiritual beings, the celestial and ecclesiastical hierarchies constitute true societies, on the model of a city ruled by a monarch.[42] Status within these sacred societies, however, is based solely upon a given being's capacity to receive the influence of the divine illuminations that stream forth from the Trinity. The greater the capacity and the more intense the participation in the divine light and love, the higher the position on the scale of beings and the greater the degree of similitude.

Objective status in a hierarchy is not to be understood as opposed to interiority, however. Roques speaks of an "essential solidarity" between the inner and outer: "The hierarchical order permits and directs the order of the intelligences; and inversely, the interior order of the intelligences is indispensable to the harmony of the hierarchies." There is thus a "profound solidarity of the two orders, hierarchical and interior."[43]

This harmony of the inner and outer aspects of a hierarchy is to be understood in terms of their common goal: assimilation and union with God. The hierarchical order exists for the sake of the divinization of the

40. *In Hex.* 21.17 (5:434a). See pseudo-Dionysius, *Celestial Hierarchies,* c. 3, n. 2.

41. René Roques, "La notion de hiérarchie selon le pseudo-Denys," *Archives d'histoire doctrinale et littéraire du Moyen Age* 24 (1949): 212.

42. Ibid., pp. 213–14.

43. Ibid., p. 216.

individual intelligences that compose it. Conversely, the level of divinization of any individual intelligence is a function of its position within the whole. Roques summarizes the matter as follows:

> Dionysian order is thus situated at once in the most authentic objectivity and in the progressive interiorization of the intelligences. It is at once static and dynamic, sociological and spiritual, juridical and mystical. To retain one of these two aspects to the exclusion of the other is to deform and mutilate it, since the one as well as the other subsists only through their reciprocal support and propulsion, in the sense of their common finality, which is divinization of the intelligences.[44]

Hierarchy is not only order; it is also action. A hierarchy is an activity, a hierarchical activity, which has as its purpose assimilation and union with God. This activity, strictly speaking, belongs exclusively to the Trinity, and it comprises both the "descending" movement of divine self-expression and manifestation, and the "ascending" movement in which the divine *influentia* of grace illumines the created intelligences and assimilates them to the divine form, their Exemplar. These fundamental aspects of the divine activity should be familiar by now. The concept of hierarchical activity introduces a further notion, however, closely related to the notion of hierarchical order. The action of a hierarchy, while remaining exclusively the activity of God alone, is *mediated* through the hierarchies of created intelligences, which act as the occasion or medium for the divine action. Bonaventure refers to this "divine law" (*lex divinitatis*) in his *Breviloquium:* "To the bodily and distant creature [namely, man], he [God] communicates his happiness indirectly, since divine law provides that lower things be led back to the highest through an intermediate."[45] Here the relatively low position of humanity, as composed of embodied spirits, is given as a reason for this mediation of the divine influence. In the *Collations on the Six Days,* Bonaventure refers to this "law" again, this time referring explicitly to pseudo-Dionysius's *Ecclesiastical Hierarchies.*[46] Here, however, the mediating role of the angelic hierarchy is mentioned. After quoting pseudo-Dionysius, Bonaventure adds:

44. Ibid., pp. 217–18.
45. *Brev.* 2.9 (5:226b). See pseudo-Dionysius, *Ecclesiastical Hierarchies* c. 5, n. 4 (504c).
46. *In Hex.* 3.32 (5:348b).

> The thearchical ray, descending upon the celestial hierarchy, illumines it and through it [it illumines] the ecclesiastical or subcelestial [hierarchy]. Everything is done by that [divine] ray, however, since the angels do nothing except serve as occasions. It is as if one who wanted the light to illumine many houses should open the windows, and then the rays would illumine all the houses; or as if one should prepare many mirrors to receive the light.[47]

The angels thus serve as so many mirrors that reflect the divine light and make it visible to those with lesser powers of vision. The light, however, remains the same divine *lux*.

If the hierarchy of the church is illumined through the mediation of the celestial hierarchy, the individual person is in turn illumined through the mediation of the church, which is "the mother of the influences by which we are made the sons of God."[48]

Finally, there is potentially at least a hierarchy within the human soul, through which it is brought back to its intended condition of likeness under the influence of grace, through the hierarchical actions of purification, illumination, and union.[49] We have already examined the topic of the soul's conversion from image to similitude. What is important here is the way in which Bonaventure's use of the idea of hierarchy introduces an element of mediation into the soul's reception of illumination. The ascending process of assimilation is mediated through the ecclesiastical and celestial hierarchies, just as was the descent of the divine light that made the ascent possible. The individual is integrated into the larger social world of the hierarchies, through the mediation of which he receives the spiritual illumination of the divine Light. For Bonaventure, the reception of the illuminations of revelation is a social event, mediated through the community of the church. The metaphysics of revelation, understood more clearly now through the notions of hierarchical order and action, can be seen to include a social ontology, having its deepest root in the sociality of the three trinitarian Persons.

Our investigation of Bonaventure's general theory of revelation reaches its culmination in this concept of "spiritual illumination" with its hierarchical activity, together with the closely related metaphysics of exemplarity and light and the anthropology of image and similitude connected with them. Together they provide the essential outlines of the

47. Ibid.
48. *In Hex.* 22.2 (5:438a).
49. See *In Hex.* 22.24–23.31 (5:441–49).

metaphysics of revelation that we have been seeking. It remains to verify our results by turning to a consideration of Bonaventure's notion of the *verbum inspiratum,* which he explicitly describes as the agent of all revelation, and by showing that this notion receives its intelligibility from the account of spiritual illumination that has been presented here.

For Bonaventure, the inspired Word is "that through which all things are revealed."[50] While the uncreated Word, as the Exemplar of creation, is sufficient to account for common illumination, revelation requires the operation of the inspired Word. There is thus a parallel between the two types of illumination, through the *lumen inditum* and the *lumen infusum,* and the uncreated and inspired Word. The inspired Word, like the infused light of spiritual illumination, clearly operates through grace in the strict sense. Indeed, Bonaventure explicitly says that grace arises in us through the inspired Word.[51] The spiritual illumination that we have described as the hierarchical work of grace is clearly the work of this inspired Word.

It would be tempting to say that the inspired Word is simply the Holy Spirit and leave it at that. But as we saw, it is significant that Bonaventure speaks not of the Holy Spirit, but of the inspired Word. The emphasis on the Word is intentional, since Bonaventure ascribes all revelation not only to the inspired Word, but also to Christ. In his sermon "Christ the One Teacher of All," Bonaventure describes Christ as the "principle of all revelation through his coming into the mind."[52] Here the agent of all revelation is clearly described as the second Person of the Trinity rather than the third. The fact is that the inspired Word effects a spiritual illumination that is at the same time the work of *both* the Son and the Holy Spirit.

It is here that the earlier analysis of spiritual illumination in terms of a metaphysics of exemplarity and a metaphysics of light, as well as the preceding discussion of the concept of hierarchy, can be seen to provide the proper foundation for understanding the *verbum inspiratum.* As *verbum,* the inspired Word is made more intelligible through the metaphysics of exemplarity, centered on the Word as Exemplar. As the Exemplar of creation, the Word is the source *in divinis* of the hierarchies of resemblances that will refract the single ray of the divine light into the myriad rays that illumine the world. It is the principle of hierarchical order. As *inspiratum,* however, the inspired Word is clarified by the metaphysics of light as it is applied to an understanding of the influence of grace and thus to hierarchical activity. Both the "formal" and the "dynamic" elements of spiritual

50. *Coll. in Hex.* 3.2 (5:343). See also, ibid., 3.22 (5:347).
51. *Collationes de Septem Donis Spiritus Sancti,* 1.7 (5:457).
52. *Sermo* IV, 2–3 (5:568).

illumination and hierarchy that we have examined above find their place in the concept of a *verbum inspiratum.* It seems safe to conclude therefore that the "interior illumination,"[53] the "illumination of the mind,"[54] that Bonaventure explicitly refers to as *revelatio,* is this "spiritual illumination" effected through the mediation of the Word. Whether this mediation be through the spiritual creation that is the Word's image and likeness, or through the Word as incarnate in Jesus of Nazareth, or again, through the Word of scripture, it is the same Spirit that speaks and through the self-same Word, the *verbum inspiratum, per quod omnia revelantur.*

With the concept of the inspired Word, Bonaventure succinctly summarizes the metaphysics of revelation that we have tried to outline in the present chapter. In this concept of the *verbum inspiratum* and the spiritual illumination effected through it, therefore, we have Bonaventure's fundamental metaphysical concept of revelation. But here, in its fulfillment in the concept of a spiritual illumination through the hierarchical activity of the inspired Word, this metaphysics points in the direction of a history of revelation. Spiritual illumination, as the transforming action of grace, occurs as an *event.* It is not something rooted in human nature, although it clearly presupposes this. It is an event that transforms the concrete existence of human beings constituting them as members of a sacral community and in the likeness of their Creator. The action of the inspired Word will thus have a *history.* The metaphysics of revelation that we have tried to discern in Bonaventure's works describes the structure of a dynamic process that is actualized only in specific cases, in concrete social and historical situations. Bonaventure calls attention to this when he writes that "God does not reveal mysteries continually, but only in accord with time and place."[55]

Bonaventure's metaphysics of revelation is thus anything but abstract or static in its implications, despite the abstract metaphysical language in which it is formulated. It is best viewed as a product of Bonaventure's attempt to interpret his own rich spiritual experience in the light of his tradition. And precisely because it is the product of living experience and presents us with a dynamic view of revelation as a gratuitous event, the metaphysics of revelation that we have discerned in Bonaventure's work points beyond itself. Because the operation of the inspired Word transcends nature and occurs as an event, only the study of these

53. II *Sent.* d. 4, a. 2, q. 2, resp. (2:138a).
54. II *Sent.* d. 7, dubia 2 (2:206b).
55. II *Sent.* d. 11, dubia 2 (2:290b).

events as they appear in concrete social and historical form — as prophecy, as incarnation, as the spiritual understanding of scripture — can lead to an adequate understanding of revelation as an actuality. Bonaventure's understanding of revelation was shaped by his interpretations of such specific instances of it. In the next chapter, therefore, we will move beyond our preliminary attempt to discern a metaphysics of revelation in Bonaventure's work in order to examine his interpretations of its actuality.

6

The History of Revelation

Given that Bonaventure describes a general metaphysics of revelation, focused on his notion of the *verbum inspiratum,* that provides a degree of intelligibility to the process of revelation taken in the abstract, it remains to be seen how Bonaventure views revelation in the concrete. If the metaphysics of revelation points forward to a history of revelation, what actual form does this take? One way to begin to address this question is to examine Bonaventure's actual use of the term *revelatio,* noting the variety of phenomena to which he applies it. The most important of these phenomena can then be examined in more detail.

REVELATIO

In the second book of his *Sentence Commentary,* Bonaventure defines *revelatio* as a certain interior illumination (*certam interius illuminationem*),[1] and later in the same book he contrasts two types of revelation, taken in a broad sense: "Revelation occurs in two ways: sometimes by an illumination of the mind [*mentis illustratione*], as happened to the holy prophets, and this is through grace; and sometimes by mere prediction, as a man sometimes reveals his own will."[2] This stress on revelation as an inner illumination should come as no surprise. It is in fact so fundamental to Bonaventure that he himself anticipates an objection: if revelation is essentially an inner illumination, of what use are the visible, external apparitions that are mentioned in scripture? This question is raised in the first book of the *Sentence Commentary:* "Of what use is the visible mission of the Holy Spirit?"[3] In replying to the objection that the certitude

1. II *Sent.* d. 4, a. 2, q. 2, resp. (2:138a).
2. II *Sent.* d. 8, dubia 2 (2:206b).
3. I *Sent.* d. 16, art. unic., q. 2 (1:280–82).

derived from revelation makes external apparitions superfluous, Bonaventure agrees that revelation is in fact an inner cognition (*interior cognitio*) but adds that external appearances to the senses can be of use in preparing for it.[4]

In fact, while revelation is primarily an act of illumination effected by the inspired Word, it is also frequently an act of interpretation, in which the illumination is applied to a specific content. Thus Bonaventure frequently uses the term *revelatio* in connection with those masters of interpretation, the prophets. Here the use of the term *revelatio* gains a new specificity, referring to the particular historical phenomenon of biblical prophecy. Furthermore, the nature of prophetic illumination is described more closely. Through revelation the prophets receive the gift of contemplation, according to the threefold vision of the body, the imagination, and the understanding.[5] This is the classification of visions that Bonaventure borrowed from Augustine, for whom it was the third vision of the understanding that was essential to revelation. In the specific case of prophecy, however, the nature of this illumination must be further defined. Whereas in most cases the grace of contemplation, or the vision of understanding, is given for the sake of the one receiving it (*ad fructum*), in prophecy this gift is given for a specific purpose (*ad hoc*). Unlike the illumination that forms a part of an individual's personal sanctification, the illumination received in prophetic revelation serves a specific purpose in the larger scheme of the history of salvation.[6] Without losing the character of interiority, illumination in the context of prophetic revelation takes on an objective, intersubjective quality. It is given for the good of the prophet's audience rather than for the prophet himself.

This can be seen as well in Bonaventure's discussions of St. Francis. In his writing about St. Francis, the term *revelatio* flowed freely from Bonaventure's pen. He tells us, for instance, that St. Francis learned his accustomed greeting, "May the Lord give you peace," through a revelation.[7] In prayer, Francis was sometimes illumined by a revelation from heaven.[8] And Bonaventure acknowledged Francis's own claim to have written the rule of the order, not through his own effort, but as if everything had been revealed by God.[9] Most importantly, he believed that the

4. Ibid., ad 2 (1:281b).
5. *Brev.* 5. 6 (5:260a).
6. See I *Sent.* d. 15, p. 2, art. unic., q. 1, ad 2 (1:271a).
7. Ibid., c. 3, n. 2 (8:510).
8. Ibid., c. 4, n. 2 (8:513). See also c. 4, n. 11 (8:516a).
9. Ibid., c. 4, n. 11 (8:516b).

Franciscan order itself, along with the rule that he as Minister General was sworn to uphold, had originated in a series of revelations given in his own time, and as appropriate to that time.[10] Here too, then, revelation exhibits both the inner character of an illumination and a social and historical character: Francis the mystic was also Francis the timely religious founder.

These references to revelation in specific historical contexts bring its objective aspect to the fore. This aspect is heightened by Bonaventure's use of the term *revelatio* in connection with angels. Angels, and specifically archangels,[11] are in Bonaventure's opinion important mediators of revelation. This viewpoint derives not only from such scriptural passages as the account of the archangel Gabriel's role in the annunciation (Luke 1:26–38), but also from Bonaventure's hierarchical view of the universe. As we saw in the previous chapter, the hierarchies of angels serve to refract the light descending from the divine hierarchy of the Trinity. In his discussion of pseudo-Dionysius's description of an angel as a "manifestation of hidden light" (*manifestatio occulti luminis*), Bonaventure explains that an angel is a manifestation of light to the extent that it shows the illuminations that it receives from God to other beings lower than itself in the scheme of creation.[12] It is interesting, however, that when this general role of mediating the divine light is specified as a mediation of revelation, the reference is usually to the archangels. Archangels occupy the middle position in the lowest of the three angelic hierarchies, being placed immediately above angels. In the *Sentence Commentary,* Bonaventure explains that unlike the angels of the lowest order, to whom is assigned the care of individuals ("guardian angels"), the archangels are responsible for the care of entire peoples.[13] Their primary role as mediators of revelation is thus understood to be a part of the care of social groups rather than of individuals, a detail that brings out the social character that Bonaventure attributes to revelation quite nicely. The role of the archangels in the process of revelation is thus a consequence of the objective and social character of the hierarchies that constitute the spiritual universe. If revelation is to have a genuinely objective character, the process of revelation must involve not only the inner illumination of the individual but also the world in which this individual lives as a historical and social being.

10. *Legenda S. Francisci,* c. 2, n. 8 (8:509b).
11. See *Coll. in Hex.* 21.20 (5:434b).
12. II *Sent.* Praenotata de Nominibus et Divisionibus Angelorum (2:239a).
13. Ibid. (2:241).

There remains one of Bonaventure's most common uses of the term *revelatio,* namely, in the description of scripture. At first this might seem inconsistent. If it is the inner event of illumination that is most properly described as revelation, then why should a book be so described? On closer examination, however, this apparent inconsistency disappears. In fact, the term *revelatio,* when used in connection with scripture, refers not to the scriptures as texts, but to the spiritual understanding of scripture, to the "spirit" rather than to the "letter."

In the prologue to his *Breviloquium,* Bonaventure ascribes both the origin and the transmission of scripture to divine revelation (*divina revelatio*) and contrasts this with "human investigation" (*humana investigatio*).[14] His use of the term *revelatio* in this connection is unremarkable. What is interesting is his extension to its use to cover the *interpretation* of scripture. In a passage from the *Collations on the Six Days,* Bonaventure seems to identify *revelatio* with the spiritual understanding of scripture. In the sixteenth collation, he attempts to draw parallels between the time of the Old Testament and the time of the church. In what seems to be a reference to his own times, which follow upon the founding of the order of St. Francis, Bonaventure says that "now the understanding of scripture will be given, namely, revelation or the key of David, either to an individual person or to a multitude, and I think it more likely to a multitude."[15] The full significance of this passage will occupy us in the following chapter. For now it is sufficient to note the equation between *revelatio* and the understanding of scripture as an ongoing process of interpretation.

If Bonaventure could use the term *revelatio* to refer to the spiritual understanding of scripture, it is not surprising to find him using it to characterize the teaching based upon this understanding. Thus in the second book of this *Sentence Commentary* he says that the doctors of the church assert their teachings *per revelationem sancti Spiritus.*[16] Gregory the Great, for instance, is described as one to whom the Holy Spirit revealed many things.[17] He goes on to say that the Holy Spirit, who gave multiple meanings to scripture, also makes its interpreters understand these meanings.[18] Scripture is endowed with a multitude of meanings,

14. *Brev., Prologus* (5:201a). It is interesting that in the previous sentence Bonaventure ascribed the origin of scripture to the influence of the Trinity: secundum influentiam beatissimae Trinitatis. See also *Brev.* prol. 5 (5:207a).

15. *In Hex.* 16.29 (5:408b).

16. II *Sent.* d. 15, dubia 3 (2:389b).

17. IV *Sent.* d. 44, p. 2, a. 2, q. 1 (4:926).

18. Ibid. (2:390a).

and these meanings are themselves referred to as revelations, indeed, "hierarchical revelations."[19]

Perhaps the most striking use of the term *revelatio* in connection with the understanding of scripture comes in Bonaventure's discussion of the Filioque controversy in his *Sentence Commentary.* According to Bonaventure, the knowledge of the true manner of the procession of the Holy Spirit — whether from the Father, as the Greeks held, or from both the Father and the Son, as the Latins believed — had its basis in scripture, its increase from reason, and its consummation from revelation.[20] Both Greeks and Latins agreed that the final authority in the matter was scripture. They differed, as Bonaventure puts it, *in ratione et revelatione.* Bonaventure argues that the Latins, in reaching their position, reasoned more spiritually and aptly, "and therefore they were elevated by their own reasonings, and were thus disposed for the understanding of scripture, and therefore were taught by manifest revelation [*manifesta revelatione*] concerning the procession of the Holy Spirit."[21]

This initial survey of Bonaventure's use of the term *revelatio* should be sufficient to illustrate the frequent and varied uses that he makes of this word. Bonaventure viewed revelation as a living experience alive throughout history and still at work in the church of his own day. At the same time, it was something more than individual experience; it was also the ongoing experience of a community. Two specific forms of revelation have emerged as being particularly prominent in Bonaventure's thought: prophetic revelation and revelation through scripture. In addition, we know that for Bonaventure the incarnation of the Word represents the central event in the history of revelation, even though he seldom uses the term *revelatio* in this connection. In the balance of this chapter we will look more closely at both the phenomena of prophecy and incarnation, saving a closer examination of Bonaventure's view of scripture and the language of revelation for the following chapter.

PROPHETIA

In the thirteenth century the nature of prophecy became an object of intense scrutiny in a number of treatises *De Prophetia,* "On Prophecy,"

19. *Itin.* 4.7 (5:308a). On the notion of the "hierarchical revelations" of scripture, see below, 136.

20. I *Sent.* d. 11, art. unic., q. 1, resp. (1:211b).

21. Ibid.

written by some of the most prominent theologians of that period.[22] It is possible that Bonaventure himself wrote such a treatise.[23] These treatises, heavily influenced by Augustine's treatment of the issue, emphasized on the one hand the supernatural character of prophecy as an essentially passive reception of divine illumination and on the other hand limitations imposed upon the knowledge of the prophet by the fact of his remaining a finite knower.

A survey of the many references to prophets and prophecy in Bonaventure's works against the background of these scholastic treatises *De Prophetia* makes two things clear. First, Bonaventure was familiar with the typical issues and positions found in these treatises and makes frequent use of some of the stock examples found there. Second, whereas the scholastic treatises were primarily concerned with establishing the *nature* of prophets and prophecy, Bonaventure has just as much to say about the *history* of prophecy, a history that in his view reaches right up to his own day. We will discuss each of these points in turn.

Bonaventure shows an interest in the nature of prophetic vision (*visio prophetalis*), and, like virtually everyone else, he discusses it in terms of Augustine's three visions:

> Vision is threefold, as is commonly said: corporeal, imaginative, intellectual. The first two have no value without the third. Thus the corporeal vision was of little value to Belshazzar in the vision of the hand, the imaginative vision of the golden statue [was of little value] to Nebuchadnezzar, and the vision of the cattle and ears of corn [was of little value] to Pharaoh, but [they were of value] to Daniel and Joseph.[24]

22. See Bruno Decker, *Die Entwicklung der Lehre von der prophetischen Offenbarung von Wilhelm von Auxerre bis zu Thomas von Aquin* (Breslau: Müller & Seiffert, 1940), and Jean-Pierre Torrell, *Théorie de la prophétie et philosophie de la connaissance aux environs de 1230: La contribution d'Hugues de Saint-Cher* (Louvain: Spicilegium Sacrum Lovaniense, 1977).

23. The treatise in question is found in Codex 186 at the Biblioteca comunale in Assisi, Italy, folio pp. 10vb–13va. Bruno Decker analyzed the contents of this treatise, *Entwicklung,* pp. 134–64, using it as the primary source for his discussion of Bonaventure's theory of prophetic revelation. A few years earlier, F. M. Henquinet had claimed to have proven the text's authenticity. See his "Un brouillon autographe de S. Bonaventure sur le commentaire des Sentences," *Études franciscaines* 44 (1932): 633–55; 45 (1933): 59–81. More recently, however, Ignatius Brady has pointed out that this attribution has not, in fact, been decisively established and that questions remain. See Ignatius Brady, "S. Bonaventura alunno della scuola francescana di Parigi," in *L'Uomo Bonaventura: Atti del XIII incontro al Cenacolo bonaventuriano dell'Oasi Maria Immacolata di Montecalvo Irpino,* September 27–29, 1973 (Montecalvo Irpino: Oasi Maria Immacolata, 1973), pp. 63–74. Brady's article is discussed briefly by Jean-Pierre Torrell, *Théorie de la prophétie,* p. 271, n. 10.

24. *Coll. in Hex.* 3.23 (5:347a).

Although the ideas presented here, and even the examples used, are, as Bonaventure himself notes, common property, the context of this passage links it with Bonaventure's own distinctive theory of the inspired Word. In the paragraph that immediately precedes Bonaventure introduces the theme of the inspired Word. After telling us that all things are revealed through this Word, he continues:

> Daniel understood the word [written on the wall]. For in a vision there is need of understanding. For unless the word resound in the ear of the heart, the splendor shine in the eye, the vapor and emanation of the Almighty be perceived as smell, sweetness tasted, and eternity fill the soul, man is not apt for understanding visions. But God gave Daniel the understanding of all visions and dreams. By what means? Through the inspired Word.[25]

Although prophecy is not explicitly mentioned here, it is hardly necessary, given the Augustinian schema of visions and the example of Daniel. In the *Breviloquium,* however, the same classification of visions is presented, and here prophets are mentioned. Bonaventure is here discussing the contemplation of truth, which, he says, "was in the prophets through revelation, according to a threefold vision, namely, corporeal, imaginative, and intellectual."[26] Here too the context is interesting. Whereas in the previous passage, Bonaventure connected the three forms of prophetic vision with the revelatory activity of the inspired Word and thereby located them within his metaphysics of revelation, here he connects them with contemplation. Indeed, he goes on to tell us that the contemplation that was in the prophets through revelation is in the just through speculation, by which he means the spiritual ascent through contemplation that he outlines in his *Journey of the Mind to God.*[27] The real contrast here is not between contemplation and speculation: these are essentially identical for Bonaventure. The contrast is rather between the mode of its presence in either case: either by revelation *gratis data* or as a result of a gradual spiritual development under the influence of grace *gratum faciens.* What is interesting, however, is not the contrast, but the parallel that Bonaventure establishes between the experience of the prophet and the experience

25. Ibid., 3.22 (5:347a).

26. *Brev.* 5. 6 (5:260a). For a third reference to the *visio prophetalis* as threefold, see I *Sent.* d. 16, art. unic., q. 2, ad opp. 4 (1:281a).

27. Ibid.

of the ordinary Christian contemplative. Bonaventure makes this parallel explicit in one of his sermons. While discussing the sevenfold spirit given to the church, he says that in the prophets there is the spirit of understanding in speculating (*in Prophetis spiritus intellectus in speculando*) and adds that the ordinary Christian should imitate the prophetic understanding in speculating (*imitationem . . . prophetalis intelligentiae in speculando*).[28] The same parallel is implied by the context of the first passage given from the *Collations*. If the preceding paragraph linked the threefold vision of prophecy with the inspired Word and thereby with Bonaventure's metaphysics, the paragraph that follows links it with the sixfold vision that provides the structure of the whole work — a work that was itself to culminate with a discussion of the visions of prophecy and rapture and that bears the subtitle "Illuminations of the Church."[29] These visions, or "illuminations," have themselves a prophetic character to which we will return below.

The *sine qua non* of all prophetic vision is of course the intellectual vision. This was the doctrine of Augustine, and it continues to be the doctrine of the scholastics. We have already seen in detail how Bonaventure explains such revelatory vision through his doctrine of the illumination of the inspired Word. In his discussion of prophetic vision per se, this primacy of the illumination of the intellect by the Holy Spirit is brought out clearly. Thus in a sermon on St. Dominic, Bonaventure says that the light of wisdom "reveals through an illumination that is spiritual and above reason, and is necessary in prophecy."[30] Similarly, in commenting on Wisdom 7.27 — "in every generation she passes into holy souls and makes them friends of God and prophets" — Bonaventure adds, *per illuminationem intellectus*.[31] This illumination takes precedence over the actual content of prophecy, which Bonaventure in one place describes as its "material object":

> Prophecy does not have, as its principal object and motive, those things that the prophet foretells; they are only its material object, toward which the prophecy is directed. Therefore the prophet does not assent to what he foretells on its own account, but because of the truth that illumines and instructs him.[32]

28. *Sermo I in Festo omnium sanctorum* (9:599a).
29. See the title page of the *Coll. in Hex.* (5.327).
30. *Sermo De S. Dominico* (9:564a).
31. *Comm. in Sapientiam* (6:159a).
32. III *Sent.* d. 24, a. 1, q. 2, ad 5 (3:514a).

Despite the prime importance of this spiritual illumination of the intellect of the prophet, however, prophecy cannot be defined in terms of illumination alone. Bonaventure was familiar with the traditional definition of prophecy derived from Cassiodorus, according to which prophecy is a divine inspiration that announces events by an unshakeable truth (*immobili veritate*). Prophecy has a content, and even if this content is not itself sufficient, prophecy without it would not be prophecy. For Bonaventure this content could perhaps best be described as a knowledge of the temporal unfolding of the created order, as prefigured in the divine Exemplar and realized under the influence of divine providence. In short, prophecy concerns sacred history, the history of creation as it emanates from and returns to its Creator. For Bonaventure, this is a history of human freedom under the influence of grace.

The content of prophecy is thus a function of the historical situation of the prophet. Indeed, there was a time when prophecy did not exist at all. Bonaventure often makes use of the threefold division of universal history into three ages, the ages of nature, law, and grace. In the first age, which was the age of the "law of nature," prior to the giving of the law of Moses, there was neither prophecy nor open revelation.[33] Although divine inspiration was nevertheless present,[34] prophecy in the proper sense began only with Moses, who was the "first author and teacher of sacred Scripture."[35] In the opening lines of Moses' final blessing before his death (Deut. 33:2), Bonaventure finds metaphorical references to the incarnation of Christ according to the three great times of sacred history, the time of the law, the time of the prophets, and the time of grace. Moses, in his view, was aware of all of this. In everything he said there was a reference to the incarnation.[36] Moses prophesied not only of the future incarnation of Christ, but also of the past, as in the creation account in Genesis.[37]

Underlying this threefold division is, not surprisingly, the Augustinian theory of the threefold vision: intellectual, imaginative, and corporeal. In the ninth of his *Collations on the Six Days,* Bonaventure introduces this theme in the same way Augustine had, by commenting on Paul's rapture (2 Cor. 12:2). Bonaventure's commentary departs from Augustine's, how-

33. III *Sent.* d. 25, a. 1, q. 2, ad 6 (3:541b).
34. Ibid.
35. *Sermo XXVIII in Nativitate Domini* (9:128a).
36. Ibid.
37. See III *Sent.* d. 25, a. 2, q. 2, ad 3 (3:549a). See also *Coll. in Hex.* 15.11 (5:400a).

ever, by introducing a new emphasis on the mediation of the visions, in such a way as to develop from them his threefold schema of the history of revelation. The context is a discussion of the firmness of faith, which is based on the witness of truth as expressed through the threefold Word: uncreated, incarnate, and inspired.[38] The first element of the firmness of faith, says Bonaventure, is the certain knowledge of the witnesses (*testificantium notitia certa*),[39] and it is in explaining this knowledge — clearly the knowledge of revelation, even though the word is not used — that he introduces Paul's experience of rapture:

> Concerning certain knowledge, it is said in the twelfth chapter of the second letter to the Corinthians, "I know a man who was caught up to the third heaven, and heard secrets," that is, certain knowledge through the ascent to the third heaven, and again, through the descent to the first, through the illuminations of all the heavens.... The threefold heaven is understood to be the threefold vision: purely intellectual, intellectual joined with imaginative vision, and intellectual joined with manifest corporeal vision. The first is found in the minds of angels, the second in the minds of the prophets, and the third in the minds of the apostles. In the agreement of these visions is the certainty of scripture.[40]

Here Bonaventure places an emphasis on the progressively more concrete mediation of intellectual vision, and thereby transforms a typology of visions into a periodization of history:

> The pure intellectual vision was in the minds of the angels and in the Legislator [i.e., Moses]. For the law was appointed [*ordinata*] through the angels; angels, who saw the pure truth in the eternal light, gave it and composed it. For this vision Moses was raised up above all prophets.... The second certitude was in the minds of the prophets.... The visions of the prophets, however, were imaginative, as in the case of Isaiah and Daniel.... The third certitude is from intellectual vision joined with the body. This [vision] was in the minds of the apostles.[41]

38. See *Coll. in Hex.* 9.1 (5:372).
39. Ibid., 9.9 (5:374a).
40. Ibid., 9.10 (5:374a).
41. Ibid., 9.11–13 (5:374).

Although Moses and the angels hold the first position here, elsewhere it is the patriarchs. In both cases, however, the historicized schema of visions is identical:

> Sacred scripture . . . is a celestial light brought down by the angels to the sacred patriarchs, prophets, and apostles. . . . Sacred scripture is the light of law in the patriarchs, prophetic light in the prophets, and the light of the gospels in the apostles. In the patriarchs, there is the brightness of merits, in prophets the brightness of merits and miracles, but in the apostles there is the brightness of merits, miracles, and martyrs. In the patriarchs there was the brightness of intellectual vision alone, in the prophets there was the brightness of intellectual vision with imaginative [vision], but in the apostles there was the brightness of intellectual and imaginative vision with certain vision, not spiritual, but corporeal.[42]

As this passage makes clear, the development from the purely intellectual vision of the patriarchs to the rich vision of the apostles, at once intellectual, imaginative, and corporeal, is a positive development toward greater and greater certitude, culminating in the apostles' experience of the incarnate Word. In Bonaventure's view, all the prophets are concerned primarily with foretelling the advent of Christ, which is "in itself the consummation of all prophetic revelation."[43] With the progression of history, the "plenitude of illumination" found in prophecy increases.[44] In his commentary on the gospel of John, Bonaventure symbolizes this historical progress by an organic image: the prophets plant the seed of expectation that later the apostles reap.[45] Elsewhere he speaks of prophecy as the light that precedes (*lumen praecedens*) the full light (*lumen plenum*) found in the teaching of Christ.[46]

What is noteworthy in all this is the emphasis placed on the concrete mediation of the prophetic vision. Here we see the actual historical realization that was prefigured by the metaphysics of revelation outlined above. In the actual order of history, prophetic revelation is found to be in-

42. *Sermo I Epiphania* (9:150a).
43. *Comm. in Lucam* 18.34 (7:468a).
44. III *Sent.* d. 25, a. 2, q. 2, f. 2 (3:547a).
45. *Comm. in Ioannem* 37.57 (6:298a). See also ibid., c. 4, q. 6, resp. (6:300a). Bonaventure discusses this question of the progressive increase in the clarity of revelation more fully under the rubric of the historical development of faith in the third book of his *Sentence Commentary*, III *Sent.* d. 25, a. 2 (3:545–51).
46. See IV *Sent.* d. 24, p. 2, a. 2, q. 4, resp. (4:635b).

separable from its content. Although spiritual illumination is the *sine qua non* of revelation, *what* is illumined is, increasingly, the concrete order of history itself, culminating (though hardly terminating, as we have seen) in the incarnation of the Word. Thus to the fundamental element of the inspired Word, the source of all spiritual illumination, must be added the equally important element of the incarnate Word, the objective presence of the Word in history, to which the inspired Word — the inspirer of the prophets, as well as the apostles — bears witness.

In an important sense, then, prophecy culminates in the incarnation, the fulfillment of the promise foretold from the beginning. In this sense, prophecy was a form of revelation specific to a particular moment in history, the "time of the prophets," a time that ended with the coming of the "Lord of the prophets,"[47] Christ. But in a wider sense, prophecy consists of any witness by the inspired Word to the Word incarnate, and just as this witness preceded the Word's incarnation in Jesus of Nazareth, so it continues its interpretative function vis-à-vis the continuing incarnate or "objective" presence of the Word in the institution of the church, in its history, and in its canonical scriptures. And so although a particular historical form of prophecy ends, prophecy itself does not. History continues, and so does its prophetic interpretation.

CHRISTUS MAGISTER

Although we discussed the incarnate Word in the previous chapter under the rubric of the threefold Word, we postponed a further discussion of the incarnate Word as revealer, pending a more complete understanding of the inspired Word and the central role that Bonaventure assigns to it in the historical process of revelation. We are now in a better position to inquire into the specificity of the role of the Word as incarnate in the process of revelation.

We have already noted that Bonaventure seldom uses the term *revelatio* in connection with Christ. *Revelatio* names more precisely the inner illumination that is the work of the inspired Word. But as we just saw, this inner illumination is, in actual historical instances of revelation, mediated through increasingly concrete forms. In prophecy it is applied to the interpretation of specific historical events, events that, for Bonaventure, foreshadowed the coming of Christ. This basic structure of the process of

47. *Comm. in Lucam, Prooemium,* n. 19 (7:6a).

revelation as a process of interpretation is preserved in the most authoritative historical instance of revelation, the incarnation, that is, the actual life and teachings of Jesus of Nazareth as the Christ. In this context, it becomes clear why Bonaventure seldom describes the incarnate Word as a source of *revelatio.* The function of the incarnate Word in the economy of revelation is not subjective, but objective. Jesus is the revealer primarily in his *public* ministry, in his teachings and in his actions. His subjectivity, his self-consciousness as at one with the eternal Word, is not made immediately and magically available to those who hear and see him. His words and deeds, as noted in the previous chapter, become revelatory in the strict sense only through the witness of the inspired Word acting within the believer. Here as elsewhere, the spiritual illumination of the *Verbum inspiratum* is absolutely necessary. We can now see more clearly, however, that what is necessary is not necessarily sufficient. As the history of revelation develops, its mediate character becomes progressively more apparent. Indeed, this is what makes it possible to speak of such "development" in the first place. As the culmination of this development, the teachings of Jesus of Nazareth — both his words and his deeds — take on a concreteness and specificity that remain unsurpassed thereafter, and therefore become authoritative and constitutive of Christian revelation as such, and especially as "incarnate" in scripture. The public teachings, therefore, although not the work of the Word as inspired, are nevertheless the definitive objective form of the Word as incarnate and thus provide for the authoritative mediation of the spiritual illumination of the Word within. Consequently, the specific role of the incarnate Word as revealer is not to inspire or illumine, to provide *revelatio* or *illuminatio,* but rather to *teach.*

Bonaventure taught, along with his tradition, that the primary purpose of the incarnation was the redemption of the human race, as well as the perfection of human beings and of creation generally.[48] Viewed more specifically as a decisive moment in the history of revelation, however, the main motive of the incarnation was pedagogical. Humankind needed a teacher that could teach it on its own level, in a form appropriate to concrete human existence. Bonaventure explains this in a sermon, beginning with a favorite text from St. Augustine:

48. See III *Sent.* d. 1, a. 2, q. 2 (3:21). Zachary Hayes has recently emphasized the importance of both of these motives and argued that Bonaventure's soteriology is best described as a theology of "redemptive completion." See his *The Hidden Center: Spirituality and Speculative Christology in St. Bonaventure* (New York: Paulist Press, 1981), pp. 152–87.

> "The one who has his seat in heaven teaches within the heart of men on earth," that is the Word, that is the foundation of all wisdom.... But in order that that teacher might enter into the hearts of men on earth, it was necessary either for men to be raised up, or for the Word to come down. Men [however] were crude and sensual, and thus it was impossible for man to be raised up to that ineffable Word and inaccessible Light and to look upon that eternal Beauty. Therefore, it was fitting either that the Word should come into the midst of men, or that men should remain in their foolishness. Therefore Christ became incarnate.[49]

Through the incarnation, the Word comes among men and women as a teacher accommodated to the conditions of his prospective pupils. Bonaventure repeatedly refers to Jesus as a teacher. He is the "true" or "most true teacher" (*verus doctor Christus; doctor veracissimus*),[50] the "principal instructor, master, and teacher" (*principalis instructor, magister, et doctor*),[51] the "teacher of truth" (*magister veritatis*),[52] indeed, the "one teacher of all" (*unus omnium magister*).[53] He is the teacher whose teaching (*doctrina*) is most efficacious (*efficacissima*).[54] This "doctrine," however, precisely as "efficacious," is something more than a set of propositions. *Doctrina* here is to be understood in its original active sense of teaching and preaching and only secondarily as what is taught. The teaching of Jesus is the full expression of his nature as the *incarnate* Word. It is a teaching not only of words, through preaching, but also of words incarnate in action. Thus Bonaventure can refer to Jesus' *doctrina operum,* the "teaching of works," as more effective than mere teaching through words: "The teaching of words without the examples of works is like stone without mortar, dry and weak.... The teaching of works inheres more tenaciously than does the teaching of words."[55] Jesus teaches as much by example as by words (*tam exemplo quam verbo*).[56] This is because people need for their instruction more than "mere words." They need concrete models to imitate: "Men need lessons and examples; for examples are more effective than words." Therefore, "the Word conde-

49. *Sermo II Dominica Tertia Adventus* (8:60a).
50. *Sermo II Dominica Prima Adventus* (9:28a).
51. *Sermo III Dominica Duodecima Post Pentecosten* (9:402a).
52. *Sermo III Dominica De Passione* (9:240b).
53. *Sermo IV De Rebus Theologicis* (5:567).
54. *Sermo I Dominica Infra Octavam Nativitatis Domini* (9:130b).
55. *De Sex Alis Seraphim* c. 5 (8:142a).
56. *Legenda Sancti Francisci* c. 6, n. 1 (8:519b).

scended to become man in order that we might be able to imitate him and reform ourselves through imitating him."[57] Indeed, "Christ's every action is for our instruction."[58]

The familiar theme of exemplarism enters in a new way here, as the basis of the practices of the community. Bonaventure makes this clear in his *Defense of the Mendicants,* where he distinguishes a twofold exemplarity of the Word: the exemplarity of the eternal Word, with which we are now familiar, and the exemplarity of the incarnate Word. The incarnate Word is "the mirror of all graces, virtues, and merits," in the imitation of which the community of the church is to be built up.[59] Jesus is thus primarily the teacher of the community of the church: "Truly and properly the Lord Jesus is called Teacher. For he alone is the teacher in heaven and earth. He teaches the entire church triumphant in heaven, and the entire church militant on earth."[60]

Thus in his descriptions of Jesus as Teacher, Bonaventure places a great deal of emphasis on his role as an exemplar of the moral life to be lived within the community of the church. In his own life, Jesus exemplified a life of "evangelical perfection," which Bonaventure, as Minister General of the Franciscans, defended as the highest ideal of the Christian life. This is not to say, however, that Bonaventure minimized the importance of Jesus' teachings through words (*doctrina verborum*). But here too the emphasis is placed on the communal and practical aspect: for Bonaventure, Jesus was not simply a teacher; he was a *preacher.* For Bonaventure, "to expound and teach the Gospel of God is to preach the divine word,"[61] and *doctrina* or "teaching" can in fact be equated with the office of preaching (*praedicationis magisterium*).[62] The original teacher of the "good news" is thus equally a preacher. In the prologue to his commentary on the gospel of St. Luke, Bonaventure connects Jesus' teaching (*doctrina, eruditionis magisterium*) with his role as a preacher,[63] and later in the same commentary he discusses the fourfold basis of the renown of Jesus' preaching: its plenitude of grace, the extent of its fame, the certitude of its teaching, and the greatness of its effect.[64] In explaining the

57. *Sermo II Dominica Tertia Adventus* (8:60b).

58. *Comm. in Ioannem* 1.106 (6:268). See also *Sermo I Dominica Prima in Quadragesima* (9:205a).

59. *Apologia Pauperum* c. 2, n. 12 (8:243a).

60. *Sermo III Dominica Vigesima Secunda Post Pentecosten* (9:444b).

61. *Comm. in Lucam, Prooemium,* n. 5 (7:4a).

62. Ibid., c. 4, n. 1 (7:88a).

63. Ibid., *Prooemium,* n. 17 (7:5b).

64. Ibid., c. 4, n. 26 (7:96a).

meaning of "plenitude of grace," Bonaventure says that perfect preaching should be conjoined with spiritual power (*virtuti spirituali coniuncta*) and quotes St. Paul (1 Cor. 2:4): "Our speech and preaching were not in the persuasive words of human wisdom, but in demonstration of the Spirit and of power."[65] Even Jesus' *doctrina verborum,* therefore, was a powerful form of action, capable of exerting an effect upon the hearer. Here too Christ serves as a model to be imitated: "a good preacher is an imitator of Christ."[66]

It will already be clear from the foregoing discussion of Jesus' role as teacher that the content of his teaching will be primarily his life itself as the exemplar of the ideal Christian life. Jesus is understood primarily as a teacher of virtue, and most especially the virtues of humility, poverty, obedience, and love — precisely those virtues that were most central to the life of "evangelical perfection" that served as the ideal for the Franciscans.[67] This is not to say that Bonaventure restricted Jesus' teaching to morality. The incarnate Word was of course also the revelation of the divine nature and of the economy of salvation. But precisely as disclosive of such transcendent realities, the teachings of Jesus are taken up into the larger process of revelation that is inseparable from the inner light of the inspired Word. This process is a process of interpretation, and in regard to Jesus of Nazareth, it is a process that comes to fruition in the composition of the scriptures of the New Testament by the apostles. For Bonaventure, these scriptures record the public teachings of the Word incarnate as received by the apostles and the early Christian community, through the light of the inspired Word.

65. Ibid., n. 27 (7:96a).
66. Ibid., c. 4, n. 97 (7:112b).
67. See Hayes, *Hidden Center,* pp. 35–42.

7

The Reception of the Language of Revelation

We have examined Bonaventure's doctrine of revelation, both his metaphysics of revelation, centered upon the hierarchical influence of the inspired Word and its spiritual illumination of the soul, and his view of the history of revelation, focused, in the final analysis, on the incarnate Word as foretold by the prophets, made present in Jesus of Nazareth, and prolonged in the communal life and official teaching of the church. Whereas we began by highlighting the importance of inner illumination in Bonaventure's theory of revelation, we came to see that its external, historical mediation was also important. In retrospect, therefore, we can see that revelation is for Bonaventure a *process* that includes both inner illumination and outer mediation as essential moments. Revelation in its concrete historical structure appears as a process of interpretation, a process that receives its metaphysical warrant in Bonaventure's notion of the threefold Word that is both incarnate objectively in history and present subjectively within the individual soul.

This process becomes actual through language. As we have seen, Christian revelation originated in the message of the *kerygma,* the preaching of the apostles as witnesses to the risen Christ. This preaching appealed both to the historical and apocalyptic expectation of the Jewish community, recorded in the Hebrew scriptures, and to the apostles' own personal experience of the risen Lord. The original apostolic *kerygma* was eventually incorporated into the canonical Christian scriptures, and it was the interpretation of these scriptures that provided the basis for the continued presence of revelation during the Middle Ages, whether in the form of spiritual commentary, preaching, or prophecy. It remains to be seen how Bonaventure himself stood in relation to this interpretative process. In this chapter we will first examine Bonaventure's view of scripture itself, as presented in the prologue of his theology "textbook," the *Breviloquium.* Then we will examine briefly his approach to the study of scripture, both as expressed theoretically in *On the Reduction of the Arts to Theology* and in his actual practice in his own scriptural commentaries. Next we will examine Bonaventure's views of preaching, here again considering both his theory of preaching and his actual practice as a preacher and as Minister General of an order devoted to preaching. Finally we will examine Bonaventure's attitudes to prophecy, not as a reality of the past but as a reality that he believed to have been present in the church of his day. Here we will see how the language of scripture, preaching, and prophecy merge in Bonaventure's most powerful expression of his Christian vision, presented in his *Collations on the Six Days.* Throughout this chapter we will be particularly interested in seeing how Bonaventure's metaphysics of revelation is related to his own concrete involvement with the language of revelation.

SCRIPTURE

In the tradition of Origen and Augustine, Bonaventure views scripture as a divinely given Book, inspired in all its parts. Properly speaking, its many writings have but one author, the divine Trinity: "The origin [of scripture] is not through human investigation, but through divine revelation, which flows 'from the Father of lights from whom all fatherhood in heaven and on earth is named,' from whom, through his Son, Jesus Christ, the Holy Spirit flows into us."[1] The Holy Spirit in particular is said to be the "author" (*auctor*) of scripture.[2] This unicity of authorship entails a unicity of meaning. The book of scripture sums up the content of the entire universe, presenting it as a meaningful whole that manifests the divine wisdom: "The entire world is described by scripture as proceeding by a most orderly course from the beginning to the end, like some beautifully composed poem."[3] Bonaventure takes this simile of the world as poem a step farther:

> Just as no one can see the beauty of a poem unless his vision embraces the entire verse, so no one sees the beauty of the order and governance of the universe unless the whole is seen. And since no

1. *Brev., Prologus* (5:201a).
2. *Comm. in Ecclesiasten, Prooemium,* c. 1, v. 2 (6:11a).
3. *Brev.* 2 (5:204b).

> one lives long enough to be able to see the whole with his own eyes, and since he is not able, by himself, to foresee the future, the Holy Spirit provided us with the book of holy scripture, whose length corresponds to the course of the governance of the universe.[4]

We have already seen that Bonaventure understood the created world as a "text," as the "book of creation" that is the expression of its "author," the divine Word. Due to sin this text became unreadable. Having lost the "eye of contemplation," people could no longer rise up through the contemplation of the creation to a knowledge of its divine ground, the Trinity. One purpose of scripture is to return to human beings the possibility of properly understanding creation as the expression of the *Verbum increatum,* the uncreated Word. But this creation has a history. It is not only the synchronic structure of creation that manifests its creator, but also its diachronic development. And whereas people are blind to the trinitarian structure of creation due to sin, they are incapable of comprehending the overall pattern and meaning of creation's temporal unfolding due to their very nature as finite, temporal beings. In order properly to interpret the significance of the present historical moment, therefore, it is necessary to locate it within the whole, and this whole can be known only through revelation, since its full course is known only to God. Thus a second purpose of scripture is to provide people with such a vision of the whole. Here Bonaventure is presupposing the notion of a predetermined divine plan of history that is a fundamental component of Jewish and Christian apocalyptic. As in earlier forms of apocalyptic thought, this divine plan is made known through a revealed book, the *liber scripturae,* which presents the entire stretch of human history, from beginning to end, as a kind of finished "poem," as a "divine comedy."

Behind the unity of the Book, however, lies the unity of the Word. Bonaventure grounds the unity of scripture in the notion of the divine authorship of the Holy Spirit, which is to say, in the inspiration of the *Verbum inspiratum.* But the unity of scripture also presupposes the unity of creation as the expression of the *Verbum increatum.* It is this expression, this "text," that scripture interprets. Furthermore, in our examination of the historical development of prophetic revelation, we saw that the history of creation is centered on the event of the incarnation, on the *Verbum incarnatum.* Thus the unity of scripture is further based upon this key

4. Ibid.

event. "All the words of scripture are summed up in this Word."[5] Here one begins to see the intimate connection between Bonaventure's theory of scripture and his theory of the threefold Word. Scripture, in its origin, is the expression of the threefold Word. It is the witness of the Word as inspired to its own objective presence in creation and in the incarnation. But this witness of the Word to itself happens within the realm of concrete human experience. In spite of the objective and universal status that Bonaventure ascribes to "the Book," he locates his theory of scripture within the larger context of his metaphysics of revelation, which presents the self-manifestation of the Word as a dialectical *process,* involving both inner illumination and objective mediation. Thus scripture per se is not to be equated with revelation. It is the necessary *medium* through which the *process* of revelation unfolds. It is the concretion of a process of interpretation that in turn makes further acts of interpretation possible. Scripture is therefore primarily an inspired *witness* that originates in the *activity* of revelation and makes the continuance of this activity possible.

The mediating character of scripture becomes apparent when we examine more closely Bonaventure's theory of the interpretation of scripture, as well as his understanding of its purpose. According to Bonaventure, scripture must be interpreted in the same spirit in which it was received.[6] Since scripture was originally given by the Holy Spirit, it is only through that same Spirit that it can be properly understood. In general this means that Bonaventure's trinitarian metaphysics of revelation, which comes to a focus in the illumination of the *Verbum inspiratum,* provides not only a theory of the *origin* of scripture, but also a theory of its *reception.* The anthropology of the human being as the *imago Dei,* which we saw to be a correlate of this metaphysics, is as well an anthropology of the human being as the reader and interpreter of scripture. Against this background it becomes clear that Bonaventure viewed scripture not merely as an "objective revelation" in the sense of a "divine Book," but also as a moment within a larger process of interpretation and spiritual transformation.

This transformative function of scripture is of particular importance for Bonaventure. The purpose of scripture is not merely to broaden the intellectual understanding of faith, but to transform the will. This function in fact determines scripture's literary form:

5. *Comm. in Lucam* 24.33 (7:595b).
6. See *Comm. in Lucam, Prooemium* 3 (7:3b).

> This teaching [contained in scripture] exists that we might become good and be saved. And this is not accomplished through mere consideration, but rather through the inclination of the will. Therefore divine scripture had to be transmitted in the way that would best dispose us. And since the will [*affectio*] is moved more by examples than by arguments, more by promises than by reasonings, more by devotions than by definitions, scripture ought not proceed by definition, division, and synthesis... but rather had to have its own proper modes, disposing different souls according to their various inclinations.[7]

Bonaventure refers to scripture's "proper modes" as being in general narrative modes (*modi narrativi*). All such modes convey particular events that cannot be formally demonstrated through rational argument. Their truth is based not on rational necessity but on their authority as divinely revealed.[8] Scripture for Bonaventure is thus primarily a narrative testimony that facilitates the spiritual transformation of the individual through the presentation of concrete norms for thought and action. Its authority in turn is grounded in just such a transformative event — the original revelatory influence of the Spirit upon the prophets and apostles.

The fundamentally practical purpose of scripture is worked out on a number of levels, however. Bonaventure accepted the traditional Christian belief in the existence of multiple spiritual meanings of scripture concealed beneath the surface of the letter. While the literal sense of scripture provided the necessary basis for the essential doctrines of the church, the spiritual senses allowed scripture to be *put to use* in the actual spiritual transformation of the individual:

> Scripture was given in order that through it man might be directed in knowing and in acting, so that he might at last arrive at those things that are to be desired. And since all created things were made in order to serve man as he travels to his heavenly goal, scripture takes up the diverse forms of created things in order that, through them, it might teach us that wisdom which guides us to the eternal. And since man is not directed to the eternal unless his cognitive power know the truth that is to be believed, his operative power do the good that is to be done, and his affective power long for God who

7. *Brev., Prologus* 5 (5:206b–207a).
8. Ibid. (207a).

> is to be seen, loved, and enjoyed, therefore sacred scripture, which was given through the Holy Spirit, assumes the book of creation by referring it to this end according to three modes of understanding, so that through the tropological sense we might have knowledge of those things that are to be vigorously accomplished, through the allegorical sense we might know those things that are to be believed truthfully, and through the anagogical sense we might know those things that are to be desired with delight.[9]

In the prologue to his mystical treatise *On the Triple Way,* Bonaventure makes this connection between the spiritual senses of scripture and the spiritual path of the individual more explicit. Referring to the moral (or tropological), allegorical, and anagogical senses, he adds: "This threefold understanding corresponds to the threefold hierarchical action, namely, purgation, illumination, and perfection." Consequently, "on the knowledge of these three depends the science of all of holy scripture, and even the merit of eternal life."[10] Here progress in the understanding of scripture is essentially identified with progress upon the spiritual path, and both are understood in terms of action: the inner, hierarchical action through which the soul is gradually conformed to its divine Exemplar. Bonaventure goes on to say that progress upon the threefold path required a threefold exercise: reading and meditation, prayer, and contemplation.[11]

It is clear that the experiential orientation of Bonaventure's theory of revelation as inner illumination is not lacking in this theory of the "objective" revelation of scripture. Inner experience and outer mediation continue to interact in a single dialectical process. This process, under the name of the *lectio divina,* had long been an essential part of Christian tradition. As early as John Cassian it was viewed as a process of personal transformation through the continuous meditation upon scripture. This tradition of the *lectio divina,* having been challenged by the new "scholastic" exegesis of masters such as Abelard, had been reaffirmed by the Victorines, who sought to unite the traditional contemplative study of scripture with the new scientific advances of the twelfth century. In this regard Bonaventure can be viewed as a disciple of the Victorines, and in particular of Hugh of St. Victor. Just as Hugh, in his *Didascalicon,* had tried to integrate the study of the arts into the framework of a scripturally

9. *Brev., Prologus* 4 (5:206).
10. *De Triplici Via,* prologus (8:3).
11. Ibid.

based theology, so Bonaventure, in his *On the Reduction of the Arts to Theology,* tried to envision the whole range of the sciences as ultimately ordered to the interpretation of scripture. In so doing, he was in effect bringing the monastic *lectio divina* into the classroom in order to fashion a theology that would remain rooted in the contemplative study of scripture.

In this short work, Bonaventure presents the whole of human knowledge as a series of illuminations, as "the generous emanation of the manifold light from that fountain of light," namely, God the Father.[12] Here we recognize Bonaventure's favorite theme of illumination. He distinguishes a series of four illuminations, each of which derives from the manifold wisdom of God: the "external light" of the mechanical arts, the "lower light" of sense perception, the "inner light" of philosophical knowledge, and the "higher light" of grace and sacred scripture.[13] This series is later expanded to six, by dividing philosophical knowledge into three: rational, natural, and moral philosophy. This sixfold schema makes possible a homology between the six illuminations and the six days of creation, a homology that Bonaventure will develop in more detail in his *Collations on the Six Days.* In either case, the point is to emphasize the primacy of knowledge derived from scripture:

> It is indeed fitting that these six illuminations can be reduced to the six formations or illuminations in which the world was made, so that the knowledge of sacred scripture might correspond to the first formation, namely, the formation of light, and so on, in order. And just as all these [created things] had their origin from one light, so all these forms of knowledge are ordered to the knowledge of sacred scripture; in it they are contained and in it they are perfected, and through its mediation they are ordered to eternal illumination. For this reason all our knowledge ought to have a place in the knowledge of sacred scripture, and this is especially true of the anagogical sense, through which illumination is led back to God, whence it had its origin.[14]

Here Bonaventure describes a program for Christian learning that remains in the tradition of the monastic *lectio divina* and that culminates in

12. *De Reductione Artium ad Theologiam* 1 (5:319a). On the Father as one inexhaustible "fountain" of light, see above, pp. 92ff.

13. Ibid.

14. Ibid., 7 (5:322a).

the soul's anagogical ascent to God. Through scripture all created things are led back to their source, and central to this *reductio* is the spiritual transformation of the individual.

It would be wrong to think, however, that Bonaventure viewed scripture solely in terms of its use in the contemplative life of the individual. Or rather, it would be wrong to think that the contemplative life of the individual is somehow isolated from the larger life of the Christian community. In his view, scripture is a social institution, and its study always takes place within the ongoing tradition of the church. It is always important to remember who Bonaventure was. He was by no means an isolated introvert, seeking private access to the divine. He was an ordained priest, an educator, a trained scholastic theologian, a respected preacher, Minister General of a major religious order, frequent guest of the royal family, and, at the end of his life, a cardinal and confidant of the pope. The spiritual immediacy that Bonaventure attributes to the individual's penetration of scripture's anagogical sense should not be set in opposition to the more institutionalized forms of scriptural study. In Bonaventure's mind it rather represents their culmination. This will become clearer when we examine the prophetic vision that Bonaventure presents in his *Collations on the Six Days.*

Bonaventure's theory of scripture, as well as his practice, are thus multifaceted. What is striking is the intimate relationship between the two. In accord with his metaphysics of revelation he views scripture as a whole as the expression of the threefold Word, and in accord with his view of the human being as the *imago Dei,* as the "reader" of the texts of creation and of scripture, he sees the study of scripture as leading ultimately to the imitation of and assimilation to the divine Exemplar, both at the level of knowledge and at the level of moral action. In accord with his essentially dynamic understanding of reality, and of humans in particular, he views scripture as essentially practical in intent. It is intended to *do* something, to persuade and ultimately to convert the unstable human soul and draw it, step by step, back to its Maker. Finally, in accord with the historical and hierarchical nature of his thought, he views scripture as addressed not only to the individual but to the church and to humankind as a whole. Scripture provides an all-encompassing vision of the whole of cosmic, human, and church history, and consequently its reception in every age entails a properly prophetic and apocalyptic element. We will return to this theme below. But first we must turn to Bonaventure's theory and practice of preaching.

PREACHING

By the thirteenth century preaching had become a central concern of a great many people. Not that it had ever ceased to be important. But by Bonaventure's day a full-scale revival of preaching was under way, and as a member of a religious order especially dedicated to preaching, in imitation of Christ, the apostles, and most particularly the charismatic St. Francis, he found himself in the midst of it. There is ample evidence of this in his work. Not only did he leave us a large number of sermons that he himself preached; he also attempted to provide his fellow friars with aids for their own preaching. Although it is doubtful that the *Ars Concionandi* included in the Quaracchi editors' critical edition of Bonaventure's sermons is really his own work,[15] there is no doubt that he himself adopted the new thematic style of preaching taught by this and other thirteenth-century preaching manuals, and further recommended this style by putting together a collection of "model sermons" intended for the use of his fellow friars. Bonaventure's commentary on Luke was also probably intended to aid the friars in their task of preaching. Add to this the fact that Bonaventure often had to come to the defense of the friars' right to preach and hear confession, in the face of opposition from the secular clergy, and it becomes clear that preaching was for him a major concern that often received his direct attention.[16] He and the friars were, in fact, at the center of a pastoral reform, supported by the papacy, that has been called the *reconquête intérieure* of Christendom.[17] Bonaventure has left us a colorful description of the times as he saw them:

> At present we are seeing the harvests of the people multiply, forests being cut down, and towns built. The inventions of sinners increase and more perplexing events emerge daily. Out of habit evil people are becoming more incorrigible and hardened in sin. Furthermore, many clerics weaken the laity by bad example, as much in morals as in faith; few among them are really knowledgeable, or capable

15. See his *Opera Omnia* 9:8–21. For a brief discussion of the problem of its authorship, see Harry C. Hazel, Jr., "The Bonaventuran 'Ars Concionandi,'" in *S. Bonaventura, 1274–1974,* ed. Jacques Guy Bougerol, 5 vols. (Grottaferrata: Collegio S. Bonaventura, 1972–74), 2:435–45.

16. In addition to his famous *Defense of the Mendicants* (8:233–330), see also his short defense of the friars' right to preach and hear confessions, *Quare Fratres Minores Praedicent et Confessiones Audiant* (8:375–85).

17. See André Vauchez, "Présentation," in *Faire croire: Modalités de la diffusion et de la réception des messages religieux du XIIe au XVe siècle* (Rome: École française de Rome, 1981), p. 10.

> of teaching as they ought. They are negligent in caring for the souls that have been entrusted to them because they are overly devoted to worldly affairs. Many of them are suspended, excommunicated, and in various ways impeded in their duty. Pastors in churches are rare, and through capricious substitutes the care of souls is put up for sale. Bishops who are given over to temporal concerns hide the fact, so that there is hardly any hope of correction. If one wants to correct the situation and remove useless bishops, one cannot find better ones to take their place. And so, since the church is now like a ship tossed by a tempest, nearly overwhelmed by the swelling waves, its rowers trembling from fear, the friars have been sent out by the highest captain, supported by the authority of the apostolic See, so that, running through the world in their little boats, those that they have found endangered by the shipwreck of sin might be snatched from the waves and carried back to the shore of salvation.[18]

Preaching was the key to this "rescue" operation, and the friars were the key to effective preaching. If those traditionally responsible for preaching and the "care of souls" were failing in their duty, if the church's "rowers" were trembling with fear (or perhaps had simply put down their "oars"), the solution was to send out new preachers. This is what St. Francis had done in sending out the first friars, in imitation of Christ's sending of the apostles,[19] and the friars' "mission" to preach had later been officially confirmed by the pope.

Bonaventure presents St. Francis as the ideal model of the preacher. Francis was the "herald of Christ," whose commission to preach had been given by God himself and subsequently confirmed by the authorization of the pope, who was himself guided in this by a revelation.[20] In his *Life of St. Francis,* Bonaventure devotes a separate chapter to Francis's preaching, which opens with Francis's own reflections on the relative merit of prayer and preaching. Although the act of prayer in many respects seems superior to that of preaching, in the final analysis Francis is led to follow the example of Christ himself. In spite of the many attractions of the inner life of prayer, he concludes that

18. *Quare Fratres Minores Praedicent et Confessiones Audiant* 13 (8:378b–379a).

19. See Bonaventure's account in his life of St. Francis, *Legenda Sancti Francisci* 3.7 (8:511).

20. See *Legenda Sancti Francisci* 12.12 (8:542).

> there is one thing to the contrary that seems to outweigh all these considerations before God, namely, that the only begotten Son of God, who is the highest wisdom, came down from the bosom of the Father for the sake of souls, so that, by instructing the world by his own example, he might speak the word of salvation to men.... And because we should do all things according to the model [*exemplar*], of what we see in him... it seems pleasing to God that I interrupt my quiet and go out to labor.[21]

Here we see Bonaventure presenting Francis's commitment to preaching in terms of his own doctrine of exemplarism as extended to the sphere of human action. But this is not all. According to Bonaventure, Francis was not content to reach this conclusion by himself. Certainty as to his preaching mission could come only through revelation, and so Francis refers the problem to his friars, and in particular—according to Bonaventure—to Silvester and Clare. This brought the intended result: "Through the revelation of the heavenly Spirit, the venerable priest and the virgin dedicated to God miraculously came to the same conclusion [*concordaverunt*]: that it was God's good pleasure that Francis should go out to preach as the herald of Christ."[22] It is noteworthy that Francis's certainty concerning his commission is here presented as requiring a degree of social mediation. The final decision is a communal one, based on Silvester and Clare's miraculous "concord" in the Spirit.

After presenting this account of Francis's vocation to preach, Bonaventure goes on to narrate a series of episodes that depict Francis's actual practice. One of these stories is of particular interest for what it tells us indirectly about Bonaventure's own view of the nature of preaching. It seems that Francis was once asked to preach before the pope, and in preparation for the event carefully composed and memorized his sermon. When the time came to deliver it, however, he went completely blank and was unable to speak. Realizing his dilemma, he invoked the aid of the Holy Spirit, and "suddenly he began to overflow with such effective words... that it was clearly evident that it was not he, but the Spirit of the Lord who was speaking."[23] Here we have the traditional Christian theme that true eloquence is a gift of the Spirit and not the product of human artifice. Preaching is ideally a spiritual event in which the human agency of

21. Ibid., 12.1 (8:539a).
22. Ibid., 12.2 (8:539b).
23. Ibid., 12.7 (8:540b).

the preacher is transformed through the *influentia* of the *verbum inspiratum.* Although it is clear that Bonaventure did not view Francis's sermon on this occasion as in any way typical of preachers in general, we shall see below that the role that he here attributes to the Holy Spirit is for him essential for effective preaching.

Another traditional theme that Bonaventure weaves into his presentation of St. Francis is the belief that the true preacher preaches *verbo et exemplo,* as much by the example of his life as by the words that he speaks. For Bonaventure, it was Francis's life, and in particular his imitation of Christ, that gave power to his words.[24] This is a theme found in both Augustine and Gregory. What is new here is the way that these ideals came alive in the person of St. Francis and the impact that this had on the church as a whole and on St. Bonaventure in particular.

Bonaventure's remarks on preachers and preaching were not confined to his references to St. Francis. General comments on preaching are found scattered throughout his works, relating both to the character of the preacher and to the act — or better, the event — of preaching itself. Preaching in general is viewed as a fundamental part of the evangelical life, the *vita apostolica* that was the Franciscan ideal. This life was grounded in the imitation of Christ, particularly as exemplified in the life of St. Francis himself. A good preacher is therefore an imitator of Christ,[25] and this imitation is perfected through a life of poverty.[26] Poverty is particularly important for the preacher because it sets an example that renders his preaching more credible.[27] Thus the preacher must strive for perfection not only in doctrine but also in his way of life,[28] since the example of his life is more persuasive that his words.[29] It was such a correspondence of word and deed that had made St. Francis so effective as a preacher, and Bonaventure, following in the tradition of Augustine and Gregory, viewed it as essential.

Bonaventure frequently comments on the nature of preaching in the *prothema* of his sermons.[30] A preacher must be characterized by humil-

---

24. See ibid., 11.2 (8:536a); 12.8 (8:540b).
25. *Comm. in Lucam* 4.97 (7:112b).
26. Ibid., 9.38 (7:228b).
27. *Apologia Pauperum* 9.21 (8:301a).
28. *Comm. in Ioannem* 21.8 (6:521a).
29. *Sermo, Dominica in Septuagesima* (9:197b).
30. For a study of these, see Johannes Baptist Schneyer, "Das Bild des Predigers bei Bonaventura," in *S. Bonaventura 1274–1974,* 2:517–30. See also Schneyer's longer work, *Die Unterweisung der Gemeinde über die Predigt bei scholastischen Predigern* (Munich: F. Schöningh, 1968).

ity, helpfulness, and nobility.[31] He should pray that he receive the gifts of an abundance of charity, the understanding of truth, and the uprightness of sanctity.[32] The preacher must be generous of soul,[33] detached from worldly concerns, illumined by the truth of the gospel, and inflamed with the love of God and of neighbor.[34]

The theme of illumination is particularly important. In order to become fit for preaching the gospel, preachers need the illumination of the Holy Spirit, as Bonaventure made clear in the case of St. Francis. It is the hierarchical action of the Spirit as it purifies, illumines, and perfects the soul, that makes the preacher fit for understanding the mysteries lying hidden beneath the letter of scripture and communicating them to his audience.[35] This belief in the necessity of such divine assistance for effective preaching had been part of the tradition since St. Paul had insisted to the Corinthians that he spoke not with the words of human eloquence but in the demonstration of the Spirit.[36] Its centrality in the preaching of the thirteenth century is evidenced by the very structure of the thematic sermon. Such a sermon was always to begin with a *prothema,* a short meditation on a scriptural text prior to the main body of the sermon. This *prothema* often included an explicit reflection on the role of divine grace in preaching, both on the part of the preacher and on the part of his audience, and ended with a prayer asking for such grace.[37] We have already noted Bonaventure's frequent references to the moral requirements for preaching in his *prothema.* The theme of spiritual assistance is also central there. "I speak badly," Bonaventure asserts, "unless the Holy Spirit is in me, and you hear badly unless the Holy Spirit opens your ears. The foundation of our art is that the Holy Spirit speaks in us and that the Spirit makes our speech hearable."[38] Or again: "We preachers and doctors do nothing by speaking aloud unless the Holy Spirit works within the heart by his grace."[39] Therefore, when beginning a sermon, Bonaventure asked the community to pray for the gift of grace so that he might be able to speak with the voice of the Lord, as had John the Baptist.[40]

---

31. See *Sermo I Dominica Prima Adventus* (9:23a).
32. See *Sermo, Dominica in Septuagesima* (9:196a).
33. See *Sermo, Dominica in Sexagesima* (9:198a).
34. See *Sermo I Dominica infra Octavam Nativitatis Domini* (9:129a). See also *Sermo I Dominica Secunda in Quadragesima* (9:215a).
35. *Sermo X in Pentecoste* (9:345).
36. 1 Corinthians 2:4.
37. See Schneyer, *Unterweisung der Gemeinde,* pp. 84–90.
38. *Sermo I in Ascensione Domini* (9:314).
39. *Sermo I de Sancto Andrea Apostolo* (9:463).
40. *Sermo I de Nativitate S. Ioannis Baptistae* (9:539).

There should be nothing surprising about this overt appeal to the Spirit in the act of preaching. Not only is Bonaventure continuing a tradition that goes back to the early church; he is also making a concrete application of his theory of spiritual illumination. Of particular interest, however, is his attention to the communal setting of preaching. The aid of the Spirit is required not only for the preacher, but also for his audience, and it is the community as a whole that prays for this assistance. This explicit reliance on the Spirit in a social context brings out quite nicely the *event* character of preaching. The effective sermon, precisely as *effective,* is something that *happens* to preacher and audience together, and as such transcends either of their own separate capacities or expectations. It is a fundamentally intersubjective experience grounded in the Spirit, as the latter becomes manifest through the actual activity of preaching, which in turn represents a "re-actualization" of scripture as the Word of God. The multiple mediations present here, both through the community and through scripture, ensure that the immediacy of the event itself, the actual reception of revelation as the direct action of the Spirit, is not reducible either to the subjective intentions of the speaker or to the subjective expectations of his listeners. Preaching is a communal and ultimately a spiritual event that grounds, even as it transcends, the individual participants. As mediating between the canonical scriptures of the community and the inner illumination of the individual speaker and hearer, the *activity* of preaching represents the most adequate realization of the Christian language of revelation. This is most especially true when preaching rises above the immediate horizon of the community to become prophecy.

PROPHECY

The line that separates preaching from prophecy can at times be a very fine one. This was the case in the early church and again in St. Gregory, with his ideal of the preacher as prophet, as the ecclesial successor of the prophets of Israel and of the early Christian communities. It continues to be the case in the Middle Ages generally, when prophecy was in most cases "prophecy by interpretation," i.e., based on the interpretation of scripture. To the extent that both prophecy and preaching were inspired acts of interpretation addressed to the Christian community, they could in fact be identified. Whereas preaching could in principle be restricted to the horizon of the present, however, and be concerned primarily with the edification of the contemporary community, prophecy never lost its associations with the apocalyptic expectations of the early church. Even as a form of scriptural interpretation it retained this reference to the divine plan of history and to the future as the necessary context for understanding the present.

Nevertheless, when preaching explicitly located itself within this context and when it was driven by the influence of the Spirit, it was an essentially prophetic activity. From Bonaventure's point of view this was clearly the case with the preaching of St. Francis, the "herald of God," and in principle with Franciscan preaching in general. In such cases the three fundamental forms of the Christian language of revelation — scripture, preaching, and the inspired speech of prophecy — were united in a single activity. The original form of such revelatory speech was the *kerygma* of the early church, the *kerygma* that was being consciously imitated by those who, like St. Francis, sought to return to the *vita apostolica,* the life of evangelical perfection exemplified by Christ and the apostles.

We have already examined Bonaventure's theoretical reflections on prophecy. Here we will look at Bonaventure's own practical involvement in prophecy through an examination of his last and perhaps greatest work, the *Collations on the Six Days,* a series of sermons delivered at Paris in the spring of 1273, the year before Bonaventure died.

It has often been pointed out that the *Collations* as we have them were not written by Bonaventure himself, but rather are reports of his words written down by individuals who heard him speak. In the present context, this fact is significant in that it underlines the fact that the *Collations* were given as *sermons;* they were *preached* to the friars of the Franciscan house of studies as *collationes,* evening sermons that were an established part of the community's life.[41] If one thus bears in mind that we are dealing with a series of sermons, it becomes apparent that the first three collations together provide a kind of *prothema* for the entire series. Each of the three begins with the same verse, Sirach 15:5, which Bonaventure gives as follows: "In the midst of the church the Lord will open his mouth and fill him with the spirit of wisdom and understanding, and clothe him with a robe of glory."[42] Bonaventure comments: "In these words the Holy Spirit teaches the prudent man to whom he should address his speech,

41. See David L. D'Avray, " 'Collectiones Fratrum' and 'Collationes Fratrum,' " *Archivum Franciscanum Historicum* 70 (1977): 152–56. D'Avray notes that the collation "reached a high point of development at the University of Paris, where a morning sermon would be followed as a matter of course, on the same day, by a *collatio.* Bachelors and even *auditores* could be called upon to give collations, so it may be inferred that they played a significant part in the training of young preachers" (p. 155). He adds that "there is evidence that university collations were regularly given at the Paris houses of both the Dominicans and the Franciscans" (p. 156).

42. *Coll. in Hex.* 1.1 (5:329a).

where he should begin, and where he should end."[43] The first three collations then go on to explain in detail that the "prudent man," namely, the preacher, should address the members of the church, that his speech should be centered on Christ, who is the source of all knowledge, and that the goal of his speech should be the multiform wisdom present in the scriptures and the understanding that comes through the illumination of the threefold Word. This illumination takes the form of six visions, and it is this series of visions that provides the organizing principle for the collations that follow. According to Bonaventure's original plan, the collations were to cover the visions of the understanding as illumined by nature, faith, scripture, contemplation, prophecy, and rapture, all in the form of a commentary on the account of creation given in Genesis. In fact Bonaventure discussed only the first four, the series being broken off when he was made a cardinal on May 28, 1273.

No attempt will be made here to summarize the contents of the twenty-three collations that Bonaventure did manage to give. What is important here is the evidence that they provide for his own involvement with the tradition of prophecy. On the one hand, they provide ample evidence of the historical and apocalyptic orientation of Bonaventure's thought, an orientation due in part to the influence of Joachim of Fiore or his followers. On the other hand, the *Collations* can themselves be interpreted as a form of prophetic utterance, especially in their presentation of the significance of St. Francis. More than anywhere else, here Bonaventure himself speaks the language of prophecy.

In order to understand this prophetic character of the *Collations,* one must view them within their historical context and in the light of Bonaventure's assessment of this context. In Bonaventure's view, his age was an age of crisis. We have already noted his assessment of the abuses present in the contemporary church, and the role of the friars in correcting some of these. To this must be added the crisis that Bonaventure believed had been triggered by the entrance of Aristotelian metaphysics into the scripturally based symbolic worldview of the medieval church. Most importantly in the present context, he saw clearly that Aristotle's denial of the Platonic doctrine of exemplarism struck at the very heart of what we have called his metaphysics of revelation, and thus by extension it called into question what for him was the very foundation of the Christian religion: the self-revelation of the Word. Bonaventure had openly criticized selected Aristotelian teachings in two earlier series of collations, first in

43. Ibid.

1267 in his *Collationes de Decem Praeceptis,* and again in 1268 in his *Collationes de Donis Spiritus Sancti.*[44] There he had singled out three errors: the doctrines of the eternity of the world, of the necessity of fate, and of the unity of the intellect.[45] In the *Collations on the Six Days,* however, he traces these errors to their source: the denial of exemplarism.[46] It is not by chance that his most forceful presentation of the centrality of Christ the Exemplar and of his metaphysics of expressionism rooted in the threefold Word should be found in the opening collations of this work, immediately prior to an extended critique of various aspects of the new philosophy. Nor was it by chance that Bonaventure chose to organize his entire series of sermons around the theme of the illuminations of the inspired Word, since it was precisely the doctrine of illumination that was called into question by the Aristotelian notion of a self-sufficient intellect. Part of the prophetic quality of these collations is thus due to this defense of the spiritual illumination of the Word, the *sine qua non* of all revelation, against a form of thought that Bonaventure believed would render such an experience unintelligible.

The *Collations* are prophetic in a more specific sense, however, and it is here that they reveal the influence of Joachim of Fiore, both his theology of history and the theory of scriptural interpretation that is inseparable from it. They first appear in the *Collations* in Bonaventure's discussion of the third vision, namely, that of the understanding based upon scripture. In his first collation on this vision, he explains that the understanding of scripture takes three forms: the traditional spiritual senses, the sacramental figures (which are essentially types of Christ and the anti-Christ), and what he calls the multiform theories (*multiformes theoriae*).[47] The latter are distinctive in being virtually unlimited in number and are symbolized by the seeds mentioned in Genesis 1:12: "Who can know the infinity of seeds, since in one seed there might be forests of forests, and consequently an infinite number of seeds? Similarly one can elicit infinite theories from scripture, which God alone can understand."[48] When Bonaventure comes to describe these *theoriae* in more detail, he notes their connection with history. The "germination" of these seeds of understanding latent in scripture "gives understanding of diverse *theoriae*

44. For a brief overview of the development of Bonaventure's anti-Aristotelianism, see Joseph Ratzinger, *The Theology of History of St. Bonaventure* (Chicago: Franciscan Herald Press, 1971), pp. 134–63.
45. See *Coll. de Donis S. S.* 8.16 (5:497b).
46. See *Coll. in Hex.* 6.2 (5:360b).
47. *Coll. in Hex.* 13.2 (5:388a).
48. Ibid.

according to the comparison of diverse times; one who is ignorant of history (*tempora*) cannot understand those *theoriae*.... Thus the knowledge of the future depends upon the knowledge of the past."[49] The comparison of diverse times mentioned here refers primarily to the comparison of the stages of Old Testament history with stages in the ongoing historical development of the church, as Bonaventure soon makes clear. After briefly summarizing the traditional Augustinian theory of the seven ages of the church, running from Adam to the end of the world, Bonaventure introduces an alternative scheme, one that he obviously prefers and that derives not from Augustine but from Joachim:

> Again, that which comes forth is compared to that from which it arises, as a tree to the seed from which it arises, and to the tree from which that seed arises. Similarly the New Testament is compared to the Old as a tree to a tree, a letter to a letter, or a seed to a seed. And as a tree [arises from] a tree, a seed from a seed, and a letter from a letter, so [one] testament arises from [the other] testament.[50]

He then goes on to delineate several ways in which such a comparison of the two testaments can be carried out. By far the most important schema of comparison is the one based on the number seven, developed at length in the following collation.[51] Bonaventure describes seven ages of the Old Testament: from Adam to Noah, Noah to Abraham, Abraham to Moses, Moses to Samuel, David to Ezekiel, Ezekiel to Zorobabel, and Zorobabel to Christ.[52] To these seven ages correspond the seven ages of the New Testament. The first five are clearly identified: from Christ to Clement I, Clement I to Silvester, Silvester to Leo I, Leo I to Gregory I, and Gregory I to Hadrian I.[53] The sixth age begins with Hadrian I (772–95) and is described as a time of "clear doctrine." Bonaventure is unwilling to say exactly how long it will last, but it is clear that he believes that he himself is living in it and that it is to be an age of crisis:

> But how long it will last, who can say, or has said? It is certain that we are now in it. It is also certain that it will last until the casting out of the "beast ascending from the abyss," when Babylon will be

49. Ibid., 15.11 (5:400a).
50. *Coll. in Hex.* 15.22 (5:401ab).
51. See ibid., 16.11–31 (5:405–8).
52. Ibid., 16.17 (5:405b–406a).
53. Ibid., 16.18 (5:406a).

> confounded and cast down, and afterward peace will be granted. But first it is necessary that tribulation should come.[54]

Elsewhere Bonaventure describes the political fortunes of the church in the sixth age — his own — and places the whole into an apocalyptic context:

> Similarly, at that time Charles [Charlemagne] exalted the church and his successors fought against it: at the time of Henry IV there were two popes, similarly at the time of Frederick the Great there were two. And it is certain that one of them wanted to exterminate the church. "But an angel, ascending from the rising of the sun, cried to the four angels: Do not harm the earth or the sea until we have signed the servants of our God on their foreheads" [Rev. 7:2–3]. Thus the tribulation of the church remains until now. And the angel of Philadelphia, who was the sixth [of the angels of the seven churches], was told, "Thus says the Holy One, the True One, who has the key of David; who opens and no one closes; who closes and no one opens. I know your works, for behold, I have placed before you an open door" [Rev. 3:7]. And he [i.e., Bonaventure] said that now for the first time the understanding of scripture, either revelation or the key of David, will be given to a person or to a multitude, and I believe more probably to a multitude.[55]

To the crisis of Aristotelian philosophy Bonaventure here adds the attacks on the church on the part of Charlemagne's successors. But not all of the "signs of the times" were negative. We know from references in Bonaventure's life of St. Francis,[56] as well as from other references in the *Collations* themselves,[57] that Bonaventure's reference here to the "angel ascending from the rising of the sun" of Revelation 7:2 refers to St. Francis. Thus what Bonaventure is doing here is employing a Joachite method of scriptural exegesis to give an apocalyptic interpretation of his own times, and most especially of St. Francis. It is unlikely that this apocalyptic interpretation of St. Francis originated with Bonaventure himself. He may have borrowed it from his predecessor as Minister General, John of Parma. Bernard McGinn has suggested that John may have been the

54. Ibid., 16.19 (5:406a).
55. Ibid., 16.29 (5:408).
56. See *Legenda Sancti Francisci, Prologus* 1 (8:504b), and 13.10 (8:545b).
57. See Ratzinger, *Theology of History,* pp. 24–55.

one primarily responsible for the dissemination of the "three classical themes of Franciscan Joachitism," which included not only this identification of Francis with the angel of the seal, but also the identification of the Franciscans and Dominicans with the two orders of *viri spirituales* predicted by Joachim and the specification of poverty as the unique mark of these "spiritual men."[58] At any rate it is clear that Bonaventure is here engaged in an act of "prophecy by interpretation," just as Joachim had been. Through his identification of Francis with the angel of the sixth seal in John's Apocalypse he is placing his own historical present firmly within an apocalyptic context, as a time both of tribulation and of hope. That hope is represented by the figure of St. Francis, the "herald of the Great King," who as both preacher and prophet heralded a new age of spiritual understanding — a new age of revelation — which, though not yet actual, lay just beyond the present strife.

Bonaventure resisted the temptation to identify the actual Franciscan order — of which he was the Minister General — with the new contemplative order of *viri spirituales* proleptically present in St. Francis. This is clear from his discussion of the contemplative orders of the church in his twenty-second collation. He identifies the friars — both Dominicans and Franciscans — with the order of the Cherubim, who occupy a position midway between the old monastic orders on the one hand, and on the other a future Seraphic order, to which Francis himself belonged but which could not be identified with certainty in the present situation: "This is the Seraphic order. It seems that Francis belonged to it. [. . .] But what this order is to be, or already is, is hard to know."[59]

Bonaventure, both preacher and prophet, thus left his audience with a warning of present dangers and a hope of future victory. Appropriately, this future was to be characterized by a plenitude of revelation. It was to be a time when all Christians would lead a common *vita prophetica;* a time of *revelatio,* when the illumination of the *verbum inspiratum* would bring Christians to a knowledge of all truth, through a deeper, spiritual understanding of scripture.

This apocalyptic vision of a future plenitude of revelation did not blind Bonaventure to the active presence of revelation in the present, however. It is significant that the *Collations on the Six Days* bear the subtitle "Illuminations of the Church." We saw in an earlier chapter that Bona-

58. See Bernard McGinn, "Apocalyptic Traditions and Spiritual Identity in Thirteenth-Century Religious Life," in *The Roots of the Modern Christian Tradition,* ed. E. Rozanne Elder (Kalamazoo, Mich.: Cistercian Publications, 1984), p. 9.

59. Ibid., 22.22 (5:440–41). See Ratzinger, *Theology of History,* pp. 39–55.

venture took the hierarchical mediation of revelation seriously. Unlike the more radical Franciscan Spirituals who predicted an end of the institutional church, Bonaventure saw the hierarchical structure of the church as an expression (in the strict sense of *expressio*) of the hierarchical action of the Spirit itself. If this Spirit inspired prophecies of the future, it did this through the mediation of the spiritual interpretation of scripture. Scripture, in turn, could be interpreted correctly only by the "hierarchical soul" who spoke "in the midst of the church."[60] It is again significant that one of Bonaventure's most detailed discussions of this hierarchical mediation comes toward the end of these *Collations,* where he discusses the vision lifted up in contemplation. We examined this section of the *Collations* earlier and there is no need to repeat that discussion here. It is sufficient to recall the intimate connection between Bonaventure's concept of hierarchy, borrowed from pseudo-Dionysius, and his metaphysics of expressionism, both of which are integral parts of his metaphysics of revelation. It was the notion of hierarchy, in particular, that provided the metaphysical foundation for the mediation of the individual soul and the objective structures of the church in the process of revelation. We have now seen that Bonaventure wishes to combine this hierarchical, social, and anagogical model of the revelatory process with the historical, prophetic, and apocalyptic model that he inherited from Joachim (and from the tradition of Christian apocalypticism in general). In fact, these two models were never really separate. The historical component of Bonaventure's metaphysics of revelation is rooted in the event-character of revelation itself. In the light of the foregoing discussions in the present chapter, however, it is clear that it is the concrete language of revelation that provides the key to these multiple mediations of the metaphysical and the historical, the social and the individual. It is through the process of interpretation that the individual finds a place within the historical and social reality of the church, and it is through this same process that the objective structures of history and society are redeemed from their mere externality in order to become objective moments of this fundamental revelatory activity. Furthermore, it is through the prophetic and apocalyptic interpretation of scripture that the present situation of both the individual and the community is related to the unfolding drama of the history of salvation. In the *Collations* we see all these themes brought together in a *tour de force* of spiritual and symbolic exegesis in which the languages of scripture, preaching, and prophecy are united in a single, complex event:

60. *Coll. in Hex.* 1.1 (5:329a).

Bonaventure's actual speech to his fellow friars at Paris in the Spring of 1273, in which he bore witness to the manifold illuminations of the Word—uncreated, incarnate, and inspired—the source of all revelation.

CONCLUSION

This brief discussion of Bonaventure's own involvement with the language of prophecy must bring our examination of his thought and practice to a close. Before turning to the comparison that awaits us in the next chapter, however, a brief review of our rather lengthy examination of Bonaventure's view of Christian revelation is in order.

We began with an examination of Bonaventure's sophisticated metaphysics of revelation, centered on his notion of the threefold Word, and in particular on the illumination of the *verbum inspiratum,* the inspired Word. Here we saw an elaborate theology of the Word that represents a kind of scholastic counterpart to the Logos-theology of the early Apologists. We then moved from metaphysics to history, and examined Bonaventure's views of revelation, not as a metaphysical possibility, but as a historical actuality. It was here that we became progressively more aware of Bonaventure's view of the actual event of revelation as a dynamic, dialectical process, a process of interpretation that includes not only the illumination of the *verbum inspiratum,* but the objective mediation of history as well, ultimately the history of the *verbum incarnatum,* the Word incarnate in Jesus Christ and in the community of his followers, the church. These two sides of Bonaventure's view of revelation, the metaphysical and the historical, were seen to be complementary rather than opposed. It was his elaborate metaphysics of expressionism and exemplarity and his anthropology focused on the *imago Dei* that prepared the ground for a fundamentally historical understanding of revelation and its reception as *event.* It was the series of such revelatory events, especially as recorded in the history of prophecy culminating in the Incarnation, that for Bonaventure constituted salvation history, which was as well a history of revelation.

Finally we turned to the actual language that mediates the process of revelation. We saw that the three forms of this language, scripture, preaching, and prophecy, remained fundamental to his actual reception of revelation in the thirteenth century. In particular, it was the language of scripture that provided the basis for the interpretative process through which revelation continued to become actual, both through preaching and, at times, through prophecy. Finally, we saw how all three of these forms of the language of revelation interacted in his masterpiece of spiritual exegesis, the *Collations on the Six Days.*

The question remains: how integrated are all these elements of Bonaventure's thought and practice? We have already argued that his metaphysics of revelation, far from standing in opposition to the actual history of revelation, in fact gave the latter a heightened intelligibility, as grounded in an anthropology of finite human being, which in turn was grounded in the exemplarity and dynamic self-expressiveness of the divine Word. But what of Bonaventure's actual involvement with the language of revelation, as an exegete, a preacher, and — in some sense — a prophet? It is precisely here that we seem to find the most intimate relationship between his theory and his actual practice, although in making this explicit we are to an extent going beyond what he explicitly tells us. It is language that for Bonaventure provides the necessary mediation for the process of revelation. It is the concrete language of scripture, especially as actualized in preaching and prophecy, that mediates the inner witness of the *verbum inspiratum* and the objective witness of both the *verbum increatum* in the created order and the *verbum incarnatum* in Jesus Christ and his church. The dialectical, interpretative process that we have found to lie at the heart of Bonaventure's understanding of revelation becomes actual only through language. There is an implicit rhetoric of revelation in Bonaventure's thought that finds expression in the intimate connection he finds between illumination, scripture, and preaching. It is in the person of the speaker, the *rhetor,* speaking through the inspiration of the Spirit *in medio Ecclesiae,* that Bonaventure finally locates the actuality of revelation as event. And it is his metaphysics of revelation, rooted in the expressiveness of the threefold Word, that gives this event, with its dialectical moments of inner illumination and socio-linguistic mediation within a concrete historical setting, its deepest significance.

As was the case with Bhartṛhari, then, for Bonaventure there is an inseparable connection between the objective mediation of revelation through language, used in a well-defined social and institutional context, and its reception by the individual as a form of illumination. Revelation becomes actual through the proclamation of the appropriate person (an ordained member of the clergy), within the appropriate social context (the church), and when grounded in the appropriate form of language (the language of the scriptures, typically available only in Latin for those able to read it). It must be noted that for Bonaventure, just as much as for Bhartṛhari, the world as disclosed, indeed constituted, by revelation is a seamless, hierarchically arranged totality in which he, again like Bhartṛhari, found himself quite well located (he died a cardinal, after all). For all the elegance of their systems, our appreciation of them must be tempered by a few critical observations. Thus, looking back over the overall shape of Bonaventure's theology of the Word, one cannot help but note not only the architectonic rigor, indeed the beauty, of the system, but also its potentially oppressive quality. The Word casts its Light into the world, but thereby also casts its shadow. For revelation to require for its mediation the objective forms of concrete historical, linguistic, and social existence is to integrate them into a cohesive and unifying vision and to safeguard revelation itself from being reduced to the level of a merely individual, interior experience. But it is equally to root revelation in the real world of human affairs with all its ambiguity. Thus the thirteenth century was not only the century of Bonaventure's cohesive Christocentric vision of Christendom but also a century that saw the continuation of the Crusades abroad and the Albigensian crusade at home — a particularly unfortunate manifestation of the unity of Christendom — and the rise of the Inquisition, set to root out those who could not be made to fit within the normative order. Revelation itself, as a concrete phenomenon, begins to display a potential ambivalence. We will have to return to this more shadowy side of the "Light of the Word" in our concluding chapter. At present, however, it is time to move on to the comparison of our two thinkers. How do they differ, how do they agree, and what are we to make of it?

PART III

Comparing Bhartṛhari and Bonaventure

8

Bhartṛhari and Bonaventure in Comparison

In the previous chapters we have examined the phenomenon of revelation as we find it represented by Bhartṛhari, a major figure in the early classical Brahmanism of India, and by St. Bonaventure, one of the most illustrious Christian theologians of the Western Middle Ages. The attempt has been made to present each thinker in his own proper historical and intellectual context. We have examined the major features of their theories of revelation and we have considered their views on the reception of revelation as they encountered it in their respective contexts. The time has come, however, to lay the two studies side by side and compare them. This is the task of the present chapter.

In comparing Bhartṛhari's and Bonaventure's ideas and, to the extent possible, their practice, we will attempt to discern — and respect — *both* what they and their respective traditions have in common and what divides them. It is often forgotten that *both* similarity and difference are intrinsic to the very idea of comparability. There is a strong temptation to privilege either similarities, seeking some common essence while dismissing all differences as inessential, or to do the reverse, finding only difference, and judging all "apparent" similarities to be either illusory or at best superficial and uninteresting. But neither the strictly identical nor the utterly diverse can be meaningfully compared. Only where there is an interplay of similarity and difference can comparison be fruitful. What is important is not to assign a privileged status to one or the other, but to understand the significance of each as we find it. What then are the specific points of similarity and difference that appear when the two studies are laid side by side? We will attempt to answer this question in the present chapter. Having compared, we will have to reflect, in the following chapter, upon the significance of the comparison.

THEORY

The initial focus of the preceding studies was on Bhartṛhari's and Bonaventure's theories of revelation, both the metaphysical conditions for the possibility of revelation and their respective theoretical representations of revelation as they found it within their own traditions. To this was then added, in each case, a consideration of the specific practices involved in the reception of revelation or, more accurately, the practices involved in the reception of the language by which revelation is mediated. In comparing these two studies we will begin at the level of their explicitly formulated theories of revelation and then move on to consider the more practical issue of reception. In order to structure the first portion of our comparison we will focus initially on four specific issues: their respective views on the source of revelation, the event of revelation, revelation's recipient, and the content of revelation.

The Source of Revelation

For Bhartṛhari, the source of revelation is Brahman, the absolute principle that is the ground of, and in some sense not different from, phenomenal existence. In the earliest Vedic tradition the term *bráhman* meant "sacred speech," and this meaning is preserved in Bhartṛhari's representation of Brahman as *Śabdatattva,* or the True Word. Brahman is the power that underlies all existence and that becomes manifest in speech. The ultimate source of revelation is thus not strictly speaking a "revealer," in the sense of a personal agent, but rather is the intrinsic luminosity of ultimate reality that is reflected in the order or *dharma* of the manifest world, and in dharmic speech in particular. For Bonaventure, by contrast, the source of revelation is understood to be a personal God for whom revelation is a free volitional act. This God is distinct from the world and is free to enter into a variety of relationships with it (or to break off such relationships).

True, both thinkers focus on the ultimate source of revelation, specifically in its character as Word, whether the True Word of Bhartṛhari or the second Person of the Trinity for Bonaventure. In each case revelation as an actual event in the world is rooted in the dynamic, self-expressive character of ultimate Reality itself. This is an important point of agreement that should not be underestimated. But here the resemblance ends. Bonaventure's elaborate trinitarian theology is designed to solve a problem that Bhartṛhari did not face. In harmony with his tradition, Bonaventure sought to present revelation as a voluntary action on the part of a personal God and to account for the person of Jesus of Nazareth, who was asserted to be the "son" of that God. He accomplished this by means of his distinction of a threefold Word, *increatum, incarnatum, et inspiratum.* Bhartṛhari, on the other hand, was concerned to provide a more sophisticated account of the insight of the ancient seers into the primordial unity of world and language and to account for both the transcendent ground of this unity and for the immanence of that ground in the world of time and space. He accomplished this through his doctrine of the True Word and its powers (*śakti*-s). We find then an intriguing similarity in their common view of reality as dynamic and self-expressive, as a reality that "overflows" (due to the Father's primacy or unbegottenness), or "shines forth" (due to the True Word's intrinsic luminosity), but quite different views of the specific character of this self-expressive activity. Bonaventure accepts the traditional Christian notion of creation *ex nihilo* and of a creator deity that is fundamentally other than creation. Bhartṛhari approaches the problem of the relation between Brahman and the world from a non-dual perspective that leaves no place for a distinct creator, nor for a "creature" in the Christian sense of the word. Behind their differences on the source of revelation lie two very different worldviews.

The Event of Revelation

Perhaps the most striking difference in Bhartṛhari's and Bonaventure's views of the original event of revelation is that for the former it is primordial and closely associated with the cosmic process of the cyclical manifestation and absorption of the universe, whereas for the latter revelation reaches its fullest form in a historical individual. For Bhartṛhari the act of revelation cannot be separated from the act of creation, or "world-construction," through sacrifice. Revelation takes place *in illo tempore,* and each subsequent revelatory event in principle participates in this original time. For Bonaventure, on the other hand, creation and revelation, though intimately related, can in principle be distinguished and in fact are chronologically distinct. Although incarnation and redemption may be viewed as a form of "re-creation" or as the re-establishment of the primordial order of creation, the temporal distance that separates creation and revelation cannot be erased.

Thus while Bonaventure represents past events of revelation as having an important historical dimension, Bhartṛhari places emphasis on the seers' visions of the essentially timeless structures of *dharma.* And while both thinkers view revelation as a socially mediated event, Bonaventure locates such social mediation in the context of a "history of salvation," a history of the interactions between God and human beings. Bhartṛhari, by contrast, locates it within the (for him) immutable structures of dharmic, Brahmanical society, themselves viewed against a cosmological backdrop.

There are similarities as well, however. Both view the event of revelation as being characterized by both immediacy and intensity. Both the inspiration and illumination by the *verbum inspiratum* of prophets or apostles and the vision of the True Word by the seers are characterized by a spontaneity that betokens the objective reality of the event. Just as *pratibhā* arises of itself, "without effort," so too the inspiration of the prophet comes from outside and is independent of the virtue (or lack of virtue) of the prophet himself. Both prophet and seer are believed to encounter ultimate reality directly, however different those encounters and that reality may be.

The Recipient of Revelation

From what has been said already it is clear that the original recipients of revelation must also be quite different in many respects. In Bhartṛhari's view, the Vedic *ṛṣi*-s were not so much historical human beings as characters in a cosmogonic myth who were present *in illo tempore* and who were the first to proclaim the hymns and perform the rites of Vedic society. The *śiṣṭa*-s of later times were members of an elite group within Brahmanical society and took their name — *Brāhmaṇa*-s — from the original name of the holy speech that they embodied, the *bráhman.* As a closed, hereditary group of specialists they also had a very specific audience, namely, the other "twice-born" members of Brahmanical society, i.e., those who were allowed to participate in the ritual life of the community. By contrast, Bonaventure viewed the early Christian apostles as independent of such a closed group, with an intended audience that was in principle unrestricted. Their status as recipients of revelation was based upon vocation rather than on birth. The contrast is less clear if we consider the preachers of Bonaventure's own day, however. The evolution of the hierarchical church, operating within a hierarchical social context, produced conditions that were in many ways similar to the Brahmanical social order of Bhartṛhari's India. Preaching came to be a right restricted to the bishops and those explicitly designated by them, and to presume to preach the gospel merely because one felt called to it could land one in serious trouble. This is a fate that might conceivably have overtaken St. Francis himself, had he shown less deference to the established church. The fact remains, however, that a figure like Francis could be taken by Bonaventure as an exemplar of the Christian preacher rather than as an anomaly. In theory at least, the preacher, as a spokesman for the transcendent divine will, enjoyed a degree of independence vis-à-vis the actual social and political order, whereas the Brahmanical *śiṣṭa* was the very embodiment of such order.

Clearly there is a difference of anthropology operative here. The concept of vocation is correlated with a certain conception of the human person as one capable of entering into a "dialogue" with a personal God. This highly differentiated notion of the individual person, which is a correlate of the notion of a personal God, has no place in Bhartṛhari's conception of the *ṛṣi* and *śiṣṭa.* The *ṛṣi*-s, as just noted, represent formal moments within a cyclical cosmic process. As for the *śiṣṭa,* while being recognizable as a normal human being, he does not "speak for" Brahman; he is not commissioned as the latter's messenger. He is rather *born* a Brahmin, as one who is "of" Brahman and who is never wholly distinguished from the absolute ground that he brings to speech. Brahman is simply not something *to* or *for* which one would speak, and the *śiṣṭa* is not such a "spokesman" or witness. His speech rather *manifests* Brahman to the extent that it is "dharmic," i.e., to the extent that it conforms to the immanent cosmic, moral, and social order of which the *śiṣṭa* is properly an embodiment.

Finally, the fact that Bhartṛhari makes no use of a highly differentiated notion of the individual subject vis-à-vis a radically transcendent God means that he will also have no need for the closely connected concept of the necessity of grace in the reception of revelation that we find in Bonaventure. Rather than a sharp break between the divine and the human that can be overcome only by the divine initiative of grace, for Bhartṛhari the divine, or rather the absolute, Brahman encompasses the human as a moment within itself. The emphasis is on continuity, and differences are differences of degree rather than of kind. Bhartṛhari's anthropological presuppositions are clearly quite different from Bonaventure's. As a matter of fact, strictly speaking we find nothing that we could label a distinct "anthropology" anywhere in Bhartṛhari's work. One might rather speak of a "grammar" of the temporal manifestation of the True Word that takes into account the limited role of human agency in this more encompassing process.

If Bhartṛhari and Bonaventure differ rather markedly in their views of the specific recipient of revelation, however, there remains a deep underlying similarity in the way they view the recipient's capacity for revelation or, perhaps we should say, his or her *need* for it. Though they may account for the fact in very different ways, both of our thinkers view the world as a whole as a changing and unstable place. Both Bhartṛhari's notion of the *śakti*-s of Brahman that account for the manifestation of the world as a dynamic system of ever-changing events and Bonaventure's interpretation of the Christian doctrine of creation *ex nihilo* place emphasis on the mutable character of all finite existence, including human existence. For both, then, revelation becomes a necessity if one is to be able to move beyond the uncertainties of the mind dependent upon the witness of the senses, restricted to mere *ratio,* or to what Bhartṛhari calls "dry reason," and know a salvific truth, be it a vision of the True Word or the spiritual illumination of the Inspired Word. Both thinkers thus place a strong emphasis on the dependence of the human knower on a higher source of wisdom and relate this dependence to an encompassing view of the instability of worldly existence.

The Content of Revelation

We saw that the content of Vedic revelation according to Bhartṛhari is *dharma,* an order that is at once cosmic, moral, and social, and the unitary ground of this manifest order, Brahman. In some respects Bonaventure's view of the content of revelation is quite similar. For him revelation involves hierarchy, the order by which all aspects of the world, the universe itself, the church, the individual soul, are conformed to their divine Maker. *Dharma* too can be seen to involve a hierarchy, the hierarchy of caste that is believed to replicate a hierarchy in nature and the closely related hierarchy of the ritual system. But the ultimate ground of the two hierarchies is, as we have seen, quite different in each case. There is a great deal of difference between Bhartṛhari's notion of Brahman and Bonaventure's notion of the triune God. To the extent that either is taken to be the ultimate content of revelation, that content varies quite markedly.

But revelation for Bonaventure has another important content, in some ways its most important content, for which there is no real counterpart in Bhartṛhari. Bonaventure's notion of revelation embraces the historical order conceived as a unique and non-reversible development. It is the divine plan of history, known from all eternity by the transcendent and personal God of apocalyptic thought, that forms the most prominent content of revelation as Bonaventure conceives it. And the centerpiece of this plan, the incarnation of the Word in the person of Jesus of Nazareth, provides an individual content to revelation that is foreign to Bhartṛhari's way of thinking. While there is certainly a cosmic dimension to Bonaventure's understanding of revelation, even a highly pronounced one, it is nevertheless true that the most decisive content of revelation is made known through the expression of God's will in the events of history rather than through the synchronic order of cosmos and society.

More could be said about specific points of divergence or convergence in the way that our two thinkers represent revelation. On the level of representation, at least, the differences are quite striking. On each issue, source, event, recipient, and content, we discover individual brush strokes of a similar color or style, but they are painted on two very different canvases and they form a very different picture. The ways in which they choose to represent the phenomenon of revelation as it is known to them from their traditions diverge in ways that reveal their respective traditions' different presuppositions about the nature of the supreme being or absolute, the nature of the world, the relation between these two (if, indeed, there *are* "two"), and the nature of the human person within that world. I take these differences in the *representation* of revelation to be major, and of major importance. But both Bhartṛhari and Bonaventure presented us with more than representations of revelation. They also provided us with their views on the reception of the language of revelation in the concrete. We must turn to these next.

RECEPTION

The Language of Revelation

When we begin to focus less on Bhartṛhari's and Bonaventure's theories and more upon their reception of the concrete language of revelation within their own historical contexts, important differences persist, but we also begin to notice more important similarities. We will examine these similarities below, but first let's note the differences.

The major differences in their respective views of the language of revelation are closely linked to the differences between the two social worlds they inhabited. Bhartṛhari's society was not a specifically religious society, not a "church" dramatically created by grace within a larger, fallen world. Brahmanical society and its language represented the social aspect of the unique dharmic order, rooted in the equally unique revelation of the Veda. Status within this society was largely a consequence of birth and was as religious as it was social. It was not the consequence of a specifically religious vocation such as inspired Bonaventure to enter the Franciscan order in 1243. Unlike the New Testament, the Veda, which stood at the heart of Bhartṛhari's society, originated not from the texts of a small sectarian community defining its identity against the pluralistic background of a more powerful and occasionally hostile imperial rule, but out of the inspired martial hymns and ritual lore of a combative people who spoke the language of the gods, a people who remind us more of the early Israelite tribes than of the early Christians. In such an environment the language of revelation remained closely tied to the social and religious order, and this continued to be true in Bhartṛhari's time. Markedly unlike the early Christian writings, it was not important that the language of Vedic revelation attain the ideality of a text through a process of "distanciation," so well described by Paul Ricoeur in regard to the Christian scriptures.[1] It was not necessary, or even desirable, to convey meanings across social and cultural boundaries. Unlike the "religions of the Book," the religion of ancient India was not to be a "world religion," but a religion restricted to a particular group inhabiting a particular place. The language of revelation accordingly served to convey the practices appropriate to a specific community rather than a religious message intended for the world at large. Thus this language and the society that produced it could coalesce in the actual *praxis* of the religious elite, the Brahmins, those "living Vedas" whose speech made present, moment by moment, the spiritual power of the True Word. Unlike Bonaventure's scriptures, the Veda was never primarily a text: it remained essentially an *activity.*

This is reflected in Bhartṛhari's thoroughly practical view of the language of revelation as a form of *dharma* and in his remarkable lack of interest — and near scepticism — concerning its referential functions. The language of revelation is more what it *does* than what it says, and as a grammarian Bhartṛhari was responsible for maintaining the "correctness" of Vedic speech, not its message. By contrast, we saw that for Bonaventure revelation finds its appropriate linguistic form as scripture, literally as something written, and more precisely in the form of a book. Indeed, Bonaventure made abundant use of the image of a book in order to refer to creation as an intelligible whole. The "book of creation" (*liber creaturae, liber mundi*), composed by the divine Author, is given its definitive interpretation through the book of scripture (*liber scripturae*). He viewed the language of scripture primarily as a form of narrative: it has a story to tell; it is meant to convey some meaning. Furthermore, this meaning has a strong historical component, since it includes the whole sweep of salvation history, culminating in the incarnation and in particular the history

1. See Paul Ricoeur, "The Hermeneutical Function of Distanciation," in *Hermeneutics and the Human Sciences* (Cambridge: Cambridge University Press, 1981), pp. 131–44.

of Jesus and the apostles. It is particularly this latter narrative, the description of the *vita apostolica,* that constitutes the message of scripture that Bonaventure attempted to bring to life in his preaching and that he brought to bear *over and against* the social and religious status quo. The notion of a book of scripture that narrates the totality of history is an idea wholly foreign to Bhartṛhari's conception of the Veda. Equally foreign is the critical function of scripture that is made possible by the "ideality" of the text. The normative function of the Veda and of the norms of Pāṇini's grammar were maintained only through the *praxis* of contemporary Brahmins, the "living Vedas." The distanciation created by writing had no place in the transmission of the sacred speech.

It is in the light of this difference between viewing the language of revelation primarily as itself a form of *dharma* or viewing it as a signifying narrative with an objective meaning that we must understand one of the major differences between Bhartṛhari and Bonaventure as students of the language of revelation. Bhartṛhari was a *grammarian;* for him the Sanskrit language, since it was uniquely rooted in the inspired speech of the original seers, was *itself* revelation. It was the True Word become manifest under the conditions of time. No more than the True Word signified something beyond itself did the language of revelation signify some revealed "object" other than itself. *Śabda* is both *vācaka* and *vācya,* both expressive and that which is expressed (or, as Bonaventure would say, both *expressiva* and *expressa*). Bonaventure, on the other hand, was a theologian. For him an interest in the Word and an interest in words were only contingently related. In his mind the medium was *not* the message. The language of revelation was not itself the *revelatum,* but only a means of signifying it. As a theologian, Bonaventure was interested in a *Logos* that was in principle independent of any particular language or grammar.

But even here we can discern important parallels. Both Bhartṛhari and Bonaventure view the language of revelation as essentially *practical.* It is there to be *used.* Both agree in viewing the original expression of revelation as an enactment of a vision or illumination through the mediation of language. This can be seen in their theories of the visionary experience and its expression in speech. Bhartṛhari's theory of this process centers on his notion of *pratibhā,* the "intuition" or spontaneous insight that is the basis of all speech-acts and that, as a kind of "instinct" or "moral sense," shows one how to act in a particular situation. We saw that the light that shines forth in *pratibhā* is the light of the True Word itself and that this illumination is as much practical or "moral" as cognitive. Indeed, just as Bonaventure explicitly contrasts the knowledge possible through the discursive intellect, or *ratio,* with that received through the illumination of the *intellectus,* so Bhartṛhari contrasts the knowledge received through the insight of *pratibhā* with the "dry reasoning," or *tarka.* The language of revelation, as grounded in such illumination, shares this fundamentally practical character. It is in this way that Bhartṛhari gives an account of the fundamental character of the language of revelation as a form of *dharma.* Accordingly, those who transmit this language to the community, the *śiṣṭa*-s, must be those characterized by *sadācāra,* "good actions." Bonaventure's notion of spiritual illumination is equally practical in nature. As an experience it presupposes the proper moral disposition of the will. This same moral qualification is evident in its expression, since Bonaventure echoes his tradition in affirming that the language of revelation must be proclaimed *verbo et exemplo,* not only in words, but also through the example that the preacher presents through his actions. For both Bhartṛhari and Bonaventure, then, the language of revelation is in the final analysis inseparable from the process of its transmission and from those persons of vision who engage in this process, whether they are *śiṣṭa*-s or preachers. Both are the moral representatives of their respective traditions, not unlike the "characters" described by Alasdair MacIntyre, who embody the moral and metaphysical ideas of their communities.[2] Even Bonaventure's emphasis on the narrative mode of scripture, so different from Bhartṛhari's emphasis on sacred speech, is motivated by his belief in the essentially practical and moral character of the language of revelation. For Bonaventure scripture should have the practical effect of facilitating a spiritual transformation of the individual, which is accomplished more effectively through the language of narrative, with its wealth of *exempla,* than through the language of doctrine. Similarly, for both Bonaventure and Bhartṛhari the language of revelation forms the necessary medium for the religious *praxis* of the community, whether this be the preservation of *dharma* or the imitation of the life of the apostles. As different as the actual form of the language of revelation is in each case, whether sacred speech or holy scripture, and as different as the specific social contexts of its employment may be, there is therefore an interesting similarity in the manner in which it is actually employed in the community as living speech and action. The comparative study of the language of revelation reveals, amid fundamental differences, a similar structure

2. See Alasdair MacIntyre, *After Virtue* (Notre Dame, Ind.: University of Notre Dame Press, 1981), p. 27, who writes that "characters" are "the moral representatives of their culture and they are so because of the way in which moral and metaphysical ideas and theories assume through them an embodied existence in the social world."

that is the structure not of revelation as an *object,* but of revelation as a *process* mediated through language. This dynamic aspect of revelation as a process merits further examination. We will examine it from two perspectives, first as a process within history and second as a process within the individual recipient of revelation.

Revelation in the Dynamics of History

Both Bhartṛhari and Bonaventure lived well after the canonical process in their respective traditions had produced a distinct body of language that was recognized as authoritative by the community. In Bhartṛhari's case this was the Veda, or *śruti;* in Bonaventure's, it was the Christian Bible. Even after the establishment of a canonical form of language, however, the ongoing community had still to preserve it, transmit it, and, most importantly, make *use* of it.

In India the story of continued employment of the language of Vedic revelation in the post-Vedic period was the story of the adaptation of the "divine speech," as a form of *dharma,* to the changed circumstances brought on by the collapse of the early Brahmanical social and political order. The Buddhist critique of the Vedic tradition and subsequent centuries of Buddhist influence necessitated fundamental revisions in Brahmanical theory and practice. On the level of theory the Brahmanical response to the Buddhist emphasis on a direct experience of *dharma* took two quite different directions. On the one hand, the Nyāya welcomed the emphasis on experience and downplayed the mediating role of language, whereas the Mīmāṃsā identified *dharma* with that which is mediated through the language of revelation and denied the possibility of any immediate experience of *dharma* whatsoever. In both cases the dialectical character of the language of revelation as moving between individual experience and social institution was lost and replaced by either a purely inward, non-verbal experience or a purely external institution.

On the level of practice, however, a new center was found, although it was now the center of a much more modest world. The language of revelation became the "correct speech" of the *śiṣṭa*-s and in the restructured ritual life of the individual householder represented both a normative institution of Brahmanical society and, as a manifestation of Brahman, a vehicle for the individual's attainment of liberation. In the actual use of the "divine speech" antinomies were avoided and the dialectical character of the language of revelation as mediating between individual experience and social institution, between immediacy and mediacy, was preserved. Because Bhartṛhari was a grammarian, it was out of this engagement with the actual language of revelation that his theory arose and allowed him to affirm the importance of the inner vision of the True Word while at the same time reaffirming the importance of tradition and *dharma*.

In the West the story of the continual transmission of the language of revelation centered on the history of scripture, preaching, and prophecy, but most especially on the history of preaching as the activity in which the institution of scripture and the inspiration of prophecy could on occasion be joined. This history was a history of gradual decline after the sixth century and then of a great revival starting in the mid-eleventh century and carrying on into the thirteenth, when Bonaventure became one of its champions.

The decline of preaching was due in large part to changes in the social conditions of the church as it entered into the European Middle Ages. The language of scripture and learning ceased to be the language of the people, and prospective preachers began to need both a knowledge of a language other than their native tongue and an ability to mediate between the official clerical culture and an increasingly rural and illiterate population. More importantly, as the clergy were slowly incorporated into the structures of the emerging feudal society, the apocalyptic themes of the original Christian *kerygma* and the call to a life of "evangelical perfection" lost much of their appeal. In addition, an audience for such a message was lacking. As a genre, preaching flourishes in situations where people feel free to respond by making fundamental choices, where the possibilities opened up by the preacher's words seem real. But such people, abundant in the urban centers of early Christianity, were rare in the rural and feudal society of the early Middle Ages after the era of conversion.

The revival of preaching was accompanied by a revival of the towns and an urban middle class. Merchants turned preachers like Waldo of Lyon and Francis of Assisi appealed to the New Testament ideal of the *vita apostolica* as a real alternative for the present. With the new urban schools there was also a revival of literacy and a growing number of people capable of reading of the *vita apostolica* for themselves. For answers to their religious questions such people increasingly turned to the scriptures and to the preachers who expounded them.

In such a historical context conflict between the traditional structures of the church and the new preachers with their sense of individual vocation was probably inevitable. In some cases, as in those of Henry of Lausanne and Waldo of Lyon, representatives of the new religious feeling found themselves excluded from the church, while in others, most notably in the case of St. Francis, there was accommodation. By Bonaventure's time, however, conflict was evident within the Franciscan order itself. Some Franciscans, the so-called Spirituals, felt that the accommodation of Francis's vision to the needs of the institutional church had gone too far. Drawing upon Joachim of Fiore's prophecy of a coming age of the Spirit, one of the more radical of these, Gerardo di Borgo San Donnino, opposed the institutional church of the past, along with its scriptures, to a coming era of spiritual immediacy.

Preaching provided a focus for this conflict. Who was to preach? And who was to interpret scripture? The secular clergy, many of whom were deeply committed to the feudal status quo? The new preachers and prophets, who spoke as the spirit moved them, interpreting scripture as a call to the evangelical life and therefore, whether implicitly or explicitly, criticizing the actual condition of the church? Was the language of revelation to be used primarily to defend the structures of the present or to call them into question? These were some of the questions that faced Bonaventure. In working out his answers on the theoretical level, and above all in his actual practice as an exegete and preacher, Bonaventure tried to find a balance between individual vocation and ecclesial office, between present reality and future hope.

•

If we compare these two historical developments and the places of Bhartṛhari and Bonaventure within them, we are struck by at least two things. On the one hand, if we view the development of the language of revelation in each case in terms of what for Bhartṛhari and Bonaventure was its fundamental character, namely, as either ritually correct speech rooted in an oral tradition or as inspired preaching rooted in a scriptural tradition, then we can discern a common historical pattern. The centuries that preceded each of our thinkers witnessed a decline in its characteristic mode of transmission, followed by a revival in which both Bhartṛhari and Bonaventure were centrally involved. In India, during the centuries that witnessed first the success of Buddhism under Aśoka and then a succession of foreign rulers often sympathetic to non-Brahmanical ideologies, the ritual use of the "divine speech" as codified by the grammarian Pāṇini was progressively restricted, as was the social and political influence of the *śiṣṭa*-s, whose job it was to preserve it. In the West the practice of preaching underwent a similar decline under the conditions of emerging feudalism, and those responsible for studying and preaching the Word of God, if they did not suffer a decline in status in the face of a new religious vision such as happened in India, certainly suffered a decline in influence as the prophetic spirit of the early preachers was supplanted by the liturgical use of Latin before an increasingly illiterate populace.

In both traditions the economic, political, and cultural revival that marked the end of this period of decline was accompanied by a revival of the language of revelation. In India Pāṇinian Sanskrit became the language of choice of the Gupta kings, and its study flourished as India experienced a "Sanskrit renaissance." In Europe there was a revival of scriptural study and most importantly a revival of preaching, as the *parole nouvelle*[3] of the mendicants was enlisted in the cause of church reform and in the construction of a new, unified, and doctrinally orthodox Christendom. In the midst of these developments we find Bhartṛhari and Bonaventure, reaffirming fundamental elements of their traditions that had been called into question, while at the same time accommodating their views of revelation to the new intellectual, social, and political conditions of the day. In the face of the Buddhist critique Bhartṛhari reaffirmed the self-expressiveness of the True Word and the traditional status of the Vedic language as a form of *dharma* intimately tied to the world of Brahmanical orthopraxy. At the same time, however, through his "yoga preceded by words," he accommodated his understanding of the power of ritually correct speech to the desire for spiritual liberation unleashed by the critics of Brahmanism and, like his more famous successor Śaṅkara, incorporated key elements of the Buddhist worldview into his own thought.[4] Bonaventure, for his part, reaffirmed the importance of the *kerygma,* Christian apocalypticism, and the prophetic vocation of the preacher, while using the tools of Greek philosophy (Aristotelian, but most especially Neoplatonic) within the context of a hierarchical society that would have been foreign to the first apostles and within a religious institution that accorded him a position of privilege not unlike that of his Indian counterpart. In each case the end result is a fundamentally new reception of the language of revelation that is deeply rooted in the central

---

3. The term is that of Jacques Le Goff, "Le dossier des mendiants," in *1274, année charnière: Mutations et continuités* (Paris: Éditions du Centre National de la Recherche Scientifique, 1977), p. 218: "Les Mendiants se distinguent ensuite parce qu'ils sont les porteurs d'une parole nouvelle. Les Dominicains affirment dans leur nom même de Prêcheurs cette fonction éminente de prédicateurs qu'ils assument. Mais tous les Mendiants — à commencer par les Mineurs — sont d'abord des hommes de parole."

4. It is interesting to note that like Śaṅkara, who was sometimes accused by his critics of being a "crypto-Buddhist," Bhartṛhari would occasionally be claimed by later Buddhist tradition as one of their own.

intuitions of the early tradition while at the same time being responsive to the contemporary historical circumstances.

It is in the context of this common pattern in the internal historical dynamic of each tradition that we must locate the second point. While on the formal level both Bhartṛhari and Bonaventure can be seen to perform very similar functions, as both revivers and defenders of their respective traditions after a period of decline and critique, on the level of content they could easily appear to be inverse images of one another. In a sense Bhartṛhari rejects what Bonaventure affirms, and vice versa. The crisis that had confronted Bhartṛhari's tradition, namely, Buddhism, provides the best Indian analogue for the very thing Bonaventure defended, namely, the critical stance of the Franciscan order, with its prophetic and (for Bonaventure) apocalyptic roots, toward the political and social structures of this world. Bonaventure, by contrast, was continually dragged into conflict with the secular clergy who, with their deep involvement in the feudal political and social structures of the medieval West, bear a certain resemblance to the Brahmanical *śiṣṭa*-s, provided with the Indian equivalent of a benefice, the *agrahāra*. If we were to imagine Bhartṛhari and Bonaventure as members of the same world we might easily imagine them more as opponents than as allies. In this they would be faithful representatives of their respective traditions and of all the distance that separates them.

Such a stark opposition is, however, a bit misleading. Both Bhartṛhari and Bonaventure sought to mediate the oppositions that tore at their respective traditions, and both of them accomplished this in large part through their practical engagement with the language of revelation. For both this language mediated a dialectical process that overcame the antithesis between experience and institution, individual and society, past and future. In the "divine speech" of the Vedic tradition Bhartṛhari found the common ground between the Mīmāṃsā and the Nyāya, between the objective institutions of *dharma* and the inner vision of the individual. Similarly, through the interpretation of scripture Bonaventure navigated a middle course both between the conservatism of the secular clergy and the radicalism of the Spirituals and between the letter of scripture as an institution of the church and the spiritual experience of the individual. In the process, both sought to re-establish for their tradition a unity and authority that had been called into question by the force of historical circumstance. Thus both Bhartṛhari and Bonaventure were engaged in historical, dialectical processes that bear a high degree of formal resemblance when viewed precisely as *concrete historical processes.* And as regards content, while they began with traditional presuppositions that, as we have seen, were in many respects quite different and even opposed, as they reinterpreted their respective traditions in the light of the historical possibilities open to them they tended to converge somewhat, Bhartṛhari tempering the ritualistic worldview of Brahmanism with a recognition of the soteriological aspirations of the individual and Bonaventure accommodating the apocalyptic vision of the early Christians to the realities of a religious institution firmly ensconced in this world. One can't help noticing, in addition, that in the process of constructing their synthetic visions both also legitimated their own positions within their respective societies, but this is an issue to which we will return in the next chapter. First we must conclude our comparisons by considering their accounts of the actual experience of revelation as a disclosive event mediated through language.

The Experience of Revelation

Both Bhartṛhari and Bonaventure developed an original metaphysics of revelation that emphasized the dynamic and self-expressive nature of reality and can be seen as a theoretical interpretation of their own *experience* of revelation as a dialectical and transformative process mediated through language. Unlike their representations of revelation as a past event, the elements of which had in large part already been established by their respective traditions, here reflection seems to have grown out of their own concrete involvement with the language of revelation in their immediate historical and social contexts. This supposition is supported by the fact that each of them goes beyond his theoretical reflections to describe the actual process of the reception of revelation by the individual, a process that is mediated by language but reaches beyond it to recapture some of the spiritual immediacy of which it was believed originally to have been an expression.

As we saw above, both Bhartṛhari and Bonaventure ground revelation in the very nature of ultimate reality, which they agree in characterizing as intrinsically self-expressive. For Bhartṛhari, the ultimate ground of revelation is *Śabdatattva,* the True Word; for Bonaventure, it is the divine Word, the second Person of the Trinity. In both cases the visible world is viewed as a product of the Word's self-expressive act. But since both agree that this world can conceal its expressive ground as well as reveal it, they identify a specific form of influence designed to overcome the world's darker potential — the illumination or inspiration that gives rise to the language of revelation.

Both Bhartṛhari and Bonaventure present this illumination against the background of the essentially dynamic and unstable character of the world. For Bhartṛhari the world is a transformation of the powers, or *śakti*-s, of the True Word. More than a set of substantially existing entities, it is conceived of as a relational system of actions, all expressing the essential dynamism of the True Word, with which the *śakti*-s are, in the final analysis, identical. In such a world true knowledge is available only through the vision of the *ṛṣi* or *śiṣṭa,* a vision rooted in the luminosity of the True Word itself. This vision makes known the stable structure of *dharma,* which alone is a trustworthy guide for human action. Bonaventure too views the world — and especially the human world — as intrinsically unstable. Brought into existence out of nothing, created things are intrinsically mutable. Only through the illumination of the Word can the mind know truth, and only through the influence of grace can human beings realize their likeness to their creator. Thus for both Bhartṛhari and Bonaventure the illumination of the Word introduces enduring order and value into an intrinsically unstable world.

In both cases, therefore, the illumination involved in revelation is transformative. This transformative influence is given its spatio-temporal extension through the mediation of the language of revelation. In Bhartṛhari's case the temporal flux of the *vikāra*-s is transformed into the ordered world of *dharma* through the action mediated by the language of revelation, the Veda as the *anukāra,* the "imitative resemblance," of the True Word. For Bonaventure, the fallen image found in the human being is reformed into the likeness of its heavenly Exemplar when the soul is converted by the witness of the Spirit as recorded in scripture. For both, this transformative process is essential to the reception of revelation. It is here that we come closest to revelation as a lived experience.

In Bhartṛhari's case this process revolved around what he called *śabdapūrvayoga,* the "yoga preceded by words," which, as we saw, probably belonged to the context of the traditional Brahmanical practice of the *svādhyāya,* the individual recitation of the Veda. Clearly it was a process thoroughly mediated through the language of revelation. It was through the practice of *dharma,* the use of dharmic speech, and especially through the ritual recitation of the "divine speech" in the *svādhyāya,* that individual householders purified themselves and opened themselves up to the inner light of the True Word.

For the grammarian the reception of the language of revelation included the penetration of its very structure as language, as disclosive of the dynamic structure of the world and as disclosive of its own transcendent ground. Through the "yoga preceded by words" the grammarian slowly moved from the external sounds of language, the *vaikṛti* stage of *Vāk,* or speech, through the inner discursive stage known as *madhyamā,* to reach a vision of the Word in its luminous reality as *paśyantī,* the Seeing One, the Word beyond words. Through a dialectic of *dharma* and vision one was led back from the external, institutionalized form of the language of revelation to its innermost core, the True Word itself.

Bonaventure recognized a process that was remarkably similar. The reception of the language of revelation began in the social and institutional sphere, in the sacramental life of the church, and especially in its preaching. For Bonaventure preaching itself had a profoundly spiritual quality and could culminate, for both the preacher and his audience, in moments of great spiritual immediacy. But the reception of the language of revelation also had a more individual dimension, and it is here that the transformative nature of the process is most evident. We saw that Bonaventure accepted the traditional doctrine of a multiplicity of spiritual meanings hidden beneath the letter of scripture. He correlated these levels of meaning with stages on the spiritual path and saw the contemplative study of scripture as a means of spiritual growth that led from purification to illumination and finally to union with the divine. The spiritual understanding of scripture was received through the illumination of the Spirit. The interpretative process was itself a form of revelation, which led through the mediation of the letter of scripture to a spiritual understanding of the Word.

Thus in both cases we find a transformative process, mediated through language, that culminates in spiritual vision. It is here, I believe, on the practical level of the actual appropriation of the language of revelation and its transformative effect upon the individual, that Bhartṛhari and Bonaventure would come closest to agreement.

Nevertheless, this process of reception by the individual should not be isolated from the broader social and historical context in which it occurs, nor from the fundamentally different conceptions of the human person within this context. The individual's reception of revelation, mediated through the language of revelation that provides the condition of its possibility, in fact constitutes a moment within the larger historical dynamic. The two levels are not opposed but in fact are interdependent. Both Bhartṛhari and Bonaventure seem to have recognized this interdependence. Whatever their differences at a theoretical level, they both seem to have experienced revelation as a concrete dialectical process that involves both the individual and his or her community, both the mediation of language and the immediacy of vision. *But precisely because of this common ground their other differences cannot be canceled out.* In each case they are taken up into the process itself, as the indispensable conditions of its possibility.

9

Interpreting the Comparison

In looking back over the comparison in the previous chapter I believe we can reach two important conclusions. First, it is impossible to say that, on the topic of revelation, Bhartṛhari and Bonaventure were simply "saying the same thing" in slightly different terms. The differences that we discovered in their theories are major and cannot be easily dismissed. Second, the similarities that we discovered in their practice, in their receptions of revelation as an ongoing *process,* make it possible to suggest that, however different their explicit theories of revelation, they are in fact both *doing* some very similar things, relative to their own respective historical contexts. These two observations raise some important questions about the significance of the similarities and differences that we discovered. How are we to interpret them, and how are we to evaluate their relative importance? In addressing these questions, I will begin with the marked divergence between Bhartṛhari's and Bonaventure's explicit theories.

DIFFERENCE: A QUESTION OF HISTORY

A considerable amount has been written of late concerning the importance of "taking differences seriously," and the differences at issue in these admonitions are often differences in theory or doctrine.[1] When we

1. I have preferred to use the terms "theory" and "representation" while discussing the thought of Bhartṛhari and Bonaventure, since I take religious doctrines to be the agreed upon teachings of religious communities rather than the theoretical constructions of individuals. Many aspects of Bhartṛhari's and Bonaventure's theories of revelation could be considered doctrinal since they derive directly from the agreed upon doctrines of their respective communities, e.g., Bonaventure's discussion of the Trinity or Bhartṛhari's discussion of Brahman. There are other aspects of their theories, however, that are much more individual and that should not be taken to represent Hindu or Christian doctrine in the strict sense. The points

look carefully at the teachings of the major world religions we find that they are in fact making quite different claims, advancing a diversity of religious aims, and if we are to respect the persons who make these claims and advance these aims we must not gloss over such differences in a well-meaning but fundamentally misguided effort to affirm some common ground.[2] As noted at the outset of this study, this demand that differences be recognized for what they are is an important one and acts as a useful corrective to attempts to affirm a universal sameness that flies in the face of the facts. In the present case Bhartṛhari's and Bonaventure's theories of revelation have been found to be widely divergent. No attempt has been made to obscure these differences or minimize their importance. But what *is* their importance? Beyond recognizing that these differences exist, what does it mean to take them seriously? Some would argue that such differences should, at least in some cases, be recognized as *oppositions,* which compel a choice: both positions cannot be true; to accept one is to reject the other (unless one judges *both* to be in error).[3] But it seems that such a position brings in its own form of "universal sameness," namely, the universality of rational criteria that are needed to reach such a judgment. And while such criteria may have a useful function within contexts where the objectification of the phenomenon under consideration is an acceptable price to pay in order to gain control over it (for instance, in the physical sciences), it is not clear that they have anything more than a minor role to play in the attempt to understand a phenomenon such as revelation, which, as we have seen, presents itself as a dynamic process rather than as an objective datum.[4] Even if there is a rather meager canon of logical principles that can be regarded as universally acceptable in the context of philosophical discourse, it is unlikely that such principles would take us very far in understanding why, for instance, Bhartṛhari assumes that revelation does not involve a personal address on the part of a personal

---

that I make below, however, appear to me to be valid whether they are applied to doctrines in the strict sense or to what, in a Christian context, one would refer to as theologies.

2. Forceful presentations of this point may be found in Paul Griffiths's *An Apology for Apologetics* and in J. A. DiNoia's *The Diversity of Religions.* DiNoia stresses the importance of recognizing the "variety of religious aims" found within the different religions.

3. I have in mind here the work of Paul Griffiths just cited, who in turn acknowledges his debt to the earlier work of William A. Christian, *Oppositions of Religious Doctrines: A Study in the Logic of Dialogue among Religions* (New York: Herder and Herder, 1972).

4. Here I believe the remarks of Paul Ricoeur are helpful. In his essay "Toward a Hermeneutic of the Idea of Revelation," he notes that a philosophical approach to revelation must begin by critiquing its own pretensions. Parallel to the authoritarian pretensions of what Ricoeur refers to as the "opaque" notion of revelation there is the pretentious claim of philosophy to "a complete transparency of truth and a total autonomy of the thinking subject." See his *Essays on Biblical Interpretation* (Philadelphia: Fortress Press, 1980), p. 95.

deity whereas Bonaventure assumes that it does. This is especially true of the *doctrines* that derive from revelation. Here such an approach would ignore the dependence of such explicit doctrines as the Christian doctrine of the Trinity or Bhartṛhari's theory of the True Word on the primary languages of revelation, with all their richness and polysemy, their practical efficacy as forms of action, and their rootedness in specific communities of interpretation. One thinks here of the cautions issued by Bhartṛhari himself against the use of "dry reason" in the evaluation of tradition, or of Bonaventure's rejection of the autonomy of reason in his theory of illumination. The end result of an approach that relies on a disembodied reason, independent of the concrete historical contexts of its use, is not likely to be the respect of difference, respect of the religious other, with which one would enter into a transformative dialectic. Rather it seems much more likely that the end result will be to exclude otherness by invoking dogma, namely, the dogma of a universal rationality propped up by the equally indefensible dogma of an autonomous thinking subject. For where does one go after it has been established that two doctrines are, from a logical point of view, in opposition? At this level of reason conceived as static and autonomous can there remain any room for movement? It seems that we are led away from dialogue as a context for mutual transformation and growth and into the realm of apologetics, indeed into the intransigence of polemics, left only to declare the winners and losers in the world contest of religions before the bar of universal reason. When reason is accepted as autonomous and universal there is no real alternative, in the attempt to understand difference, than to resort to argument and, when arguments fail to convince (as they almost certainly will in this context), ultimately to fall back on either indifference or force. In neither case is there true mediation.

To simply let the differences be, however, in some sort of relativistic acceptance, is equally unacceptable. For certainly this is to fail to "take differences seriously." Here too the ultimate result would seem to be the same: either indifference or, when that becomes impossible, resort to coercion. In the end, neither universalist attempts to adjudicate who has "got it right" nor a relativistic tolerance bred of indifference and self-satisfaction is acceptable. In both cases differences remain unproductive, and this it seems to me is the main issue. To borrow a phrase from Paul Ricoeur, I would argue that we must allow the differences between theories or doctrines, rooted as they are in the historical experience of those who produce them, to become productive, to "give rise to thought," rather than allow them to close thought off through forcing a choice of either/or.

It is precisely the incompatibility of Bhartṛhari's and Bonaventure's *theories* of revelation, viewed within the context of the striking similarities in their reception of revelation within their own respective historical contexts, that discourages us from taking their theories at face value, as two "opposing" attempts to describe a single object "out there," and rather encourages us to seek an explanation of their differences beyond the realm of theory, in the presuppositions that inform their theoretical formulations and the historical conditions that underlie these presuppositions. Indeed, an outspoken advocate of the apologetic approach just criticized has pointed to the possible need of such a procedure in the conclusion to an article that attempts to adjudicate between Christian and Yogacara Buddhist notions of "maximal greatness."[5] It is this historical approach that has been pursued here, and thus it remains to ask whether our study of the histories of Bhartṛhari and Bonaventure can help us understand the significance of the differences between their theories of revelation.

What then truly separates Bhartṛhari and Bonaventure in their views of revelation? We have examined *what* some of the major differences are, but it remains to ask *why* they are. How should we understand them? Did one simply "get it right," whereas the other "got it wrong"? I believe we should begin to address the question of their differences by making the fundamental observation that the representations that people make of the divine, or of anything else for that matter, are rooted in the same historical, social, and linguistic contexts as are the people who construct them. There are no "pure" theories or doctrines any more than there are "pure" experiences, and therefore the differences that one observes between two sets of religious doctrines, in this case the differences between Bhartṛhari's and Bonaventure's theories of revelation, cannot be separated from the differences one observes between their respective historical, social, and linguistic contexts. It would be unwise to assume at the outset that two theories from two separate cultures represented two attempts to respond to one and the same question, posed in equivalent

5. See Paul J. Griffiths, "Buddha and God: A Contrastive Study in Ideas about Maximal Greatness," *Journal of Religion* 69 (1989): 502–29. The significant thing about this article is its ending. Griffiths acknowledges that there seem to be irreducible differences in intuition underlying different notions of "maximal greatness." He admits that "finally (and this last task is likely to be of more interest to the intellectual historian than to the philosopher), an attempt needs to be made to show how and (nonphilosophically) why Yogacara intuitions about maximal greatness differ from others within Buddhist traditions" (p. 529). This question could well be expanded to the question of why Buddhist and Christian intuitions differ. Thus Griffiths here seems to acknowledge that the grounds for understanding the fundamental differences between religious traditions are non-philosophical. Differences are not decidable merely through logic, but lead on to differences of intuition and their grounds.

terms, or to somehow describe one and the same object "out there," as if either Bhartṛhari or Bonaventure were free to rise above his tradition, his language, his most fundamental presuppositions to address the other directly beyond the limits of time and space. Both were thoroughly embedded in their respective contexts, and these contexts were in turn the result of the histories of their respective traditions and of the worlds in which they developed. In order truly to understand and appreciate the differences between their theories of revelation, then, we must begin by understanding and appreciating the differences between these respective histories.

Different Worlds: Tribe and Sect

The most profound differences that divide Bhartṛhari and Bonaventure are rooted in the fundamentally different worlds that provided the setting for the original revelatory events of their respective traditions. These events and their original reception determined certain pre-understandings of the nature of revelation that became permanent parts of each tradition and to a degree determined all later reception of revelation. It is what Bhartṛhari and Bonaventure took for granted, what for them was "obvious," that most divided them. The fundamental differences that concern us here are thus not simply functions of Bhartṛhari's or Bonaventure's personal viewpoints. They are functions of the different worlds that produced the objective possibilities for their later reflection and praxis. These worlds were quite different.

We know today that Vedic revelation originated historically in the inspired visions of the *ṛṣi*-s, the poet-seers who composed the liturgical hymns that make up the Ṛg Veda.[6] These seers were attached to the semi-nomadic tribes of Aryans who migrated into northwest India sometime around 1200 B.C.E. Successful in battle as they penetrated the northern plains of the Indian subcontinent, the Aryans represented the world in their hymns as the scene of a continual contest between gods and demons, with the gods — the prototypes of the ideal Aryan warriors — always coming up victorious. The maintenance of the world order was a continual task, a struggle, but the task was manageable. The sacred hymns of the *ṛṣi*-s presuppose this basic optimism. Reality can be expressed in speech; indeed, only what is spoken is real. Language is endowed with power. In it the underlying order of the world, the *ṛta,* becomes manifest,

6. See, for instance, Jan Gonda, *The Vision of the Vedic Poets* (The Hague: Mouton & Co., 1963).

becomes real, and this happens especially through the speech of the sacrifice, the *bráhman.* Revelation here was immanent in the inspired speech of the *ṛṣi*-s, which in turn was immanent in the rituals of the individual families of the Aryan tribes. In this rural and oral culture the dimensions of the world were determined by the memories of the seers of the tribe. What these venerable seers uttered was the measure of the real. Knowledge of the past and the imagination of the future were all but identical in a culture that left no permanent trace of itself as it migrated through time and space, save for the Vedic hymns themselves.

How different the situation of the early Christians. The consciousness of the early Christians was determined by the historical panorama that had already been put into place by the prophetic and apocalyptic writings of the intertestamental period. Time was not structured by the rhythms of nature and family life but by the divine Plan, recorded once and for all in the heavenly Book. The early Christians inherited the scribal culture of the ancient Near East and the tradition of apocalyptic thought that was the product of literate national traditions in crisis.[7] The early Christian message of the advent of the "Kingdom" of God in the person of Jesus the Christ, the Messiah or "anointed one," a term traditionally applied to kings, presupposed not only the existence of the national histories of the ancient Near East, focused on the figure of the Near Eastern king, but also an elaborate narrative of God's successive interventions in these histories: the call of Abraham from Ur in Mesopotamia, the sojourn of the Israelites in Egypt and their eventual exodus, the conquest of Canaan and the establishment of the monarchy, the exile at the hands of the Assyrians and Babylonians, redemption from exile through Cyrus, the king of Persia. Furthermore, as Collins has noted, the subsequent demise of the national monarchies throughout the Near East under the Greeks and then the Romans led to an experience of loss of meaning and of alienation that provided the apocalyptic context for the early Christian hope in the imminent return of the Messiah.[8]

The contrast with the early Vedic period is striking. Neither the Jews of the intertestamental period nor the early Christians were in direct control of their political destinies. Neither were capable of actively constructing

---

7. On the Near Eastern tradition of apocalypticism that influenced the early Christians, see John J. Collins, "Jewish Apocalyptic against Its Hellenistic Near Eastern Environment," *Bulletin of the American Schools of Oriental Research* 220 (1975): 27–36. On Near Eastern scribalism, see also Jonathan Z. Smith, "Wisdom and Apocalyptic," in *Map Is Not Territory* (Leiden: E. J. Brill, 1978), pp. 67–87.

8. John J. Collins, "Jewish Apocalyptic against Its Hellenistic Near Eastern Environment," p. 34.

their world as the Vedic Indians had done. On the other hand, although the world of the early Christians was in a real sense not their own, it was vast by comparison with the rather small-scale cosmos of the Aryans. Great expanses of time stretched out before them, both into the past and into the future. This was not a world to be constructed; it was a world from which to gain deliverance. Revelation came not as the inspired language of the sacrifice, intended to manifest and sustain a primordial order, but as the inspired language of apostles and prophets, leaders of an apocalyptic sect who called the established order into question and who found guidance through the interpretation of texts fixed in writing, texts in which to discern a divine plan, foreordained and immutable.

Few contrasts could be more stark than that between the immense world of Near Eastern apocalypticism and the comfortable world of the Vedic sacrifice, unless it could be the contrast between the beings that inhabited those worlds. The "three worlds" of the Vedic Indians — earth, atmosphere, and heaven — were peopled by innumerable natural and preternatural beings, some of them divine, some human, and some halfway in between. In heaven and in the atmosphere that lay between heaven and earth there were numerous gods and ancestors, all with their part to play in the world process, none with an exclusive claim to divinity. On earth, the human sacrificer actively participated in this same process, playing a role that was no less essential than that of the gods. The general picture was one of the intimate interaction and interdependence of realms that were never wholly separate. Movement between them was the rule more than the exception.

In the world of early Christianity, by contrast, there was a clear demarcation between the heavenly world and its secrets and the human world. The divine and the human belonged to essentially different realms, and the initiative in establishing contact between the two lay exclusively with the divine. Further, the divine itself was conceived of as a single all-powerful creator God whose relationship with his creation was viewed on the analogy of a father's regard for his children or of an all-powerful king's control over his subjects. There was here nothing analogous to the reciprocity of gods and humans based upon the Vedic practice of sacrifice.

The differences between the original recipients of revelation in these two settings must themselves be viewed against the background of the worlds they inhabited. The Vedic *ṛṣi* with his ritually potent speech contrasts with the early Christian preacher announcing the secrets of a divine plan realized in history in much the same way as a world sustained by ritual sacrifice differs from a world governed effortlessly by a transcendent and omnipotent creator. Both seer and preacher were to an extent products of their respective worlds. The function of each in the reception of revelation becomes unintelligible if uprooted from the historical moment that provided its objective possibility. We have had numerous occasions to observe the practical and social character of revelation as a historical process. Both the Vedic seer and the early Christian preacher must be viewed as integral parts of this process, as foci *within* it. In this sense, both brought to speech a vision that was appropriate to the times. But they did not do this as an act of accommodation on the part of detached and privileged subjects, nor was their vision a merely passive reflection of an already established world "out there." Their speech arose from an active and transformative engagement with the world as they experienced it. In the Vedic world revelation could be realized only through the structures of a relatively undifferentiated tribal society, whereas in the Mediterranean environment of the early Christians its reception was mediated through the structures of a differentiated, literate, and pluralistic society. Whereas it is the preacher — whether Christian, Cynic, or indeed Buddhist — who thrives in this latter sort of world, it is the seer-poet, the master of sacred speech, who thrives in the former.

Several of the most important differences that distinguish Bhartṛhari's and Bonaventure's views of revelation derive from these more fundamental differences that determined the origins of their respective traditions. In India, in the later Brahmanical tradition to which Bhartṛhari belonged, revelation continued to be experienced as a form of sacred speech that was the exclusive possession of the seers and sages of the tribe — the *śiṣṭa*-s, the less charismatic counterparts of the original *ṛṣi*-s. The speech of such persons continued to be understood as a manifestation of the order *(ṛta, dharma)* immanent in the sacrifice and in the ritually constructed world of Brahmanical society long after the original historical conditions of the Vedic *ṛṣi*-s had faded from memory and Brahmanical society had been shaken by the preaching of the Buddha. Similarly in the Christian tradition to which Bonaventure was heir the experience of revelation continued to be determined by the presence of scripture and the divine plan permanently inscribed within it. The preacher continued to be one called to proclaim the "good news" to all who would listen, news of a transcendent world of divine mysteries and of a future judgment, even though the radically different conditions of later feudal society would tend to lead in another direction. That revelation should be passed down in the form of sacred speech was something that Bhartṛhari accepted as given, just as surely as Bonaventure accepted as given the idea that revelation is passed down in the form of sacred scripture. These were major differences that both Bhartṛhari and Bonaventure accepted as given. They provided them with a pre-understanding of the nature of revelation that neither of them ever seriously questioned and that therefore determined their thought all the more decisively. What for us appear to be differences intimately related to objective social, cultural, and historical conditions of entire civilizations, for Bhartṛhari and Bonaventure were differences in the objective nature of revelation *per se*.

Take for instance the difference noted above between Bhartṛhari's (and his tradition's) understanding of Brahman and Bonaventure's (and his tradition's) understanding of God. The concept of *bráhman* has its roots in a tribal and oral society. Louis Renou translates the term *bráhman,* as it appears in the early Vedic tradition, as "formula" or "hymn," a form of activity that is most clearly manifested in speech.[9] According to him, what comes to speech in the *bráhman* is the fundamental mystery of the world order, "the equation between human behavior and natural phenomena, the connection between rite and cosmos."[10] Jan Gonda too notes the general meaning of *bráhman* as "hymn" and observes that the term "generally applies to power or powerful objects or concepts connected with the ritual, the priests and the gods."[11] He goes on to compare it with such well-known notions of supranormal power as the Melanesian concept of *mana,* noting in passing the attempt of Hubert and Mauss to identify *bráhman* and *mana.*[12] Such a concept belongs to the tribal world of an oral culture where words and things remain bound in a primordial unity, and it is this understanding of the cosmic dimension of speech that underlies Bhartṛhari's notion of Brahman as the True Word.

Bonaventure's concept of God, by contrast, is the product of a long historical process that saw the gradual differentiation of a tribal deity, Yahweh, from a host of similar tribal deities to become, by the time of the Babylonian exile, the monotheistic deity of the Israelites.[13] This process in turn must be understood against the background of the political unification of the state of Israel under the monarchy, whose royal imagery made important contributions to the figure of Yahweh, and the experience of extreme social dislocation during the years of exile, during which

9. Louis Renou, "Sur la notion de *bráhman,*" *Journal Asiatique* 237 (1949): 9.
10. Ibid., p. 13.
11. Jan Gonda, *Notes on Brahman* (Utrecht: J. L. Beyers, 1955), p. 14.
12. See ibid., p. 16, and Marcel Mauss, *A General Theory of Magic* (New York: Norton, 1972), pp. 116–17.
13. On this process, see Mark S. Smith, *The Early History of God: Yahweh and the Other Deities of Ancient Israel* (New York: Harper and Row, 1990).

the notion of Yahweh as a monotheistic deity makes its first unambiguous appearance. Another significant factor in the emergence of Israelite monotheism may have been the use of writing, which encouraged a universalization of religious norms.[14] In any case, the monotheistic concept of deity that Bonaventure inherited, like the notion of Brahman inherited by Bhartṛhari, was the product of a set of specific historical conditions that have left their indelible trace.

The Christian pre-understanding of revelation involves more than the monotheistic deity of classical prophets, however. As noted above, it also involves an apocalyptic element. The very term "revelation" comes to us as a Latin translation of the Greek *apokalupsis,* which refers to an "unveiling" of what is hidden. The notion of an apocalypse in the literal sense of a sudden unveiling of long-kept divine secrets is deeply embedded in the Christian conception of revelation. In general the apocalyptic writings reveal an understanding of the world that is quite different from the one we find in the classical prophets, not to mention the Vedic seers. The authors of the apocalypses were most probably learned scribes who wrote of visions of a mysterious, transcendent world beyond the present world of confusion and strife. This transcendent world is preeminently a world of secrets, secrets that concern not only the nature of the divinity, his "divine court," and the celestial world, but also the divinely ordained plan of history and its impending end. Human history is portrayed as a closed predetermined whole with a predetermined end. The apocalypse, or "revelation," makes this end known in advance and warns of the judgment that is to come.

This general approach to the phenomenon of revelation is the product of a long historical development that includes not only the political developments noted above but also the invention of writing and record keeping. Jonathan Z. Smith has suggested that the concern for interpreting heavenly mysteries typical of apocalyptic thought should be connected with the much older Near Eastern tradition of Babylonian scribalism, "an unbroken tradition from the Sumerian period to the sages of the Babylonian Talmud."[15] Thus already by the time of the Exile, Ezekiel is given his commission as a prophet by being given a written scroll to eat, a scroll presumably written by a Divine Author. And in Daniel (as earlier in Exodus 32:32) we find not only the fates of individuals written in a heavenly

14. See ibid., 148–49, where Smith refers with approval to the work of Jack Goody, *The Logic of Writing and the Organization of Society* (Cambridge: University of Cambridge Press, 1986), pp. 39–41.

15. See his "Wisdom and Apocalyptic," p. 70.

book of life, but a mysterious hand, presumably the hand of God himself, writing letters on the wall of the royal palace for Daniel to interpret (Dan. 5:1). Perhaps the most striking example of a heavenly text containing the divine plan is found in the Apocalypse of St. John, with its famous image of the scroll sealed with seven seals. In each case we find the remarkable notion of a heavenly text wherein are written, by none other than God himself, the destinies of specific historical figures. Revelation is then the making known of such information. Nothing of the sort is present in the India that Bhartṛhari knew, nor *could* it be, and for obvious reasons. There was no ancient tradition of scribalism in India. And without a tradition of record keeping on the part of rulers analogous to what happened in the ancient Near East, it was quite unlikely that the notion of a heavenly book could play a prominent role in the mediation of revealed knowledge.

A similar observation can be made as regards the personal and dialogical character of revelation in Bonaventure, where the Word of God is addressed to individuals in history, and the more "impersonal" character of revelation as found in Bhartṛhari, where it would be meaningless to speak of revelation being "addressed" to anyone. In each case these differences in perspective are rooted in their larger traditions. Just as revealed *scripture* played no role in ancient India so too the kind of reader or interpreter of scripture presupposed by Bonaventure was largely nonexistent there. The speaker and hearer of the language of revelation in ancient India was not the highly differentiated and self-conscious subject that Bonaventure, influenced by both Christian and Greek traditions, took for granted. In fact, ancient Indian thought has no equivalent for the Christian notion of the person as a locus of ultimate value.[16] The focus is rather on the processes of which the individual is a part. This is reflected, as we have seen, in the relative unimportance of the grammatical subject in the traditional science of Sanskrit grammar that Bhartṛhari represents. The person, inasmuch as it was endowed with a specific identity, tended to be understood in terms of position within a hierarchically ordered matrix of interrelationships. The reality of the person was a function of these relationships, a situation not uncommon in tribal societies. Even with the

16. This point has been argued, from differing perspectives, by Gaspar Koelman in his study of the classical system of Yoga, by Louis Dumont in his study of caste, and by Madeleine Biardeau in her major study *Théorie de la connaissance et philosophie de la parole dans le brahmanisme classique* (Paris: Mouton & Co., 1964). For the complexities of the "history of the person," both in India and elsewhere, see the colloquium *Problèmes de la personne,* ed. Meyerson (Paris: Mouton, 1973), and more recently *The Category of the Person: Anthropology, Philosophy, History,* ed. Michael Carrithers, Steven Collins, and Steven Lukes (Cambridge: Cambridge University Press, 1985).

breakdown of the old tribal order and the "discovery of the individual" in movements of renunciation such as Buddhism, the status of the individual remained deeply problematic. Any assessment of the differences between Bhartṛhari's and Bonaventure's "personal" and "impersonal" theories of revelation must take this larger context into account.

The point that I am trying to make in all this is that the major differences that we find between Bhartṛhari's and Bonaventure's explicit theories are rooted in the differences between the two worlds that they inhabited and the objective possibilities for expression that those traditions made available to them. Neither thinker simply "chose" from a list of universally available options the view of revelation that he believed most adequately approximated what revelation "really" is. Many of the most fundamental features of their approaches were predetermined by their traditions, which developed for the most part independently of one another and under very different conditions. Consequently, to suggest that Bhartṛhari and Bonaventure were "saying the same thing" would be to ignore their respective histories, to overlook, in effect, who they actually were.

The Broader Context: World History

In pursuing these larger differences between traditions further, one is led onto the ground — some would say the shaky ground — of world history. Why did the early Indian tradition present a set of possibilities so markedly different from those presented to the early Christians? Why, in other words, was the early Indian tradition so different from the early Christian tradition? Why the differences in the civilizations of which they were a part? It seems to me that, grandiose as they may sound, these questions must be accepted as relevant to the more specific question of why Bhartṛhari and Bonaventure disagree on the nature of revelation.

To a degree these questions lead us off into imponderables that are best left alone in the present context. But I believe it is a mistake to say that we can make no response at all to such questions or that they are simply irrelevant. To be sure, a response must not entail grand world-historical schemes of salvation history that ultimately depend upon the biblical view of history as somehow conforming to a divine plan. Nor can we resort to the equally metahistorical Indian view of the progressive degeneration of civilizations and religious traditions through long world cycles. The origins of such speculative views are precisely what need to be understood. But I believe that we can speak meaningfully about certain objective factors in world history that contribute to establishing the parameters of what it is possible to say about revelation at any given time.

From a world historical perspective one can see that the traditions to which Bhartṛhari and Bonaventure belonged not only originated in radically different circumstances but that this was in part a result of sheer historical (or perhaps ecological) accident. Simply put, the ancient Near Eastern civilizations that developed in Mesopotamia and Egypt were able to survive and exert a powerful influence on the worldview of the Israelites and later the Jews and Christians. In India, by contrast, the early civilization of the Indus valley, in many ways similar to the ancient Near Eastern civilizations, collapsed, perhaps due to changes in the natural environment prior to the arrival of the Indo-Aryans who carried with them the earliest hymns of the Ṛg Veda. As a consequence, the predominantly oral culture of the Aryans was able to achieve a hegemonic position in what came to be known as Aryavarta, the land of the Aryans, in northwest and north central India. Although the heritage of the earlier urban culture of the Indus valley was not wholly lost and continued to exert an influence on the development of the Aryan tradition,[17] the Vedic paradigm of revelation as sacred speech transmitted orally within the families of a tribal culture established the essential parameters of how one was to think about revealed knowledge in the Indian subcontinent.[18] Much later, in the fifth century C.E., even after the reurbanization of northern India, the advent of Buddhism, the imperial experiment of Aśoka, and the "Hindu renaissance" under the Guptas, Bhartṛhari still adheres to this basic paradigm.

By contrast, in the ancient Near East it was the scribalism of the literate elite of the ancient city states of Mesopotamia that provided the most influential paradigm for revealed knowledge. As noted above, we can speak of an unbroken tradition of scribalism that goes back to ancient Sumer. Although the ancient Israelites seem to have existed for some time at the margins of power and perhaps even originated as a confederacy of tribes united against the urban centers of power, the impact of this scribal

17. Perhaps more of an influence than has generally been thought. See for instance the work of Asko Parpola, in particular his article "The Pre-Vedic Indian Background of the Srauta Ritual," in *Agni: The Vedic Ritual of the Fire Altar* (Berkeley: Asia Humanities Press, 1983), pp. 41–75.

18. On the prestige of this Vedic paradigm in India, see Brian K. Smith, *Reflections on Resemblance, Ritual and Religion* (New York: Oxford University Press, 1989), chapter 1: "Making Connections: Hinduism and Vedism." I have myself discussed this question in more detail in my "Language, Ritual, and Society: Reflections on the Authority of the Veda in India," *Journal of the American Academy of Religion* 90 (1992): 57–77.

paradigm on the later Jewish and Christian conceptions of revelation is unmistakable and emerges clearly in the Jewish tradition in the period after the Babylonian exile, as we have noted.

One is tempted to contrast a tribal or perhaps shamanistic model of revelation with an imperial or monarchial model and say that while the former attained a hegemonic status in ancient India, the latter became dominant in the ancient Near East. Such a contrast no doubt overly simplifies the matter, but it does help us focus on an important fact, namely, that fundamental features in the way that revelation was represented in these two civilizational areas were determined to a large degree by historical, social, and political forces that were beyond the control of the individual religious thinkers and even the individual religious traditions that were influenced by them. The "history of revelation," if we may speak in this way, thus cannot be understood simply (if at all) as the history of God's mighty (kingly) interventions in the histories of nations, as is traditionally done in a Christian context. Such a view, from the perspective of world history, represents *one* local interpretation of *one* history, but cannot legitimately be expanded to embrace, in the present context, the Indian case. The history of revelation, that is to say, the history of the different experiences, doctrines, and institutions that together constitute revelation as a concrete phenomenon, must be understood within the context of world history as a whole, a history that did not, with apologies to Samuel Noah Kramer, begin at Sumer. What began at Sumer is a particular kind of history, which led to particular ways of representing the interactions between the divine and the human. India by and large took a different path, no less legitimate in its own right. The history of revelation should be seen as a history of diversity that is inseparable from the profound and wonderful diversity of the human race and the world it inhabits. If there is to be a grand narrative that will locate this diversity within a unifying context, it will not be the narrative of Augustine's *City of God,* nor its secularized revisions in Hegel or Marx. It will much more likely be a history of the earth that puts the multiple histories of civilizations back into the natural and ecological context of the planet as a whole and questions the role of the human species, and of human religion, within that context.

Revelation and Ideology

Such a panorama of cultural and religious diversity against the backdrop of world history was not shared by either Bhartṛhari or Bonaventure, however, nor is it widely shared by official representatives of religious traditions today. To suggest that the revealed doctrines of different religious traditions are dependent to a significant degree upon the contingencies of such things as history and politics — and even upon such basic matters as ecology — seems to undercut the very idea of revelation as authoritative truth. As noted above, what for us appear to be differences dependent upon the objective social, cultural, and historical conditions of entire civilizations were for Bhartṛhari and Bonaventure differences in the objective nature of revelation per se, and in this they are far from atypical. Implicit in the very idea of revelation is the claim that it is true and authoritative. Thus, unlike differing styles of dress or varieties of cuisine, which are readily accepted as cultural variables, as part of the rich variety of human experience, to think of revelation as a cultural variable seems to undermine its very reality.

We will return to the question of the truth of revelation below, when we examine the similarities that we discovered between Bhartṛhari's and Bonaventure's receptions of revelation. The question of the *authority* of revelation, however, is more closely related to the issue of difference, which is our present concern. It is in making authoritative claims about specific disclosive events, about the canonical forms of their mediation and their relationship to specific communities, that an ideological function of revelation comes into play. This ideological function of revelation brings it into potential conflict with any attempt to interpret the differences in the various doctrines of revelation as functions of a dynamic ongoing process deeply rooted in the contingencies of history.

From the moment that a religious community confers an authoritative "canonical" or "scriptural"[19] status upon the records of the disclosive events that lay at the origin of a distinctive religious tradition, they become crucial for the community's own identity. Indeed, the act of "canonization" is in an important sense a communal act of self-recognition and self-affirmation. At the same time, as now entrusted to the community in its objectified form, as a *depositum fidei,* authoritative revelation becomes implicated in the community's legitimation of itself and may

19. David H. Kelsey has noted that to be authoritative is part of what it means to call something "scripture," and something becomes "scripture" as a result of its function within the community. In reference to the Christian tradition, Kelsey writes: "biblical texts are taken as 'scripture' in virtue of their *doing* something. On further examination it is apparent that what they do is shape persons' identities so decisively as to transform them; and it turns out that the texts do this when used in certain ways in the common life of the church." See his book *The Uses of Scripture in Recent Theology* (Philadelphia: Fortress Press, 1975), p. 90. I believe that what Kelsey says here in regard to scripture applies equally to the language of revelation in general.

even become a means of domination of those outside the community. It is here, it seems to me, that the ideological aspect of revelation becomes the most profound and significant, for, as Paul Ricoeur has noted, all ideology is finally about the legitimation of authority.[20] While the representations of revelation may be recognized by a given community as authentic expressions of its experience and praxis, at the same time, precisely as objectified representations, they may become the means by which that community or its leaders seek not only to legitimate themselves, but to impose their own authority in situations where representation and praxis no longer correspond.

There are then often strong motives for disregarding or rejecting the contingencies involved in the representation of revelation within a particular religious community. Examples of this can be found in both Bhartṛhari and Bonaventure. As we have noted, both occupied positions of privilege within their respective traditions, and both owed their positions to institutions that were legitimized by appeals to divine revelation. Neither would have welcomed the view that his representations of revelation were constructions dependent upon a wide variety of factors, some of which were wholly unknown to him or beyond his control. On the contrary, within their respective traditions we find a similar pattern in the way that both the hymns of the Vedic seers and the early Christian writings are gradually transformed from being the first-order expressions of primary situations of disclosure, rooted in a recognizably human and historical world, to being viewed as in a sense divine artifacts, received from on high without any significant involvement of human agency. In the case of Hinduism, this transformation is complete by the time of the early Mīmāṃsā, which denies that the hymns of the Vedic seers were in truth their compositions and claims that they were instead non-human (*apauruseya*) in origin, without temporal beginning or end. In the case of Christianity, the gospels suffer a similar fate when, for example, in Irenaeus, the four individual gospels, the products of diverse local communities over several decades, each with its distinctive image of the life and teachings of Jesus, are identified as "the" gospel, with a fourfold form that is the result, not of historical chance, but of divine necessity. In each case the formulation of canonical scriptures and the institutionalization of the means for their authoritative transmission and interpretation is not only a process of disclosure, an attempt to bring religious truths to ex-

20. Paul Ricoeur, *Lectures on Ideology and Utopia,* ed. George H. Taylor (New York: Columbia University Press, 1986), p. 192.

pression, but also and at the same time a process of closure, a social and inevitably political process of constructing totalities that itself raises important issues of legitimacy and power. The human temporality of the original disclosive situation is sacrificed to the temporal needs of the institution. While both Bhartṛhari and Bonaventure each in his own way made some resistance to this process of reification, through their common emphasis of the importance of experience in the reception of revelation, both were nevertheless deeply influenced by it, Bhartṛhari accepting the Mīmāṃsā doctrine of the non-human origin of the Veda and Bonaventure accepting the *liber scripturae* as a divinely willed unity inspired in all its parts.

Our consideration of the differences that separate Bhartṛhari and Bonaventure thus brings to light two very different aspects of revelation considered from a comparative perspective. Revelation as a concrete historical phenomenon appears to be deeply rooted in the contingencies of history, and yet it is precisely these contingencies that the various *doctrines* of revelation are concerned to erase from view. This leads to the question of whether a fully historical and comparative understanding of revelation is possible, one that acknowledges the historical rootedness and contingency of all forms of revelation but in doing so somehow avoids undermining the central claim of revelation to be true. The consideration of this question brings us back to the similarities that we discovered in Bhartṛhari's and Bonaventure's reception of revelation, which remained apparent even in the midst of the significant differences that we have been discussing. How do we understand these similarities and what do they suggest about the claim of revelation to be true?

SIMILARITY: THE QUESTION OF TRUTH

It might be helpful to begin by reviewing the more important similarities that we discovered. As regards the language of revelation itself, we saw that both Bhartṛhari and Bonaventure agreed in viewing it as eminently practical, as originating in some type of spiritual experience that is in a sense re-enacted in its transmission and proper reception. In each case revelation appeared neither as an exclusively subjective experience nor as an objective fact, but as a dynamic process mediated through this language. This process entailed both historical and personal aspects. In their respective historical settings, both saw the proper reception of the language of revelation as the key to defending the integrity of their traditions against both internal decline and external critics and as a way of avoiding the extremes of objectivism and subjectivism. And both saw the reception of the language of revelation on the part of the individual as the key to his or her spiritual transformation. Thus by focusing on the centrality of the *language* of revelation as facilitating a dynamic *process,* both sought to reconcile the institutions and norms of the community and the spiritual transformation of the individual.

Both Bhartṛhari and Bonaventure agree, then, that revelation is a dynamic process mediated through language that has both an objective and a subjective aspect. The similarities that we observe are thus primarily similarities in the structure of this process. When we begin to fill in this structure with specific content, differences very quickly reassert themselves. Nevertheless there are some intriguing similarities even on the level of content. One of the most striking of these, as we saw, is the common assertion that reality is at its core self-expressive and that it is this self-expressiveness that underlies the spontaneous events of disclosure, illumination, or "revelation" that for them are a fundamental fact of human experience. Thus the common process that they describe is not a merely empty structure, but one that gives concrete form to the human encounter with the Real. At the same time, the fact that such an encounter does entail such a dialectical structure removes it from the realm of the merely subjective and places it squarely within the ongoing processes of history and society.

A consideration of the similarities between Bhartṛhari and Bonaventure thus leads to a perspective on the phenomenon of revelation that is deeply dialectical. Such a perspective recognizes the immediate and irreducible quality of religious experience as an essential moment in revelation, but also recognizes that such experiences are received as revelatory only within particular "situations of disclosure" that determine the objective conditions of their possibility. Furthermore it calls attention to the fact that the social mediation of such experience through language and action is an essential part of the revelatory process itself. Revelation is essentially dialectical, occurring amid concrete historical situations and remaining tied to them. It can be understood only *through* the temporal forms of its mediation, as a form of "mediated immediacy," a dialectical *process* of disclosure.

Thus, in the case of Bhartṛhari and Bonaventure at least, revelation occurs *pro loco et tempore,* in specific contexts of time and space. It is not some reality hidden "behind" phenomena. Nor is it to be identified with an inner spiritual experience that is in principle separate from its subsequent expression. Both experience and expression are moments of a single ongoing process of disclosure. This is the same as to say that precisely *as* an experience, revelation is dialectical and intersubjective. It is revelatory only to the degree that it is shareable. Only where the spiritual experience of the seer or prophet is rooted in the collective experience of the community and can be recognized and appropriated by the community as authoritative for them as a group can we speak properly of revelation.

Revelation is also *practical;* it is mediated *verbo et exemplo.* As expression it is also enactment. The visions and inspirations of seers and prophets are expressed as much through actions as through words, which is to say that here there can be no clear separation of word and deed. The language of revelation serves to mediate social practices that are essential to the continued appropriation of revelation by the community. It is through these practices that revelation remains actual as a social reality.

The question, however, is whether revelation viewed from this perspective can be true. Is it not reduced to being little more than an epiphenomenon, a changing expression of the changing experiences of individuals and groups without a mooring in something permanent, something that could guarantee objective truth? Can one historicize revelation as a process rooted in the uncertainties of history without undermining its central claim to be true, without which it ceases to be intelligible as "revelation"?

It is all too easy to fall into a series of dichotomies, holding that revelation must either be wholly objective, transcendent, and unchanging or be merely the expression of subjective experience. But the structure of revelation as a process, or better in its reception as an *event,* suggests that such dichotomies should be avoided, provided of course that we are to give the historical *actuality* of revelation precedence over its theoretical representations. Neither an objectivist nor a subjectivist position seems capable of doing justice to both the question of the irreducibly experiential or immediate element in the process of revelation *and* the equally irreducible moment of objective mediation. What is needed is a concept of truth as disclosure that roots both the subjective and objective moments in the experience of truth in the self-manifestation of reality itself.

One such understanding of truth as disclosure, as distinct from theories of truth as either correspondence or coherence, has been formulated by the philosopher Martin Heidegger and further developed by, among others, his student Hans-Georg Gadamer. While I would not want to suggest that either Heidegger or Gadamer has said the last word on this matter or that the hermeneutical tradition that they represent is our only resource for addressing the issue, a brief consideration of Gadamer's understanding of truth may serve as an illustration of the sort of approach that seems to me to be most relevant and helpful here.[21]

Gadamer's elaboration of a Heideggerian notion of truth as disclosure, through his investigation of the irreducibly historical and linguistic character of human understanding and the self-presentative character of Being as it is disclosed in language, culminates in a description of truth as disclosive *event* that is directly relevant to the problem under consideration here. Far from opposing history and truth, Gadamer understands truth to be embedded in, indeed made *possible* by, history and the historicity of human existence. As an event, truth is something one experiences. But this experience (in the sense of the German *Erfahrung*) cannot be understood as simply "subjective" experience (*Erlebnis*), since all experience is a part of the historical context in which it occurs. Gadamer makes this clear in his criticism of Wilhelm Dilthey's view of the role of experience in understanding:

> Since he [Dilthey] started from the awareness of "experiences" [*Erlebnisse*], he was unable able to build a bridge to the historical realities, because the great historical realities of society and state always have a predeterminant influence on any "experience." Self-reflection and autobiography — Dilthey's starting-points — are not primary and are not an adequate basis for the hermeneutical problem, because through them history is made private once more. In fact history does not belong to us; we belong to it. Long before we understand ourselves through the process of self-examination, we understand ourselves in a self-evident way in the family, society and state in which we live. The focus of subjectivity is a distorting mirror. The self-awareness of the individual is only a flickering in the closed circuits of historical life. *That is why the prejudices of the individual, far more than his judgments, constitute the historical reality of his being.*[22]

21. Obviously a fully adequate examination of either Gadamer's thought or of disclosive models of truth generally is far beyond the scope of the present work. For a full discussion of the model of truth as disclosure in Heidegger, Gadamer, and Paul Ricoeur, see James DiCenso, *Hermeneutics and the Disclosure of Truth: A Study in the Work of Heidegger, Gadamer, and Ricoeur* (Charlottesville: University Press of Virginia, 1990). There is a strong Neoplatonic element in Gadamer's thought that in part accounts for the similarity between his understanding of truth as disclosure and Bonaventure's notion of truth as dependent upon a kind of illumination. On the Neoplatonic element in Gadamer, see David Carpenter, "Emanation, Incarnation and the Truth-event in Gadamer's *Truth and Method,*" in Brice Wachterhauser, ed., *Hermeneutics and Truth* (Evanston: Northwestern University Press, 1994), pp. 98–122.

22. Hans-Georg Gadamer, *Truth and Method,* 2d rev. ed. (New York: Crossroad, 1992), pp. 276–77.

Gadamer is not rejecting experience per se, but only an ahistorical model of experience. What he is saying, and what seems to be borne out by the foregoing study of Bhartṛhari and Bonaventure, is that individual experience — in our case the experience of revelation — must not be located outside the hermeneutic continuity of human historical experience, but must be grasped *within* the dialectical process of history itself. This means that the study of the experience of revelation, and ultimately the question of the *truth* of revelation, cannot be separated from the question of the forms and process of its mediation. The media of revelation are not merely *post facto* expressions of a prior and essentially autonomous or *sui generis* subjective experience. They constitute the conditions of the possibility of the experience itself and thereby enter into its constitution. All revelation is at the same time interpretation.

Gadamer attempts to clarify the nature of the experience of truth by analogy with the experience of play. According to Gadamer, the mode of being of play is not determined by the player but by the play itself. "All playing is a being-played."[23] The subjectivity of the individual player is transformed by the to and fro movement of the play itself. Similarly in the experience of a work of art, one does not experience a mere "object"; one is taken up into the process of self-presentation that is the proper mode of being of the beautiful.[24]

Such an analysis of experience escapes the pitfalls of subjectivism not by reverting to an equally problematic objectivism that would posit a knowledge of objective reality independent of the concrete conditions of human existence, but by developing a "hermeneutical ontology" guided by the phenomenon of language. In elaborating this ontology Gadamer extends his description of the mode of being of the beautiful to our experience of understanding mediated by language and ultimately to our experience of truth:

> The metaphysics of the beautiful can be used to illuminate two points that follow from the relation between the radiance of the beautiful and the evidentness of the intelligible. The first is that both the appearance of the beautiful and the mode of being of understanding have the character of an event; the second, that the hermeneutical experience, as the experience of traditionary meaning, has a share in the *immediacy* which has always distinguished

23. Ibid., p. 106.
24. See ibid., p. 116, and his later discussion of the mode of being of the beautiful, pp. 477ff.

> the experience of the beautiful, as it has that of all evidence of *truth.*[25]

In making his first point, Gadamer points to the way that beauty "charms" us, prior to our adoption of a conscious orientation to it. In a similar way, that which is "clear" asserts its own rightness prior to any giving of proofs. Drawing on the Neoplatonic metaphysics of light that was also important for Bonaventure's theory of spiritual illumination, he argues that the hermeneutical experience shares this immediate appeal, giving it an event-character. Further, this event-character is related to our finitude. In asserting its own truth, the tradition that addresses us disturbs our horizon, challenges us, and is experienced as an event, in a way that parallels our experience of beauty.

Gadamer introduces his second point in the following way:

> If we start from the basic ontological view that Being is *language — i.e., self-presentation* — as revealed to us by the hermeneutical experience of being, then . . . just as the mode of being of the beautiful proved to be characteristic of the being in general, so the same thing can be shown to be true of *the concept of truth.*[26]

Thus the mode of being of the beautiful is also the mode of being of the true. Truth is self-presentation. In applying this understanding of truth to the case of language and interpretation, Gadamer recalls that "words that bring something into language are themselves a speculative event. Their truth lies in what is said in them, and not in an intention locked in the impotence of subjective particularity."[27] Then he returns to the example of play:

> What we mean by truth here can best be defined again in terms of our concept of *play*. . . . What we encounter in the experience of the beautiful and in understanding the meaning of tradition really has something of the truth of play about it. In understanding we are drawn into an event of truth and arrive, as it were, too late, if we want to know what we are supposed to believe.[28]

25. Ibid., p. 485.
26. Ibid., p. 487.
27. Ibid., p. 489.
28. Ibid., p. 490.

Gadamer's description of the hermeneutical experience may help us better understand the experience of revelation as a dialectical process of disclosure that unfolds *within* the ongoing "play" of history and, most importantly, through the mediation of the language of revelation. Gadamer's "de-centering" of the subject through the analysis of play and later through the analysis of "effective historical consciousness" and the experience of language itself offers an important corrective to the tendency to isolate the individual recipient of revelation or the religious subject in general from the concrete conditions of history, as a kind of disembodied knower of the religious "object." Gadamer makes it clear that the individual is "always already" located in the larger processes of history and tradition, and that one always arrives "too late" to achieve some "pure" perspective on the world. Religious truth cannot be objectified so as to be understood apart from the concrete conditions under which it is disclosed. As James DiCenso has noted, under a disclosive model of truth, "to ask about truth is, simultaneously, to ask about the structures that inform our modes of being-in-the-world."[29] In the present context of a study of revelation, this suggests that the dialectical character of revelation as a historical process defines the phenomenon *as such* and is not merely a description of a *post facto* "expression" of a prior, ahistorical experience hidden deep within the caverns of subjectivity. In short, Gadamer's philosophical hermeneutics can aid us by clarifying what is entailed in viewing religious truth in a consistently historical manner.

In the passages quoted above, Gadamer does not hesitate to speak of "truth." For Gadamer, truth is disclosure, or "self-presentation," and this disclosure is a temporal process. Truth makes a claim on us within the context of our finite historical existence. It is an *experience,* analogous to the experience of the beautiful. I would suggest that the striking similarities in Bhartṛhari's and Bonaventure's descriptions of the actual reception of revelation, through which the individual moves from a naive experience of the world as given, as objective, *in se,* as *vikāra,* to the disclosure of the world as relational, as *expressio,* as *anukāra,* point to an experience of truth in this sense. If so, then the historical conditions that determine the character of revelation as a dynamic process need not militate against its truth. On the contrary, they can be seen as making truth possible.

One consequence of such a view of revelation is that it casts a crit-

29. DiCenso, *Hermeneutics and the Disclosure of Truth,* p. 147.

ical light upon any claim to "possess" the revealed truth, as some kind of fixed content, independent of the historical conditions of its reception. A revelation that is "fixed" for all time, locked into a particular set of representations, is no longer revelation but ideology, which has lost its dynamism, its event-character. Such an ideology may be useful for reinforcing the separate identity and legitimacy of individual religious communities. But this practical usefulness must remain subject to critique if the light of revelation is not to be extinguished. Consequently claims for the uniqueness or finality of any revelation betray a fundamental misunderstanding of the character of revelation itself, which is always an opening, a disclosure, and is never final. Indeed, as understood here, the conditions of finitude and hence of change and impermanence are introduced into revelation as an *essential* element.

This abandonment of finality or absoluteness is of course consistent with the thinking of a "pluralist" such as John Hick, who explicitly abandons the Christian claim to uniqueness and finality, and in this sense the view of revelation presented here would seem to support Hick's call for a "Copernican" revolution in theology. But whereas Hick grounds his pluralism on the Kantian notion of a noumenal reality that is the identical referent of all religious experience yet that itself remains unknowable, I am uneasy with the dualism that is implicit in this view, as well as in the very similar attempt of Wilfred Cantwell Smith to distinguish a single, universal "faith" from the "cumulative traditions." It seems that a more relational understanding of reality and its self-presentation in revelation is called for, one that breaks free of an analysis in terms of a noumenal, unknowable object and phenomenal, subjective experience. In the actual *event* of revelation, there is no self-same "object" "out there" that remains beyond our purely subjective powers of knowing. Rather, revelation as an event can perhaps best be understood as the disclosure of a reality that is itself dynamic and relational. There are of course many resources for working out such an understanding of reality, not only in the thought of Bhartṛhari and Bonaventure as examined here or in the thought of Heidegger and Gadamer, but also, to take but one example, in the thought of the Islamic mystic Ibn 'Arabi and his notion of the "heart that is receptive of every form." According to Michael Sells this notion in turn presupposes "a dynamic notion of identity between the particular and unique forms of manifestation and the unity beyond all form and relation. In this perspective, to deny either the plurality or the unity is to fall into reification and binding and to lose the dialectic."[30] It seems to me that Ibn 'Arabi's notion of the "heart that is receptive of every form" is richly suggestive of the sort of approach that is needed. From a very different quarter one might also mention John Keenan's engaging attempt to employ, in a Christian context, the Mahayana Buddhist conception of emptiness as the key to a non-essentialist understanding of religious truth.[31] Pursuing such suggestive ideas would of course take us far beyond the limits of the present study. Nevertheless, such understandings of truth as disclosure, as plural and historical in its very nature, as involving a "dynamic notion of identity" between the immanent and transcendent rather than their dualistic and static separation, as finally being "empty" of all essence, seem to me to be best suited for making sense of the multiple claims to revealed truth that we encounter in the history of religions and of the dynamic character of revelation itself as a concrete historical phenomenon. Such a view of revelation does indeed "take differences seriously" while at the same time making them productive. For it places revelation and the doctrinal claims based upon it squarely back into the dialectic of history and into the realm of the ongoing human practice of understanding. The similarities discovered between the actual reception of revelation on the part of Bhartṛhari and Bonaventure thus point to a dialectical and historical understanding of truth mediated through concrete linguistic practices in which difference constitutes a necessary moment of alterity rather than the contradiction of a statically conceived "objective" truth.

SIMILARITY IN DIFFERENCE: FROM REVELATION TO DIALOGUE

If such a historical understanding of truth is possible, then the truth of revelation can be freed from the reified status to which its ideological usefulness so often destines it. Rather than being used as an instrument for communal self-assertion and the exclusion of difference, revelation, as an ongoing process, is returned to the sphere of authentic human existence in its historicity and its openness. Rather than closing off dialogue between religions such as Christianity and Hinduism, as the authoritative justification for the immutability of some established

30. See Michael A. Sells, "Ibn 'Arabī's Garden among the Flames: A Reevaluation," *History of Religions* 23 (1984): 314 and passim.
31. See John P. Keenan, *The Meaning of Christ: A Mahāyāna Theology* (Maryknoll, N.Y.: Orbis Books, 1989).

doctrinal difference anchored in the past, revelation itself becomes the ultimate *ground* of such dialogue, representing the possibility of a shared process of spiritual transformation that holds the promise of a common future.

In this dialogue both similarity and difference will need to be taken seriously. And as we have seen, attention must be given not only, or even primarily, to the similarities and differences that can be observed between the explicit representations of different religious communities. Of primary concern must be the historical experiences and practical forms of life that underlie such explicit representations, for it is only in approaching the task of dialogue at this level that we can hope to transform static oppositions into productive differences that can fuel both a critique of the ideological pretensions of religious communities and most importantly, beyond such a necessary critique, a common quest for spiritual growth and enlightenment.

The critical dimension of this task will need to pay close attention to the histories of the different religious traditions, within the context of a global history conceived not merely as the history of great nations and empires, or even of great civilizations, but more fundamentally as the history of the evolution of human life within its natural environment, its interactions with and transformation of that environment, and the subsequent evolution of human society and human forms of knowledge and representation. In such a context the history of "revelation," with its "axial age" connotations, would have to be re-examined as a moment within a much longer history of human religious experience. Nor can this broader historical perspective remain purely retrospective. It must also embrace our present as the product of this longer history, not so much the present of the academy as the present of our "new world order" of fragmentation and violence, often religiously inspired and legitimated. It is this real, practical world, which is the historical, social, political, and economic location of those who would enter into dialogue, that must be taken into account in any attempt to discuss the "meaning" of a particular religion's claims to truth or the nature of their authority.

The post-critical dimension of this task will become possible only through such a critique, through the openness that it makes possible. Only through the honest recognition of a radical pluralism, through the acknowledgment of the historical character of religious value and truth, and through the firm rejection of the demonic pretension to "possess" such truth can a new "dynamic sense of identity" emerge from the ossified and opposing identities that fuel present communal conflicts, identities often justified on the grounds of "revealed" verities. Such a post-critical commitment to dialogue will constitute not the abandonment of truth that is feared by those who still cling to the forms of its appearance, but a reaffirmation of the truth that, as Gadamer might say, charms us even before we can say what it is.

Index

Abraham (biblical figure), 181
Aklujkar, Ashok, 31, 32
Althaus, Paul, 9
ancient Near East, 181, 188–89
angels, 117
Apocalypse of St. John, 186
apocalypticism, 149–51, 170, 181, 185
apostles, 85, 125, 131
Aristotelianism, Bonaventure's criticism of, 146–47
Aristotelians, radical, 90
Aristotle, 63, 90
Aryan tribes
  oral culture of, 188
  worldview of, 180–81
Aśoka, 22–23, 52, 169
assimilation (*assimilatio*), 94, 97
Augustine, 87, 116, 120, 123, 132, 142, 189
authority. *See* religious authority
axial age, 2, 201

Baaren, Theodorus Petrus van, 15
Barth, Karl, 9
benefice, 171
Bhartṛhari, 16
  and Buddhism, 40, 170–71
  and critique of reason, 52
  on doctrinal language, 50–51
  as grammarian, 28–34
  historical context of, 22–24
  intellectual context of, 24–28
  on language as representational, 59–60
  and Mīmāṃsā, 33
  and Nyāya, 33
  and Patañjali, 31
  on the sentence, 61–64
  on the stages of speech, 47, 174
  on tradition, 49–57
  on the True Word, 35–40
  on the Veda, 40–43
  on the Vedic seers, 43–49
Biardeau, Madeleine, 22
Bonaventure, 16
  doctrine of illumination of, 108–13, 137
  and the Franciscans, 89–91
  historical context of, 81–84
  intellectual context of, 84–89
  on preaching, 139–44
  on prophecy, 119–26, 144–52
  on scripture, 132–38
  theology of the Trinity of, 92–96
  and use of term *revelatio,* 115–19
  on *verbum incarnatum,* 102–5
  on *verbum increatum,* 98–102
  on *verbum inspiratum,* 105–13
book of creation, 100, 133, 136, 164
Brahman, 36, 158, 161
  historical context of, 184

Brahmanism, 25, 167, 170
Buddhism, 23–24, 30, 167, 169, 170

Candragomin, 32, 77
canon, 23
  and communal self-definition, 190
Cardona, George, 31
Cassiodorus, 86, 123
Christians, worldview of early, 181–82
Clooney, Francis, 4, 11
Collations on the Six Days, 145–52
Collins, John J., 181
comparative theology, 4
comparison, 157
  phenomenological approaches to, 15–16
  and the study of revelation, 14–16
created existence, as mutable, 100–101
creation *ex nihilo,* 99–101, 159, 162
Crusades, 154

Daniel (biblical figure), 120–21, 124, 185–86
dharma, 43, 49, 52, 159, 162, 167, 183
  and knowledge, 54–56
DiCenso, James, 198
differences
  cannot be cancelled out, 175
  as oppositions, 177–78
  as productive, 178–79
  vital to comparison, 176
Dilthey, Wilhelm, 195
DiNoia, J. A., 11, 16, 177
"dry reasoning," 56, 166

ecology, 1, 189, 190
Eliade, Mircea, 7
emanations, in Trinity, 94
empires, religious legitimation of, 1–2
emptiness, 200
expression (*expressio*), 95, 97
  and creation, 98

feudalism, 169
Francis of Assisi, St., 89, 116, 146, 149, 161
  as preacher, 140–42
Franciscans
  establishment at Paris, 89
  spirituals, 169

Gadamer, Hans-Georg
  on the beautiful, 196–97
  and hermeneutical ontology, 196
  on play, 196
  on truth as event, 194–98
Gerardo di Borgo San Donnino, 90, 169
God, 92–96, 158, 161
  as all-powerful creator, 182
  historical context of, 184–85
  as Light, 105–7
  self-communication of, 92–93
Gonda, Jan, 184
gospels, as fixed canon, 191
grace, as spiritual influence, 106–7
grammar (*vyākaraṇa*), 23, 28–32
  as spiritual path, 68–75

grammatical tradition, decline of prior to Bhartṛhari, 31
Gregory the Great, 86, 144
Griffiths, Paul, 3, 11, 16, 177, 179
Gupta Empire, 22–23

Hanson, R. P. C., 88
Heidegger, Martin, 16, 194
Hein, Norvin, 76
Hick, John, 10, 199
hierarchy, 108–11, 151
hierophany, 7
Hindu Renaissance, 23
Hugh of St. Victor, 136

Ibn 'Arabi, 199
ideology, and revelation, 189
illumination, 105, 108–13, 115–17, 166, 173
  in prophecy, 122, 160
image of God
  human person as, 100–101, 107
  in Trinity, 94
Indus Valley civilization, 188
innascibilitas, 93
Inquisition, 154
interreligious dialogue, 12–13, 200–202
intuition (*pratibhā*), 46, 64–67, 160, 165
Irenaeus, 87–88
Israelites, 188

Jaimini, 25
Jesus Christ, 103–4, 159, 162
  as King, 2, 181
  as moral exemplar, 128–29
  as preacher, 129–30
  as revealer, 126–30
  as teacher, 127–30
Joachim of Fiore, 90, 146, 169
  and Bonaventure's interpretation of scripture, 147–51
John Cassian, 136
John of Parma, 149

kāraka-s, 61–64
Kātyāyana, 30
Keenan, John, 200
Kingdom of God, 181
Knitter, Paul, 11
Krishna, 76

land grants, 24, 171
language
  as dharma, 68–75, 166
  primacy of the sentence in, 61–64
  as representational, 59–60
  and vision, 67–75
language of revelation, 4, 16–17, 58, 68–75, 131–52, 163–67, 193
  as communal, 166
  as mediating oppositions, 171–72
  as practical, 165–66
  as sacred speech, 165, 183
  as scripture, 183
  as text, 165
learned scholar (*śiṣṭa*), 30, 47, 54–56, 161, 169, 183
lectio divina, 136–37
Logos theology, 17, 18

McGinn, Bernard, 149
mahāvākya, 50

mana, 184
Mauss, Marcel, 184
"mediated immediacy," 193
Mensching, Gustav, 15
Mesopotamia, 181, 188
Messiah, 181
metaphysics of revelation, 97, 105, 108, 111–13
  and anthropology, 100
  and history, 113
  and *verbum inspiratum,* 113
Mīmāṃsā (school of Indian philosophy), 25, 33, 191
Moses, 123–24

Nāgārjuna, 40
Neoplatonism, 93
Nyāya (school of Indian philosophy), 26, 33

Oṃ, 27, 49, 50
Origen, 88, 132

Pāṇini, 29–30, 169
Paramārtha, 23
Patañjali, 29
Paul, St., 86, 124, 143
person, Christian and Indian concepts of, 186–87
pluralism, 199, 201
powers of Brahman (*śakti*-s), 37–39, 159, 162
  and knowledge, 54
  and language, 60–63
Prajāpati, 70
preacher, in early Christianity, 182–83
preaching
  in Christian tradition, 84–85
  as communal, 144
  decline of, 168–70
  and the Franciscans, 139–40
  as prophecy, 145
  revival of, 168
  and *vita apostolica,* 142
prophecy, 116, 119–26
  in early church, 85–86
  and history, 123–26
  in the Middle Ages, 86–87
  scholastic treatises on, 119–20
pseudo-Dionysius, 93, 105, 108, 151

Rahner, Karl, 10
reality, as self-expressive, 37–38, 93–96, 159, 193
reason
  Bhartṛhari on, 52–57
  and intuition, 56
religious authority, 7–8
religious diversity
  in history, 1–3
  as theological problem, 2–3, 10–12
Renou, Louis, 184
revelatio (term), 115–19
revelation
  content of, 162–63
  as dialectical, 193
  as event, 152–53, 159–60, 194
  experience of, 172–75
  as a historical phenomenon, 3–4
  as a historical problem, 5
  in history, 167–72, 189, 193
  as ideology, 189–92, 199
  as interpretation, 126–27, 151, 152
  as intersubjective, 194

language of. *See* language of revelation
monarchial model of, 189
as personal vs. impersonal, 186
as practical, 194
as process, 4, 17, 18, 131, 134, 151, 152–53, 176, 193
recipient of, 160–62, 163–75
and religious authority, 7–9, 190
representations of, 15–16, 163, 179, 191
shamanistic model of, 189
source of, 158–59
as a theological problem, 9
as transformative experience, 172–75
truth of, 192–200
Ricoeur, Paul, 164, 177, 191
Roques, René, 109–10

Śabara, 25
śabdabrahman, 37
Śabdatattva. See True Word
sacred, the, 7
sacrifice, five great sacrifices, 72
salvation history, 187
Śaṅkara, 40
Sanskrit language
as Divine Speech, 27, 34, 71, 167
as *lingua franca,* 23–24
as powerful speech, 28
Sanskrit Renaissance, 170
Scheler, Max, 8
scribalism, 185–86, 188
scripture, 164–65
authorship of, 88, 132–33, 164
in early church, 87–88
as form of revelation, 118–19
as narrative, 135
as social institution, 138
spiritual meanings of, 135–36, 174
and threefold word, 134
as transformative, 134–39
secular clergy, compared to *śiṣṭa*-s, 171
seers. *See* Vedic seers (*ṛṣi*-s)
Sells, Michael, 199
similarity, between Bhartṛhari and Bonaventure, 192–93
similitudo expressa, 97
smārta Brahmins, 51
Smith, Jonathan, 185
Smith, Wilfred Cantwell, 10–11, 199
Söderblom, Nathan, 8
spiritual influence (*influentia*), 105, 106–7
śruti, 21, 45–47
Sumeria, 189
svādhyāya (personal recitation), 72

theology of religions, 10
and pluralism, 10–12
Thiemann, Ronald, 9
Threefold Word, 95, 97–113, 159
totality, 1, 153, 192
tradition (*smṛti*), 46, 49
tribal religions, 1
Trinity, the, 92–96, 158
True Word (*śabdatattva*), 35–37, 40, 41, 48, 73–75, 158, 159
as light, 65–66
truth
as disclosure, 194–99
of revelation, 192–200

Ultimate Reality (*tattva*), 37, 38–40
unity, of Brahman, 38
Upaniṣads, 36–37

Vākyapadīya, 31–32, 34, 35
Vasurāta, 23
Vātsyāyana, 26
Veda, 21, 164
  as *anukāra* of Brahman, 40–43
Vedic gods, 182
Vedic seers (*ṛṣi*-s), 24–25, 43–49, 160–61, 180, 182–83
vikalpa, 40, 50, 59
vita apostolica, 168
Von Campenhausen, Hans, 87–88

Wach, Joachim, 8
Wheelock, Wade, 28
William of Saint-Amour, 90
Word of God
  as exemplar, 99–101
  in Trinity, 95
  as *verbum incarnatum,* 102–5
  as *verbum increatum,* 98–102
  as *verbum inspiratum,* 96, 105–13
world cycles, 46, 187
world history
  as context for comparison, 187–89
  as context for dialogue, 201
worldviews, early Indian and Christian contrasted, 180–82

Yahweh, 184
Yāska, 44
yoga, preceded by words, 69–75, 173

Other Titles in the Faith Meets Faith Series

Toward a Universal Theology of Religion, Leonard Swidler, Editor
The Myth of Christian Uniqueness, John Hick and Paul F. Knitter, Editors
An Asian Theology of Liberation, Aloysius Pieris, S.J.
The Dialogical Imperative, David Lochhead
Love Meets Wisdom, Aloysius Pieris, S.J.
Many Paths, Eugene Hillman, C.S.Sp.
The Silence of God, Raimundo Panikkar
The Challenge of the Scriptures, Groupe de Recherches Islamo-Chrétien
The Meaning of Christ, John Keenan
Hindu-Christian Dialogue, Harold Coward, Editor
The Emptying God, John B. Cobb, Jr., and Christopher Ives, Editors
Christianity through Non-Christian Eyes, Paul J. Griffiths, Editor
Christian Uniqueness Reconsidered, Gavin D'Costa, Editor
Women Speaking, Women Listening, Maura O'Neill
Bursting the Bonds? Leonard Swidler, Lewis John Eron, Lester Dean, and Gerard Sloyan, Editors
One Christ — Many Religions, Stanley J. Samartha
The New Universalism, David J. Krieger
Jesus Christ at the Encounter of World Religions, Jacques Dupuis, S.J.
After Patriarchy, Paula M. Cooey, William R. Eakin, and Jay B. McDaniel, Editors
An Apology for Apologetics, Paul J. Griffiths
World Religions and Human Liberation, Dan Cohn-Sherbok, Editor
Uniqueness, Gabriel Moran
Leave the Temple, Felix Wilfred, Editor
The Buddha and the Christ, Leo D. Lefebure
The Divine Matrix, Joseph A. Bracken, S.J.
The Gospel of Mark: A Mahāyāna Reading, John P. Keenan
Salvations, S. Mark Heim